Albert Gallatin Riddle

Alice Brand

A Romance of the Capital

Albert Gallatin Riddle

Alice Brand

A Romance of the Capital

ISBN/EAN: 9783744673686

Printed in Europe, USA, Canada, Australia, Japan

Cover: Foto ©Thomas Meinert / pixelio.de

More available books at **www.hansebooks.com**

A ROMANCE OF THE CAPITAL.

BY

A. G. RIDDLE,

AUTHOR OF "BART RIDGELY," "THE PORTRAIT," ETC.

CLEVELAND:
COBB, ANDREWS & CO.
1875.

ENTERED, according to Act of Congress, in the year 1875, by
D. APPLETON & COMPANY,
In the Office of the Librarian of Congress, at Washington.

PREFACE.

As the author proceeded in the composition of these pages, he became aware of some of the difficulties inherent in the material which he was attempting to use. It may be supposed that its weight and inflexibility were too much for his hand to fashion and combine into the harmonious unity of a narrative having life and movement, and the charm of interest, which can alone attend the fortunes of individuals.

In committing these labors to the public, he has no wish to deprecate any criticism which they may challenge, as a work of art. He is quite aware that he is responsible, alike for the material selected and his method of dealing with it.

Whatever fortune may attend him, he ventures to hope that, as sketches of life, of men and things, at the capital, at the period immediately following the war, the importance of which has not been appreciated, with something of the color, spirit, and atmosphere of that time, his work may be found to possess much interest.

A. G. R.

CONTENTS.

CHAPTER	PAGE
PREFACE	3
I.—BANG-BORUMS	7
II.—ALICE	12
III.—THE CIVIL SERVICE	17
IV.—CIVIL-SERVICE REFORM	22
V.—THE DEFIANCE AND THE MEETING	29
VI.—DREAMS AND FLOWERS	36
VII.—FRANK MAKES A FOOLISH SPEECH	42
VIII.—TEAZER AND TWEEZER	46
IX.—THE HEART OF MIDLOTHIAN	51
X.—ST. ARNAUD HEARS MR. DRYBOW	59
XI.—THE VANES	73
XII.—MRS. CROLY OPENS THE CAMPAIGN	85
XIII.—THE KING OF THE LOBBY	88
XIV.—MR. RHYMER'S CROWNING MERCY	92
XV.—AN OLD FRIEND OF CAPTAIN BRAND	94
XVI.—THE DETECTIVE	99
XVII.—THE NEW ALLY	103
XVIII.—MRS. CROLY AT HOME	110
XIX.—MRS. THOMPSON HAS A CALL	117
XX.—WHO WOULD BE A MEMBER OF CONGRESS?	123
XXI.—THE YOUNG REPRESENTATIVE	127
XXII.—LOVE AND POLITICS	135
XXIII.—AT THE CHIEF-JUSTICE'S	145
XXIV.—MASON SEES THE GODDESS OF LIBERTY	158
XXV.—ROCKS AND PIG-IRON	164
XXVI.—IN A MIST	173

CONTENTS.

CHAPTER	PAGE
XXVII.—Mrs. Lozier's Party	175
XXVIII.—Where Frank was	179
XXIX.—Another Crown	183
XXX.—Harbeck's Little Supper	187
XXXI.—Alice serves a Notice to quit	191
XXXII.—The Croly's Grief	194
XXXIII.—The President and his Ministers	204
XXXIV.—Sap and Bark	210
XXXV.—The Story of Haym Salmon	219
XXXVI.—A Mine prematurely sprung	224
XXXVII.—Ellen	225
XXXVIII.—Hannibal in Rome	233
XXXIX.—An Idyl of the Summer Sea	243
XL.—Minnie's Message for the Angels	251
XLI.—The Lovers	257
XLII.—Summer at the Capital	267
XLIII.—Some Beginnings of the End	272
XLIV.—Mrs. Croly's Last Appearance	277
XLV.—Old Nancy's Notion of an Angel	283
XLVI.—The Trial	289
XLVII.—Grayson's Views	296
XLVIII.—Le Grand	300
XLIX.—Valerie's Leave of her Lover	303
L.—Surprised	306
LI.—The King takes the Field, and is checked	309
LII.—Melodrama	314
LIII.—The King checkmated	321
LIV.—Margie's Vision	325
LV.—Mr. Smith's Last Appearance	330
LVI.—Mrs. Harbeck explains	336
LVII.—Grayson's Ride	342
LVIII.—How Mike executed Orders	445
LIX.—Mrs. Harbeck has a Call	352
LX.—Frank	358
LXI.—Frank's Story	361
LXII.—The Tables turned	364
LXIII.—Ellen at the Capital	374
LXIV.—A Spring Day on the Potomac	376

ALICE BRAND.

CHAPTER I.

BANG-BORUM'S.

A WASHINGTON boarding-house it was, of the antebellum period, a thing as well defined as any word in the dictionary. The war had ploughed out slavery, but had not struck deep enough to uproot Bang-Borum's. The Old Dominion and chivalry went out together, but the Washington boarding-house was planted on the Old Red Sandstone, and could only die out in consuming seediness and odor.

Bang-Borum was of course from the older Virginia, in some generation whose "high-toned" could keep a wayside tavern, and there was a time when one might call for board or lodging-room at almost every house in the national capital without fear of offense, however careless of his references he might be.

The unvarying three-story, red-brick, narrow front, with decaying wooden steps over the basement area to the front door, and the open drooling trench from one corner across the sidewalk to the reeking gutter, always full, with its fixed stench, which was only lost in the more pungent fragrance into which it oozed.

In the vestibule one encountered an odor older than

the last freshet, and that might survive a deluge, while the corridors, stairways, and several floors, had each a fragrance of its own. Nearly every room had its distinctive flavor, and might have been named from it, and all mixed and mingled in the dining-room with a permanent perfume from the kitchen, forming a compound quite torturing to a sense not acclimated by the smells and odors of the streets.

There were creaking stairs and reeking walls, from which the faded paper was starting in bulging blisters, or peeling in rotten tatters. The whole might have been mistaken for a hospital for infirm and disabled furniture, crippled chairs, sick tables, scabby carpets, leprous sofas, broken-hearted ottomans—the drift and *débris* of auction sales—of fossils, rejected of pawnbrokers and receivers of stolen goods.

A brass plate on the door bore the compound Bang-Borum. What the legend once signified was lost in the antiquities of the Ancient Dominion, and may, like so many distinguished quarterings, have descended from Pocahontas. The place was usually called "Borum's," and was presided over by a female divinity, one once sharing the name in common with a supposed male Borum, who had, however, given no conclusive evidence of his sex. It was a time-honored dispensary of dyspepsia, roaches, and kindred entomological specimens. Whatever doubt may have existed as to the Bore*man*, none was ever felt as to the Bore*woman*—the chief in the war upon suffering humanity. The first had found ample scope for all his powers, in the ever-losing battle to maintain the place as head of the house, which resulted, like most similar struggles, in the permanent position as the antithesis of that governing extremity. His only success was that mysterious legend, Bang-Borum, on the door-plate, with the "Mrs." omitted. The result of which on the world was, the impression that there was but one Borum, who exhibited many of the unquestionable peculiarities of a female. The other Borum never quite understood it. He had his way with the plate. There it was. The name was his—came from him. She was Borum, because he was—or had been, for now she seemed to be the whole of it. This was apparent to him. The last certainly known of him, he was observed intently studying this dingy plate, and in vain endeavoring to understand the meaning of it. This I am glad to say was before my time, and, as we must commence and remain a few days at Bang-Borum's, it would be painful to witness his chronic discomfiture. Poor Borum! his is not the sole instance of a vain attempt to realize the traditions of his sex, in the face of that logic which decrees that where the brains are, there shall be the head also.

And yet Borum's held one almost bright, sweet place, which in some way managed to maintain a cheerful aspect of warmth and color, pervaded with a healthy air. Some charm, in spite of Borum, managed to hide the frayed carpets of two rooms, tone up the weakness of the chairs, and counteract the griminess of the walls. Flowers somehow found help to keep fresh in a vase, and some actually grew in two little pots in the windows. Two or three small but rare pictures hung on the walls, and a dozen little nameless graces and things of woman's invention and taste, which come of a nature purer than art, and higher than mere culture, and capable of giving the soul of beauty and grace to a corner of the Borum retreat, were disposed about the rooms, showing that, although it was approached through the Bang-Borum portal, it was in fact the domain of another spirit.

In the larger of the two rooms, in state, sat Mrs. Thompson in a creaky rocking-chair, with her feet on an ottoman, flashy, frowsy, and forty, attended by two lady admirers who came to "set" with her, as one of them appropriately called it. Mrs. Thompson's voice had drawled and died away, when with an effort she resumed: "Well, it is a comfort to know that these things was permitted for our shortcomin's, an' for our good; though the massy knows what I've did;" and, closing her washed-out eyes, she looked as if she would have preferred to realize the "good" in more convertible funds. "Yis, she takes after her father in her workin' ways—a regular Yank never gits the mean, workin' spirit out on 'em; and, as if we hadn't gone down low enough, she must take this place in the Treasury; I tho't I should 'a died. You see, I know'd nothin' 'bout it till 'twas all did."

"Well, now—I think," remarked one of her friends, "that seventy-five dollars a month is not a bad thing."

"Yis; but then—I'm a Biggs, an' the Biggses never did work," was the sufficient answer.

"Then Alice is not a Biggs? I tho't she was your own niece."

"Bless your soul—no! My husband, who's as good as dead, was a cousin to her step-mother. Her mother an' step-mother was both on 'em Craiks, you see, an' cousins; and the Craiks, though a high-toned Southern family, warn't Biggses, by a right smart. Yer see, 'er father, Commodore Brand, married Helen Craik in the ole country somewhere. The Craikses were all in the ole country, both families. Well, the commodore, then a lieutenant, married Helen, an' when she died, leavin' this Alice a baby, he, like a real Northerner, married her cousin. The Craiks was rich, an' some years after, her father resigned his office, an' went to live on his first wife's plantation, called Magnolia, a spul-endid place! near Vicksburg. Her father an' mother was dead, an' she had mor'n a thousan' niggers, an' no end o' horses an' mules, an' raised cotton, an' a heap o' sugar, an' every thing. For some reason, Commodore Brand never went North, an' Alice was raised mostly at the South. Her step-mother died first, an' then, jest afore the war, she lost 'er father, an' was left with the plantation, an' niggers, 'an things; an' she not mor'n sixteen. I never sawn her father; my husband took me thar just after he died, an' went on down the river, as I told yer, an' never come back. Men is dreadful unsartin'. Wal, the war come, an' General Grant an' his army of Yanks an' murderers, an', for a time, our General Pemberton made his headquarters to our house, an' one o' his aides, General Gardé, took a great fancy to Alice; but she was jest as full o' her father's Northern blood as she could hole, an' stood up for the North, an' all we could do an' say, she held out, an' quarreled with General Pemberton an' all on 'em. She had 'er father's boat-flag, an' sword, an' plume, in 'er room, an' when the general threatened to confiscate all the property, she tole him to do it.

"Wal, yer see, we had to fall back inter the city, an' insisted on taking Alice with us, an' she refused to go, an' General Gardé staid with some soldiers to take us in ; an' Alice still refused; an' jest as we had got 'er out an' started, the Yanks come up. It was jest at dark. Oh, dear! I fainted clar away! The Biggses always did. I only remember the guns, an' a clash, an' shouts; an' when I come-to, we're all back in the house, with Yankee soldiers guardin' on't; and Alice was as wild as a mad thing. Wal, the house stood on high ground, an' the mean Yanks tore it down, an' dug a fort thar, an' settin' all the niggers to work, an' took all the corn an' cotton, mules an' horses. They gave 'er some sort o' papers for 'em all; but Lord! when we come yer, the Linkinites only paid for the corn —the mean, thievin', 'ornary creters, an' we never had a red for the niggers, an' cotton, an' things ; and never will have. I don't wonder the Lord took off Linkin; I only wonder that Seward lived, and Stanton was spared; an', as if there could be no end to our misfortins, they put poor Alice in the Treasury to earn her livin', an' I thought she would never git that. Oh, dear! it's a comfort to know that these is permitted fer our good"—sinking back in despairing exhaustion a moment, and then, springing to her feet, with her scrawny person alive with energy— "Massy on us—thar's the dinner!" as the Borum dinner-bell sent its cracked clangor up from the reeking depths, " and me a Biggs!"—as, followed by her companions, she escaped from the room.

A bright-faced yellow girl tidied up the room, and placed a low chair by the cheery grate, whose ruddy light dispelled the gloom of an early winter evening.

A light step, a lithe form, and a young girl's face lingered on the threshold, seeming to bring additional brightness; but, as she stepped flaggingly to the chair into which she rather dropped than sat, and placed her chilled feet to the glowing grate, almost a sigh was breathed out, and her eyes for a moment lost the power of seeing castles and knights in the fire.

It was Alice Brand.

CHAPTER II.

ALICE.

VACANTLY she looked into the fire, yet saw neither knights nor castles. The deft hands of the bright-eyed girl placed a small table near her, with its neat napkins and cloth, and the most tempting bits of the Borum kitchen, with Alice's own small tea-urn, unheeded. How lonely seemed the solitary girl, and what a strange whirl had been the last two or three years! There was her beautiful Magnolia, in that semi-tropical clime, which Nature and wealth, had made a paradise, with its memories and riches rudely dissolved—swept from around her, by the torrent of war; her people scattered, even her old mammy lost to her. And how bravely she' had given them all up, all for the memory and flag of her father! And then there was the gathering up of the few valuables left after the scattering, and the journey North, the arrival at Washington; the friendly greeting of the President, and the certainty of a speedy adjustment of some of her losses. But the war, tempest, and earth-shake, would not hush, that a slender girl should be heeded and her plaint heard. Time elapsed; her papers and claims, vouchers of the quartermasters, even the signature of Grant, were rudely huddled up and bundled into forgotten pigeon-holes, and she parted with many of her little treasures, left the great hotel, took rooms, and was finally at Borum's, clogged by the feeble, helpless Thompson, whom she called aunt, and whose silly weakness she would not know. Finally, came at the last her place in the Treasury, which would but barely pay the Borum bills.

Here was something to do, a way opened, and how gladly she tripped away to the room; and she did not see the glances and stares with which they looked her through and over, or note the manner with which the twenty women in the great room greeted her—the scanning of her dress, face, and style—the Southern girl—by those curious, critical Northern women. Yet there were many true and noble women there, as she came soon to know; widows, and daughters, and wives, uncomplainingly struggling, as women, born to nothing, thankfully take and sacrificingly accept, what man, born to empire, scornfully rejects. And their women's hearts warmed to the lonely child, whose quick sensibilities went out to meet them. Among them was Mrs. Harbeck, a dark woman, with resplendent eyes, and regal brow, out of place in that room of work, and woman's talk; who kept herself apart, high and aloof, who came and went, or went and did not come, as she would; and worked as she would or wouldn't. There was a mystery about her somehow. Who she was, where she came from, or how she came there, no woman knew. The chief of the division treated her with the utmost deference. The aristocratic Kramer, whose frown withered, and whose smile was life to many, stood abashed in her presence. Gentlemen managed to gain entrance to the room, apparently to see her; she was of a style to impress and attract men, and earn the fear and hate of women. She, too, kindly bent her dark brows on the Southern girl, so strangely thrown amid alien surroundings.

Alice soon mastered her duties, and did not attach herself to any of the little woman bouquets, into which the ladies naturally grouped themselves, and the month went very pleasantly away and she received her pay—the first money she received for any thing she had ever done, with a strange and delightful sense of independence, and of its value. Never was there such money before, and what a world of things it would buy!

Then came a change. She was promoted; taken from the main room to that of the chief, to act as his secretary. How queerly her associates looked at her, and exchanged glances, and there was a little shadow of regret or something, in the great eyes of Mrs. Harbeck! She did not think of it then, but it all came to her now. She had been in the room of the chief before; one of the interior rooms, which opened to the central court; not unpleasant, and rather sumptuously fitted up, with mirrors and many things of woman's devising, indicative of the chief's tastes, or of his surroundings, or of something.

Here Alice had her little table, partly hidden by a screen, but adjoining the desk of the chief, and she found upon it every morning a fresh bouquet. She had little to do, and was told to come and go at her pleasure, and she didn't like it. The atmosphere was unpleasant to her from the first, and, finally, condensed into little nebulous atoms outlining themselves into shadowy forms. She didn't like the chief, handsome man that he was, with his rings and ringlets, and soft ways, and for whose smile, caps had almost been pulled by her associates of the great room. He annoyed her in a thousand nameless ways; little accidental things, meaning nothing, or intentional, and meaning what? And this had been going on for three weeks. How coldly, unseeingly and unknowingly, she sat in that room, through those cheerless days, never noticing the flowers, never looking or speaking unless compelled, and unapproachable in her reserve!

It seemed at times that the chief brought in men with queer atmospheres about them, for no purpose but to stare at her. She could feel their eyes, though she never saw them. She would remain this month out, and then she would certainly leave that room. Another incident came into her mind. Indeed, it lingered pretty constantly on the horizon of it. Then she had so few pleasant things to think of, and this was wholly pleasant, and, as it arose fully before her now, she could see knights and castles in the fire.

One day there came into the chief's room two young men, the younger and taller of whom the other called Frank, and in return was called Mason; while the chief called the former Colonel Warbel, and the latter general, and who was now a member of Congress from one of the Western States. They came in for some information of the chief, about a matter connected with some of Colonel Frank's soldiers, whose pay or bounties he was adjusting. The name Warbel struck her. It was very familiar to her. An officer called Warbel commanded the advance that rescued her from General Gardé, on the night when he attempted to compel her to go to the city. She was determined not to go, and his servants and men carried her out, and were placing her in the carriage, when the attack was suddenly made, and a hand-to-hand fight in the grounds occurred, in her presence; some of which she saw, and all of which she heard. She was alarmed, frightened, and filled with a wild, strange thrill; and men were killed about her, and the rebels were compelled to retire; and she heard the next morning that the attacking party was led by Captain Warbel, and, when he spoke in the room, she fancied that it was the same voice she heard when the fight was over, though she was not certain that she saw him.

In a day or two after, Frank came again, and had to remain while she copied a short paper; and, instead of standing near her, or talking loudly and consequentially, and posing, as men do, went away, and stood looking into the court; and, when the copying was finished, he gave her a bright, respectful look, with thanks, and went his way. And many times he came after that, and now in the most respectful way bowed to her as he came and went, till she wondered, each morning, if he would come that day, and, if he did not, she wondered why. And his coming, somehow, seemed to annoy the chief, whose civility to him appeared forced. Once, when he went away, something her superior muttered about "puppy." Surely he must be the officer who rescued her and her household from the rebels; and she longed to ask him about it, and could not. Of course, he did not know her name, and may never have known the name of her father, but it was pleasant to connect him with that event of her life.

Two days ago he came again to her room, and this time a paper was to be copied, and she was alone; and her hand would not obey her will, and the color came to her face, and a moisture to her eyes, with a tremor to her hand; and the youth offered to make a copy, which he did, and she read the text to him, which he wrote very slowly, in a bold, strong hand, repeating many of the words after her; and, occasionally, darting quick, bright looks at her, full of respectful admiration. Somehow, this little work in common, which ran through many minutes, seemed to make this youth and maiden old and almost intimate acquaintances, though each knew absolutely nothing of the other. They had met by one of the world's busy waysides; and the burden of the young girl had become oppressive—was, momentarily, too heavy for her, and the stronger youth had carried it for her; and went with her out of the forest; and, at the margin, they had lingered for a moment, and parted with regret. How pleasant and hopeful the world had become to her! The next day he did not come, nor yet to-day. Perhaps he had left Washington, and how blank the world seemed!

All this time, Millie, the bright girl, stood a little apart, awaiting. "Would Miss Alice have her dinner, please," and the young girl, for the first time, seemed aware of her presence, and its occasion.

CHAPTER III.

THE CIVIL SERVICE.

In a large and somewhat profusely-furnished, dimly-lighted room, in Eleventh Street, just north of the avenue, sat Mrs. Harbeck, at a later hour of this same evening. Many rich and some curious things were arranged in disorder about her. Many pictures hung or leaned against the walls, two of which were turned toward it. She was in that *negligée* that might attend arrested dressing, with abandoned robes suddenly resumed. Some effort to reduce and confine the masses of black hair had ceased, and it was left like the tresses of night, to darken shoulders and bosom, with a fiery-eyed stone burning above her brow, and another sending its smouldering gleam from the black folds that robed the bust. One hand toyed with the strings of a guitar, which seemed instinctively to wail out little moans of melody at the approach of her fingers. Somehow the music would not suit itself to her mood, and ceased wholly. Perhaps she had not heard it. The softened light toned down her almost fierce beauty, though the straight, dark brows still met over the eyes, whose light had in it something of that scorn which the scorner shares.

It was not an hour of repose or reverie, nor one of memory or thought. Broken fragments of strong emotions filled the soul, with only flashes of thought lighting up their abysses.

A servant brought in a card, which the lady laid down without looking at it. A moment later:

"Pleas', mum—the gentleman waits."

"Let him wait."

And still later: "Shall I say you are engaged."

"No!" and then, taking up the card, "show him up."

"Mr. Kramer," and the chief of the division advanced into the room. A slight quiver, and the lady turned without rising to meet her visitor, whose profound bow, as he came confidently forward, she acknowledged with a nod. Coldly she extended her hand, which he took with both his, and would have bent to, when it was withdrawn. Without inviting him to a seat, the eyes of the lady seemed to go through her visitor, whose assurance seemed proof. "Well?" interrogatively from him.

"My lesson was lost, I see—

> Bescented and bechained,
> Bejeweled and becaned—

got up with as little reference to appearance as to expense.

Can you never rise to the form of a gentleman? That person would be rather goodish if—"

"Thank you."

"It was not necessary to hide its vulgarity, and show that it held a tailor's soul, or none," she continued.

"Take care, my lady! I won't stand every thing," with real anger.

"Ha-ha-ha! It won't stand it, will it? What will it do? Go back like a bantam-cock, and ruffle its feathers among its Treasury hens? It shall."

A hot expression came into the visitor's face, as in changed voice, "Really now, my dear lady—"

"Don't 'my dear lady' me!" with severity. "I'm not your lady—dear or otherwise."

"I'm unfortunate to-night," with some manliness; "but we may as well come to an understanding. I'm weary of this."

"Put an end to it, then. I always was," in a dreary voice.

"What do you demand? Have I not done what I promised? Have I not paid—"

"Paid! Paid for what? For me?" springing to her feet with flashing eyes, under which the chief's went down, withered, and then in a changed voice: "You made certain business arrangements by which, for money, you were to betray the Government, and defraud its creditors and people, I believe, and m&&&& done what you promised, though you are quite&&&& of treachery to your own treason"—and dropping&&&&ead and voice, "And I believe I was to s&&&&o occasional visits from you."

"What is y&&&&d?" truculently.

"My demand? and here?" and, going to one of the reversed pictures, she changed it, and touching the burners she flooded it with light, revealing the noble head and bust of a man in first maturity, wearing the naval uniform.

"Look upon this. This was my husband. He died a suicide, betrayed into the rebellion, and, as he thought, his honor betrayed," her voice fell, "by me, his wife. What is my demand?" with a low tragic hiss, and, after a pause, in a voice from which all life had died—"I ought to go cheap now. Did you not understand the terms? So far as I was concerned, you were to take your chance, poor as it was, of winning my—my—regard. I cannot name the word love in your presence."

"I've been deceived, then—fooled—fooled and sold—sold like an ass!" with energetic rage.

"If sold at all, it was as asses go—certainly," coolly.

"I'll see Le Grand; I'll—"

"Hush! You profane even that name, bad as it is."

"And you? Oh, you're for presidents and senators to buy railroad grants, or foreign missions, I s'pose," with a sneer.

"I was not bought with a place in the Treasury, nor with a threat of losing it. Go on, Mr. Kramer. And this brings me to a thing which I want to say to you. Send Alice Brand back to the large room, with the rest of us."

"Alice Brand! Alice Brand! Good! good! Ha! ha! ha!"

"Ha! ha! ha-a-a—a—h—h! Did you ever hear Hermann laugh as Mephistopheles?" Kramer thought he heard the evil one himself.

"So this is the price, is it? We are jealous, ain't we? Isn't she a delicious morsel, **though**? I thought you would come round. Shall it be a **bargain**?"

"George Kramer! You harm a hair of that young girl's head—you think harm of her, if you **dare!**" laying a finger on his arm and looking him fully in the eye.

"And what will be the dreadful consequences?" in a little persuasive voice. He felt secure now. "Will we go to the President?" in the same tone.

"I will go to the Secretary of War—to Stanton."

"And what will we tell?" in his natural voice, a little shaken.

"What will I tell? What won't I tell? Perhaps give the names of senators' ladies who help make up your entertainments. Perhaps what that auburn-haired lady paid for her place. Possibly, why that officer's widow was dismissed on a charge of impropriety, and because she would not be what you charged her with being."

"Well, that will be interesting. What else?"

"Let me see—was it forty thousand dollars which you and two others of your gang received, when the Alabama corn claim was paid for the third time? I can tell in a moment;" taking some papers from a small cabinet. "I have it in your own hand."

"Hell and fury!" exclaimed the chief, springing forward. "Ward said those papers were burned." He was instantly quivering.

"No. I was wrong. Fifteen thousand dollars for the chief, and fifteen thousand dollars for the other two. And then," going on, "you were to furnish from the rolls the names and descriptive lists of at least forty-five thousand colored soldiers entitled to bounties and back pay, for ten per cent. of the proceeds of the attendant forgeries and personations. That, however, will be divided among several, I suppose—" pausing as if in thought.

"My Lady Macbeth—"

"Don't Lady Macbeth me," said the lady, turning again fully upon her visitor, and meeting on his face a dogged, sullen, hard expression, which she had never seen in it before, and which rather amused than cowed her. "Lady Macbeth could only excite another to murder, and then go mad"—drawing near him with an air and manner that the stage never knew—"I have committed worse crimes than murder; I can strike with my own hand and never even regret the blow. See here," and turning the other picture revealed a beautiful boy-face of five. "I was this boy's mother, and I rejoiced when he died. Now go, George Kramer!"

The hard, determined look never left his face, nor did he quail or falter under those last words and her superb action, but, with a haughty inclination of his head, without a word, he strode from the room.

As the hostess turned back from his exit, with every nerve at greatest tension, and the strong light fully on the faces of her husband and son, the hand of the former seemed to withdraw from its rest in the bosom, and the lofty brow to cloud. An instant, the illusion was perfect, a shriek died away in a gasp, and she sank to the floor before them.

CHAPTER IV.

CIVIL-SERVICE REFORM.

On the following morning, Alice was at the breakfast-table as usual, equipped for the department, with cheery words for all, each of whom paused and observed her until recognized. The more observing noticed a shade of languor, and just a tone of less vivacity, and eyes and hearts went with her as she passed out. Thoughtfully she tripped away up G Street to the Treasury; entered at the central ingress from Fifteenth, and passed the central corridor, and up the west staircase, as was her wont. At the top of the stairway, on the third floor, she met Mrs. Harbeck, who greeted her with warmth, and asked her if she would like to return to her old desk.

"Oh, so much!" was the answer. She lingered a moment, but Mrs. Harbeck passed without further word, and, as Miss Brand entered the room, she found the chief already there, which was unusual for him at that hour. There was something a little distrait about him, Alice thought, and he started at her entrance, and addressed her almost confusedly. The day was unusually quiet, and the chief was absent much of the time, and, when present, seemed preoccupied, and Alice observed that both the day and night watch, of that part of the building, came in, and that the chief went out of the room with each of them.

The day was gloomy outside, and darkened early, and long before the hour of release, at three, the gas was lighted. About that time the chief handed her a manuscript to copy, saying that he wished it done that day, and, directing her to remain till his return, went out. She bent to her task with deft fingers, and wrote on. Slowly the sombre daylight was burned out by the gas, and the stillness with something of the loneliness of night was about the girl. Suddenly the door opened, and day with sunshine came in surrounding the form of Colonel Frank, who stepped in with his cheery, elastic way. A glance about the room, and hat in hand he approached the electrified girl, as if she had been a princess.

"I see that Mr. Kramer is out," he said.

"Yes; he has been absent for some time."

"I declare it is almost three!" as if surprised. "It is an awful day out—rains cataracts. I—I have an umbrella in the building, Miss Brand, which I must give you to go home under; and—and," hesitating, "I believe you—you may—will you permit me to carry it for you?" The eyes of the girl fell, but her color rose.

"Does it rain so very, very hard?" faintly, without raising her eyes.

"Perfect cats and dogs; you never saw such a rain." Few had. Was there ever so blessed a rain? and were youth and maiden ever so grateful for a deluge in winter?

"I shall certainly await you at the front entrance; and it is now three." This quite settled it, and man's imperiousness was never less like tyranny. When he went, sun and warmth went with him. Alice could not write or even read the manuscript. It was clear the copy must wait; she looked to the door, walked about the room, put her sack on, and rolled a white cloud of something around her wealth of wavy golden-brown hair, and waited. Once the click of the door met her eager ear faintly, but it did not open, and she went and looked into the gloomy court, already prematurely dark, and, glancing about its walls, saw no lights in any of the windows. How still it was! The tide of hastening feet had ebbed from the corridors, dashed down the stairways, and divided into various currents, flowing away for the night; and already resounding booms, coming faintly from afar, indicated that the heavy doors were being closed. Shadows seemed to steal into the room. She would remain no longer. Frank might think she had gone another way; she stepped to the door, turned the knob, but it refused to open. She gave it a sudden and strong pull, but it had become a part of the wall—it was locked! A shudder just touched her, and, instinctively raising her eyes to the transom-light over the door, she saw that it had been covered with paper on the inside. She sprang to the door communicating with the large room, always closed—it, too, was locked! One moment her breath refused to come, the air darkened and the room swam. It was but for a moment. The girl who had not fainted in battle, who had felt a sort of frenzied ecstasy as the shots and shouts cracked and clangored about her, would not be easily deserted by her better self. One more breath came hard drawn, and with it the soul of her warrior father and the spirit of her Southern mother. She did not think—it flashed upon her. This was no accident, but preconcerted, and that flash lit up all the little points and dark ways of the past weeks, and she felt like a young lioness in the hunter's toils.

Deliberately she walked to the window and threw it up, and calculated the granite wall that fell sheer and dark below. She would not shriek or call. She went again to the corridor-door, and, seizing, shook it with all her strength. It scarcely made a noise, so nicely was it fitted. With a paper-weight she struck the resounding panels with all her force. Surely the watch, some messenger, laborer, belated clerk, or girl at chamber-work, would hear that; or were all sent away, or in conspiracy against her, to prison her in the heart of this granite castle? Then she looked about for means of barricading the doors, which opened inward, and then clasping her hands she sank on her knees, and committed herself to Heaven. As she arose, the knob of the door was turned with a force that resounded like the quick blows of a hammer, and then it was shaken with a violence that threatened to force it, and a loud, excited ringing voice called out: "Who is here? What is the matter?"

It was the voice and tone heard in the battle, in answer to her prayer.

"It is I—Alice Brand." The first word was loud and clear, the last faint and low. "I'm locked in here," and this was lost in a sob.

"Courage! courage! I'm Frank Warbel!" in a still excited voice, broken with a cheery gladness.

Frank, when he left the room, struck up "The Soul of John Brown," which in his exuberance he treasonably exchanged for "Dixie," and, after breathing out "Away down South in Dixie," found himself still on earth; and, whistling a more patriotic air, gained the doorway on Fifteenth Street, and was charmed to find the rain increasing. The clerks and messengers were already leaving the building, pausing in shrinking huddles on the margin of the flood, to adjust wraps, coats, and umbrellas, and then plunging out—or rather in. Frank sent a draggled colored boy to Fowler's stable on New-York Avenue, near by, for a carriage, and turned to watch and scan the crowd, as they came in flocks or singly. Once or twice he thought he saw Alice, but the crowd thinned, drizzled to single persons, then to lingering stragglers, and then ceased. It was growing dark, and he, too, heard the resounding doors. He grew impatient, and then suspicious. She had gone out another way, to avoid him. She had not said that he might attend her, nor even that she would come out at that door. All right. If she preferred to walk home in that rain alone—all right. But she had not gone; and, telling the coachman who had come at his call, to watch for any lady who might come out, and to say to her that he was to take her home—"Mind, a lady, Miss Brand," he dashed into the building through the long corridor, and flew up the darkened stairways to the chief's room. The transom-light was darkened and the room silent. Of course she had gone. His heart sank. Mortified, and his man's self-love wounded—half-angry, he sauntered slowly down the stairways, reached the lower floor, and had just turned toward Fifteenth Street, when half a dozen sounds, as of sharp blows, summoned him back. In a moment he was at the door, which, refusing to open, he shook in his impotent eagerness, and called out as above. Ere Frank could answer Alice, another step rapidly approached, and a voice roughly called out: "What the devil is the matter? what's going on here?"

"That's what I'm trying to find out," was the answer, spoken with decided spirit. "There's a young lady locked up here, it seems."

"What business is that of yours?"

"I've *made* it my business, Mr. Kramer!" haughtily answered Frank, who had discovered the chief in the dim light from the sky. "Miss Brand is inside."

"Oh, Miss Brand! Miss Brand! How could that have happened? Oh! I remember. I told her to remain, and forgot to come back, and I suppose the watch locked the door accidentally. I usually do some night-work here, and that's why I'm here now," fumbling with the key for its place of entrance. He was some time in finding it, and rattled at the lock for half an age, as Frank thought, before it yielded. Frank had his hand on the knob, and Kramer politely stepped back for him, as the guest. The door opened, and with a glad and broken "Thank God!" Alice sprang toward him. Frank eagerly drew her arm in his, and they started in unceremonious haste for the near stairway, now lit up from the open door of the room.

"Miss Brand—Miss Brand," said the chief, from the shadow, "I'm very, very sorry, that this—this—accident—"

"No matter, to-night," came back from Frank, halfway down the stairs. "The accident won't happen again." Slowly and uncertainly the poor girl stepped down. When the lower floor was gained, with a little gasp she would have fallen, but Frank took her lightly in his arms, and dashed through the now lighted lower corridor. As he gained the open door at the east front, the strong air revived her, and when he placed her in the carriage she was able to sit.

"Drive to Borum's as fast as possible!" cried Frank to the coachman, who little needed such an order on such a night.

"What a weak, cowardly thing I am!" said the half-revived girl, apologetically, "and I am as grateful and thankful to you as if I had been in real peril."

"Thank you," said the charmed youth. "Let me think that you really thought that you were in peril in the enchanted castle of an ogre, and that I broke the spell and rescued you. And you certainly had cause of alarm. If young maidens are wont to be locked up in that old granite Bastile, the matter ought to be looked into."

The young girl looked at him, to see what might be the real meaning of his words. But it was too dark to see his face.

"I've not felt very well for some days, or I would not have been so overcome at this little mishap," she said; for the fear that he could suspect that she had been the object of a design was very painful to her. She half felt that she had been breathed upon; had for a moment been under the wing of a nameless shadow, that had in some way soiled her.

The inspiration of Frank's presence and high spirit bore the brave girl up, and she almost sprang from the carriage as it stopped at Borum's. But, when she entered the lighted hall, noisy with the voices of the throng just from the dining-room, the lights whirled and darkened, and a moment's confusion ensued. Frank saw her on a parlor sofa, and dashed back up G and down Fourteenth to F, where, three or four doors below, was the office of Dr. Bland, a famous army surgeon, and now hardly a less famous physician, whose acquaintance he had made at the commencement of the war, and to whom he communicated on their way to the Borums' all he knew of the affair. The doctor found Alice quite herself in her own room, and comprehended the case—a fearful shock. He saw that one of her fine fibre needed rest and repose, and, with a careful examination—and nothing could be more invigorating and assuring than his manner—with some slight prescription, and a few words to anxious attendants, he left. On his way out, in the corridor, a querulous voice from an open door summoned him to another room, where, a smelling-bottle and bandaged head, and limp form extended on a bed, with two lady friends by her, lay Mrs. Thompson. Of course the first sight of the sinking Alice was notice to her to go into hysteria, but, as the appliances were not at hand, and attention was directed another way, the success was not encouraging. The presence of a doctor, however, was a needed help, and by the time he was leaving Alice she had reached a very satisfactory stage.

"Doctor," said the new patient, "I am a Biggs, and the Biggses—"

"I see you are," with his dark face growing darker; "and the Biggses are a very numerous family, with incurable ailments, which always come on at inopportune times," was his ready response.

"How you do understand my case, doctor! Will I git well, d'ye think?"

"The Biggses seldom die!" with marked disgust. Having placed his fingers on her skinny wrist: "Let me see your tongue—not the other end of it. It's a bad tongue; I think we will quiet it for a time, however," quite confidently.

"Yis, somethin' soothin' and quietin', doctor. How you do understand my case!"

And, with a hasty prescription, he left.

CHAPTER V.

THE DEFIANCE AND THE MEETING.

Frank Warbel was a warm-hearted, impulsive, proud, generous boy; a little sensitive, and inclined to take more than was intended, sometimes, which usually manifested itself in a silent, indifferent coolness, and he was not apt to inquire whether the hurt was intended. Once, quite early in the service, he hesitated to pass, with a part of a troop, a bit of brush and straggling trees; and the tone in the inquiry of his superior, for whose approach he lingered near the margin, seemed to imply censure, and Frank's reply was an order to charge. As the spurred horses dashed into the brush, the discharge of two light field-pieces, and the rattle of the supporting infantry, flashed in their faces, and a moment later five or six horses, with empty saddles, ran back. A bugle-clang, a white puff of smoke, a moment's mingle of yells, shout, and sabre-clash, and it was over. The Union support was at hand, and just beyond the abandoned guns Frank was found insensible, under his dead horse, severely wounded.

Until nineteen, his life was passed in the family of an uncle, in the beautiful village of Aurora, on the shore of Cayuga Lake. In his second year at Yale, the whole world was startled by the first gun at Sumter. In Frank's class, his best-loved, best-trusted friend, was Hampton Gordon, a brave, handsome, fiery Southron, of Frank's age. Both were favorites, resembled each other, and both had the same resolution. Each evidently championed the cause of his section; both were well informed, and both had the same fiery dash in argument and declamation, and each was the leader of his party. Many and fierce were their encounters, until the almost constant contest cooled their attachment, and at last, when the reverberation of the bombardment of Sumter reached and made the walls of Yale tremble, an open, fierce quarrel ensued, when the haughty young Southron told the equally haughty Northern that he would have an opportunity to meet him in the first battle, if the North dared face the South; and, after the manner of old chivalry, he dashed down a glove in token of defiance. Frank spurned it contemptuously with his foot, and answered back that he would not have to wait for him. The wag of the class picked up the glove, and, finding an old slipper, nailed them to an elm, near where the defiance was made, with an apt Latin quotation. Both left the college immediately—Hampton to hurry South, and Frank to enlist in the first company under the three months' proclamation. Before the expiration of that time, he became the member of a company of cavalry for the three years' service. Years elapsed before the pledged meeting took place—not until after Grant put impossibility between him and communication with Washington, crossed to the east side of the Mississippi, cut his own line, and invoked that fiery whirlwind of war that baffled Johnston and consumed Pemberton, at the bloody battle of Champion Hills; but, near nightfall, as Frank was aiding in gathering the Confederate wounded, on the ground of the hottest fight where he had been engaged, he passed a form in gray which he supposed to be lifeless. A moan drew his closer attention, and, raising the dying officer's head, he recognized his classmate. He placed his canteen to his parched mouth, and knew that he was recognized. "Frank," said the dying youth, with a faint smile, "I know the fault wasn't yours. I knew you would come. Tell my poor old uncle—" his head drooped over the supporting arm, and night came into the still-open eyes.

Frank had the mangled form tenderly cared for, and saw it as decently interred as the hurrying horrors of the war would permit, and carefully marked the place of burial. He took from his friend's person the miniature of the dead youth's mother, who, alone of her sex, held his heart. This, with his watch and sword, he soon afterward found means to forward to Hampton's uncle, of whom he knew at Washington. In the autumn following the war, he visited the capital, partly on the repeated invitation of Colonel Gordon, his friend's uncle, and partly to adjust his own accounts as a regimental commander, and to aid in the collection of the claims of his officers and men, and see the capital of the new republic.

He found Colonel Gordon a fine, manly bachelor; a

thorough Southern gentleman of the olden time; a little weak, but genial, full of quiet, sparkling ways, little fossilized bits of youthful spirits, and young-man notions, that forever linger in the air of a bachelor. He had been many years a resident of Washington, had once taken office under Taylor, adored Clay and Webster, those antipodes and enemies, was a friend of Senator Pierce, and a great admirer of Corwin; remained a Whig, read the *Intelligencer*, and practically sympathized with later Democracy. He could but remain by the Government in any hands; was almost heart-broken at the death of Hampton, who was his heir; and took an immense liking to Frank, and soon had a vague idea of subrogating him to the place and rights of his nephew.

He had a beautiful residence on Fourth Street, North, where he had elegantly-fitted rooms, in one of which he compelled Frank to install himself, with a place at his table, furnished from a neighboring restaurant. For Frank, nothing could be pleasanter or more fortunate; and his easy, pleasant manners and ways, the sparkle and vivacity of his conversation, extent of reading, and fine tastes, joined with his advantages of person, made him not only a very pleasant companion to the elder man, but one of whose companionship he was proud; and he was anxious to introduce him to the real Washington circles, than which none in America are more pleasant.

The discipline of the army and habit of command but overlaid Frank's naturally vivacious temper with a manly gravity, which hardly concealed its effervescence; while below, lay the quick, proud, sensitive spirit, ready at a moment to take control, regardless of consequences.

Thus far Frank had sedulously devoted himself to the accounts of himself, officers, etc., and was rapidly realizing the impossibility of getting things done. The vast arrears of all the accounting bureaus, weakly waging a losing war against a world of intricate accounts; the insufficiency and inefficiency of the department service; the constant interference of powerful Senators and members of the House, procuring cases to be taken up out of their order; or the more patent and scarcely less concealed causes that found openings in some bureaus; the swarms of rapacious and incompetent claim agents, whose ordinary weapons were fraud, false personation, forgery, and perjury—all together tended to render the accounting bureaus of that time scenes of the most extraordinary usages and abuses known to modern civil service. Not much of this did Frank know, and little of it did he suspect. He only knew that he constantly met delays, stoppages, and inertia.

The "stoppages" in quartermaster and ordnance accounts were more than marvelous; and "differences" accumulated beyond comprehension, and then as marvelously and incomprehensibly disappeared. In a sort of ironical despair, at the end of an ineffective day's wanderings and stair-climbings, through the departments, he declared to Colonel Gordon that "there was but one thing that any man had ever done the whole of, closed it out, and completed in Washington, in one day; and that was, to take a drink. But for that the facilities are wonderful to astute minds. Why, yesterday, your friend Morgan, rather at your suggestion, volunteered to aid me—to show me some of the 'short cuts,' as he called them, and how to come in on parties from unexpected approaches, through back-doors, and take them by surprise. Never was such a place for unexpected ways, back-doors, and unusual approaches, and never such a man in it. He found whiskey everywhere, in every room and corner—under stairs, in cupboards and boxes. He would go into the least likely of places, and find a bottle. From around behind doors he would bring one. He would turn over a board on the sidewalk, and bring up a bottle. I am obliged to you for suggesting his valuable aid; but, really, I can hardly profit by his researches," and more he ran on.

In the early forenoon following the incidents of the last chapter, he was surprised by a call from Kramer, and the coolness of his reception a little dashed the assurances of the caller. "I thought I would call, colonel, and explain the little incident of last evening, at the Treasury. I—"

"It's hardly necessary; no explanation is due to me. I thought you did explain to the lady, last evening," was the discouraging response.

"Yes; well, you see, that might not be satisfactory; and I thought I would—"

"State some other thing, perhaps?" with a touch of sarcasm.

"Well, not exactly that. You see I was taken a *leetle* by surprise last night, I must own," smiling.

"Apparently, we all were, a little," dryly.

"I called on Miss Brand this morning, and—" hesitating.

"She did not see you, of course?"

"No, she was ill; just a little shaken up, I suppose; and I came to you."

"Well, now, Mr. Kramer, did it never occur to you that the only thing to be said or done about this is to say and do nothing? I know of but three who know any thing about it; and I know the least of the three," with emphasis.

"I don't understand you."

"See if I can reach your apprehension. There is a lady involved, incapable of suspecting evil to herself till forced to. She was locked in your room, and wellnigh beat the door down; and yet no watch, messenger, or laborer, no servant, chambermaid, sweep, or room-cleaner, was in all that part of the building to hear it. They don't go at three, do they—all of them? and when you went back to your night-work," with emphasis, "you found a stranger at your door. Of course, it was an accident; but, was it known, the chief of that division would, doubtless, find an equally worthy field for his enterprise elsewhere? You can, I think, understand that. I shall not try to have you comprehend the considerations due to the young lady. The real object of this visit is to get from me, if you may, how I came to be at your room when this accident occurred. Well, sir, that was by the same kind of accident. *I went on purpose.* Beyond this, Mr. Kramer, your errand is likely to be 'the pursuit of knowledge under difficulties.' What I know is mine; what I suspect—you must be stupid, indeed, not to guess at. My regard for the lady will keep me silent. It remains to be seen what influence prudence has over you. Good-morning, Mr. Kramer."

No self-control, no assumed coolness, no swagger was equal to an indifferent air and manner on the part of Kramer, as he listened to this deliberately-pronounced *exposé* of the case. Once or twice he turned as if to go. But the sullen, hard look came into his face, and he truculently rejoined: "I ought to have arrested you last night; and I'll not be bullied. I don't scare worth a cent."

The face of the young man turned pale, and a little water came to his eyes; and, with a forward step, "Go, ere a vacancy occurs in your bureau;" and, without word or menace, Kramer withdrew.

CHAPTER VI.

DREAMS AND FLOWERS.

Late on that same morning, Alice awoke from a seemingly quiet sleep. When she came under the charm of the prescription, she fell off to slumber, and awoke from a dream that in some way lingered about her. She was in a rocky solitude upon a perilous cliff, over an impending chasm, from which there seemed no escape; and, as her terror grew extreme, a golden mist, with the perfume of flowers, came like a cloud about her feet, while above and around her the air was radiant with sun and filled with the notes of birds. She thought the cloud condensed and hardened, until it would sustain her, and, as she stepped upon it, she was borne away by it, when she awoke. As she languidly and reluctantly opened her eyes, Millie was standing by her, with a fresh and beautiful bouquet, having a single half-opened rose, whose virginal cup had just the glow of faintest color, surrounded with white camellias, and interspersed with mignonette and heliotrope. The wondering girl extended her hand for it, and dipped her face into its incense, and looked up to the attendant askingly.

"He brought it," was the response.

"He brought it? Who is he?" with a sparkle in her voice.

"Well, he told me not to tell—it was that handsome colonel, or general, or captain, who brought you home. I told him I'd tell."

"So you think he's handsome?" looking down. "What else did he say?"

"He wanted over 'n over to know all how you was;

an' I tole 'im; an' he said he'd come this afternoon an' inquire."

"Indeed! He takes liberties," again pressing his flowers to her face.

"'Course 'e do. I hope 'e will," was the laughing response.

Toward evening came a little, rather formal note, with Frank Warbel's compliments, who hoped she was quite restored; and he would be very happy, if her health permitted, to make personal inquiries the next morning.

"Say to him that I hope to be well enough to see him in the morning," was her answer.

The next day came, warm with sun and vapor over the muddy, reeking city; and, at the earliest allowable hour, Frank was shown into Alice's little parlor. She had many things to say, and, long the mistress of a large establishment, she was entirely secure in the propriety of receiving him in her only room, as a matter of course.

As the young man stepped in, he was just a shade embarrassed by the tallish, dignified, and beautiful woman, just at her earliest best, surrounded with the supports of her own home, that seemed almost grand and sumptuous, so rich did her presence make all her belongings, who now came forward so graciously to receive him. Was this the shrinking though brave Treasury girl, who had swooned in his arms, and whom he had actually borne through a long corridor? Warmly she came to where he paused, and gave him her hand with the frankness of her nature. "I'm so glad to see you; I intend to think how I can thank you," with a low, rich voice.

"If you knew how gladly I rendered the slight service, you would know how unnecessary thanks are," was the well-spoken answer.

"They are nevertheless due you," said the pleased

maiden; for she knew that the ardor of his words was not mere gallantry.

As they took seats, she remarked: "I believe the doctor said, last night, that 'confinement and bending over her desk all day had induced a vertigo, with which she was taken in her room.'" To which her visitor bowed, as quite decisive and satisfactory; and that was all the reference made by either to the incident of the evening before.

Was there ever any thing of it which transpired to the public? Something like an echo of something, somewhere, nobody knew what about, or whom; as when the half-awakened sleepers in a great house listen with the consciousness of sound in their ears of a distant footfall, the bang of a blind, the fall of a sash, or closing of a door by an air-current, on which, in the weird night they muse for a moment, with a half-startled sensation, and which succeeding sleep brushes forever from their memories.

"Colonel Warbel, are you a lawyer?" laying one hand on a small cabinet.

"If you want one, I am sorry I am not."

"I believe you were in the Vicksburg campaign?" after a little hesitation.

"I was."

"On the day that the rebels finally drew within their lines, there was just at night a little battle and skirmish between one of the Union advances and General Gardé's men, where he had temporary quarters."

"Near where Fort Brand was constructed, on the grounds of a beautiful residence?"

"Yes."

"I was there. The rebs lingered rather than made a stand, and we dashed upon them. I remember to have passed a carriage that they seemed to want to defend. The coachman was off, and the horses plunged fearfully."

"Yes. I was in that carriage, and—"

"You! you, Miss Brand, in that carriage?" interrupting her in amazement.

"Yes; that was on my own grounds; that was my residence; it came to me from my father and mother. You see, General Gardé had made my house his quarters, and, when compelled to retire, he was determined to take us— my aunt Thompson and myself—into the city; and I was more determined not to go. My father was a naval officer, and I had his notions about the flag," with emotion. "Resistance was useless; but my obstinacy delayed them until you came up."

"And you were under our fire—between two fires!" with a sort of scared bewilderment. "And you did not faint? And I was so near you then!"

"No, I didn't faint, but I was awfully frightened. Of course I got back to the house, and my servants returned." The young man with a kindled eye looked for a moment into the transparently deep eyes of the maiden. How wonderful is young faith in Providence! What romance it was to them, that their orbits had so strangely touched! The eyes of the girl fell, and the gaze of the youth was charmed.

"And Fort Brand was named for you?"

"For my father, I suppose. Our estate was called Magnolia." After a little pause she told how her people were scattered; her property, what the rebels had spared, was plundered and appropriated by the Union generals— the accumulated crops of two years, cotton, sugar, etc.; that finally, with the vouchers and papers given her by them, after making provision for mammy, her old nurse, and her husband, with Millie their niece, and Aunt Thompson, she made her way to Washington; and of the delay and disappointments there; and, after much difficulty, she had received a place in the Treasury—"which," she concluded by saying, "I have just given up." To which her visitor bowed, as if that was a matter of course. She handed Frank a bundle of papers as copies or duplicates of those received. His eye, practised with such papers, enabled him to take them in at a glance. "And so," a little depressed, "you are a great heiress?"

"I believe," as if she understood the feeling that inspired the remark, "that I am the poorest heiress in America. If I could only receive enough from all this to build me a little home, and gather up my poor, scattered people, and give them each a cabin, I should realize my only wish."

"Of course, these must be paid some time," holding up the vouchers.

"Will you take them for me, and put them into competent hands, Colonel Warbel? Something I must do." What a sweet trust and confidence were in her voice and manner—precious to him!

"Gladly—oh, gladly!" with a little impetuosity. "My friend Mason, who is an able lawyer, is in Congress, and Colonel Gordon will aid me to secure the best counsel in Washington; though I know something of the delays of the departments. But we will slay even these dragons," with a fine enthusiasm.

"What is this?" he said, after another overhauling of the papers, reading from a large sealed envelope—"'Rachel Withers's will.' Who's Rachel Withers?"

"That? oh, that is quite another matter. May I tell you of it? Though perhaps I ought to consult myself also. That is a secret of the dead—I fear a sad heart-history, of this poor Rachel, which involves my dear father also, and in some way refers to me." She then explained that her father, Edmund Brand, was a native of Connecticut; that she had old letters showing that there was an engagement between the two; that estrangement, for some act of hers, had separated them; and that her father sailed for the Mediterranean, where he met and very soon married her mother, etc.; that this Rachel, who must have died many years ago, was an heiress, and in her will gave to her some property situated in Washington; that just before her father's death one of the executors visited them, and brought this will; and it seems that others had bought or claimed the property, "and my father would have nothing to do with it, and said that I ought never to claim it. Indeed, I had forgotten all about it. I never read the will, and knew little about it."

"I think I will take it along with the rest, and have it looked into. It may be a clew to Kidd's money," smiling. "He probably buried as much up the Potomac as anywhere."

And then a little pleasant talk of little nothings, so delightful with those who find words the least interesting things of an interview whose great charm is mutual presence, which some words must make the continuance of possible. But ere long came a shuffling step and a querulous voice, when Alice sprang forward with—"My aunt Thompson!" to whom she presented her visitor. "Yis, you see, Colonel Wobble, though I'm a Biggs, she calls me her aunt; but she hain't got a drop of that blood." Which Frank thought a possible good thing for Miss Brand, notwithstanding the halo which she received from being that young lady's nominal relative. He was in that admirable frame of mind when a young lady's repulsive aunt becomes an object of tender interest to a young man so beautiful to behold. He heard all about "the Biggses" and many interesting details of the aunt's illness of two nights ago, and the invaluable discovery of a doctor who understood her case; which Alice bore with charming endurance, and which was prized by Frank, as it served to excuse his remaining beyond an already prolonged visit. The young people parted with the delightful mental assurance that there was an absolute necessity of their meeting often, and without reserve—so much important business, you know!

CHAPTER VII.

FRANK MAKES A FOOLISH SPEECH.

On the following morning Colonel Gordon accompanied Frank to the law-office of the Bardlaws, near the city hall. They found the senior at his table, banked around with papers of every imaginable form, shape, and age, in a confusion only equaled by the House of Representatives in its normal state. He was then the admitted head of the Washington bar, about sixty years of age, on whose large, well-modeled head the hair grew thin, with finely-cut, intellectual features, and a smouldering fire in a dark eye, and a form that still retained much of the strength and agility which distinguished his youth. Nothing could exceed the suavity of his ordinary manner, or his haughtiness when aroused—a thing not difficult to achieve. His learning, marked ability, and conceded integrity, gave him great influence with the courts, and secured him the confidence of his numerous acquaintances, while a large circle of friends held him almost in reverence. Colonel Gordon was among the first of this circle, and young Warbel was kindly received, and introduced to the junior Bardlaw.

Miss Brand's cases and claims were placed at once and unconditionally in the hands of the Bardlaws, who decided to request that the pending claims should be at once rejected in the departments, to enable a suit to be brought upon them in the Court of Claims; while, for the destruction of the homestead, relief should be asked of Congress.

Bardlaw, senior, examined the will with the utmost

care, and pronounced its execution valid to pass lands in the District of Columbia, and then read aloud the provision in favor of Alice Brand.

"*Item.*—I give and bequeath to the eldest daughter of Edward Brand, lieutenant in the Navy of the United States, and his wife Helen, *née* Craik, and to her heirs, all that certain piece of land, situate in the city of Washington and District of Columbia, known as Square No. 368 of said city plot: it being the same devised to me by my uncle, John Withers, by will duly recorded in the probate records of said District, and to which reference is had for a more particular description. And in default of such daughter surviving me, then my said executors are to dispose of said real estate, and to pay the proceeds to the American Board of Foreign Missions."

"Why, this property is now worth from three to five hundred thousand dollars! It is situate between M and N, northwest," consulting a map, "and between Ninth and Tenth, and much of it is marked as standing in the name of Rymer, one of the executors. With the establishment of two things, apparently, this property can be recovered —the proof of this will, and that Alice Brand is the daughter of Edmund and Helen Brand." Frank was dispatched to bring that young lady to the office, to aid in the consultation. A very pleasant errand he made of it, and a very favorable impression the young lady made for herself on her admiring counsel. She said that, as she understood, she was born abroad; that her mother survived her birth but a few days; and that, within the year following, her father married a cousin of her mother, who, with other friends of her mother's, was of the same party; and that her father and step-mother returned to the United States when she was about three years old; that she knew of no survivor of this party. Her step-mother died some ten years ago, before which time her brother had removed to Texas, and had not been heard from. All the others were dead, except her nurse and her husband, who accompanied her mother to Europe, and who she supposed were still on the plantation near Vicksburg, which was called Magnolia.

In answer to questions, she said that her family records, with many papers, placed in a box to be shipped up the river, with other effects, had never arrived, nor had she ever obtained any clew to them.

The names, and a full description of her nurse and her husband, were taken, with the place where they might be found.

Upon an examination of the District record, the Rachel Withers will was found recorded, with two witnesses only, and it appeared that John Rymer had declined the office of executor, which was accepted by Reuben Williams, whom Alice remembered as the man who was at Magnolia. A further examination disclosed that Rymer had procured various quit-claim deeds from the alleged heirs of Rachel Withers of said square, and that he had sold several lots to various parties; from all of which the experienced Bardlaw inferred that this was a scheme by which the claim of Alice, if ever made, was to be in some way defeated, though it was not apparent to him how it could succeed, as he declared that "its ingenuity was not at all equal to its depravity." And at the same time a pretended sale of the property under the will would obviously be for a nominal sum, and thus defraud the legatee.

The junior Bardlaw undertook in person to go in pursuit of the nurse and her husband. Inquiries were made in Connecticut for witnesses to prove the will. Notices were given to the occupiers of the square, and suits in the old form of ejectment—John Doe *vs.* Richard Roe—were commenced. A petition was filed in the Court of Claims for nearly five hundred thousand dollars *vs.* the United States, and General Mason took charge of a memorial and bill in the House of Representatives, and within a week all the important steps had been taken; the Bardlaws advancing the funds necessary to meet the initiatory charges.

What a week that was to Frank! How many times he had to call on Alice, and with what quiet, cheerful grace and warmth she always received him, and forgave the alleged annoyance of his call! Of course it was all business. It is true that, under the direction of Mr. Bardlaw, Frank had been constituted her "true and lawful attorney in fact," irrevocably; but somehow he could do nothing, even under the advice of Mr. Bardlaw, without consulting his principal. And now the suits were commenced; and really, save to talk it all over and over, there was no excuse for calling. The young people were not a little surprised to find how many things, tastes, likings, and antipathies they had in common; and Frank had quite the usual way of looking into Alice's eyes, and she had the old way of avoiding his gaze. Then he could not forget that she was a great heiress, and once he was so imprudent as to utter the thought, and a good deal more, and mischief came of it. They had been summing up the chances of success, and Frank had quoted the last and fullest assurances of Mr. Bardlaw, and, closing the case out conclusively, he relapsed into a pensive silence. At length, "And so you see, you are a great heiress," as if it was a thing to be deplored.

"Well?" was the interrogating response of the heiress.

"Well, then I shall not dare to—to love you."

He was standing, and as he spoke he turned and walked toward a window, his voice falling into broken murmurs, agitated by an emotion which he could not control. He was frightened with the unnatural sound, and more by the burden which it involuntarily conveyed. He stood by the window a moment, and when he turned back his face was pale and a moisture was in his eyes. When he raised them again to Alice's face, she too looked very grave, though her eyes were averted. He thought that he had offended her, and, approaching her with an almost abject respect—"Forgive me, Miss Brand, I know my folly must offend. It was not premeditated."

"It was a foolish speech, Mr. Warbel," was the reply; and, however deeply offended, she managed not to betray it in her voice or manner the least bit.

"Forgive me, and I will not repeat it," in a voice scarcely less agitated than that which had uttered the folly. Alice looked up surprised. Frank silently bowed, and went out. It is possible that they parted with just a shade of misapprehension, if not misunderstanding. When next the young man sent up his card, Millie was directed to show him into the Borum parlor, and in some way the air of constraint which the possibly now conscious maiden brought with her into the room may have deepened it, and admonished the young man that the day of unquestioning confidence and freedom of approach had disappeared. His call was short and his manner constrained, and his departure quite unexpected to both, perhaps.

CHAPTER VIII.

TEAZER AND TWEEZER.

Teed and Tazewell—Timothy Titus Teed and Thomas Tazewell—Tweed and Teazle, Teazer and Tweezer, or Tweedle-Twaddle, as facetious opponents or envious rivals occasionally designated the firm, occupied no common place in the needs and economies of the capital. The senior of this alliterative firm was found several years ago already established in it, " practising law and its kindred Christian vices," as with nice accuracy and a proper appreciation of words he defined his calling. " Not attractive in person, but with winning ways," as he said of himself; broad and high-shouldered, with frouzy red hair, bristly beard, and nose with an upward tendency, he yet had some learning and much acute vigor, with a coarse, robust way of putting things, made pungent at times with a rude, irreverent wit. Without a nice appreciation of morals, and sometimes forgetful of statute law, and a tendency which gravitated to the vicious side of a case, and which usually excluded him from one destitute of such elements; shrewd, artful, and full of resources, with no limit to expedients but the limit of invention, and none to effort but the bounds of ability, the field of his professional labors was both wide and fertile, in a capital full of the seeds and rank growths of the droppings and plantings and sproutings of all the corrupt hands of the republic, in the national hot-bed and stimulating atmosphere. With him, a favorite method of supply was to purchase. " When a fellow wants a thing, why, let him buy it. That's the way. Then he has it;" and the knowing ones had a notion that he was as ready to sell also.

He had an idea, also, that any thing could be bought through the two Houses, " with money enough, you know."

On the day after service of process in the ejectment cases, the chief of the T. firm, in his especial office—one of several rooms on F, between Thirteenth and Fourteenth— was approached by his valued client Rymer, with a more lugubrious, saintly expression than usual. Long rather than tall, long, dark, cadaverous face, with lank, black hair, and an habitual expression, which epitomized the New-England catechism and the whole duty of man, with an added tinge of the final doom of the ungodly, on the present occasion.

"Well," said Teed, without other greeting, "what's up now?"

"All's up!" with hollow voice, rolling his eyes up, and throwing the declaration and summons on the table.

The quick eye of Teed ran over the papers, and a smile hovered on his lips and died under his beard.

"Yes, I should think pretty much all was up. That will has turned up, and an heiress has come up, and you have gone up—unless you come down—with about a hundred and fifty thousand dollars!"

The pallor of the cadaverous face became ghastly.

"God's will be done!" with solemn resignation.

"Rachel Withers's will is likely to be done. The other party seldom manages to have His way."

This irreverent speech went unrebuked. Rymer had momentarily ceased to take even an interest in the honor of God.

"This all comes of your infernal stupidity," said Teed, deliberately. "If I owed the executive of the Brimstone Republic ten tons of pure fool, he'd take you in full, and pay back the difference in an orthodox church. Now, see here. You and Rube Williams were executors—two Down-Easters. The estate was large, and this Capitoline Square was to be the plunder. You settled the rest according to law, and paid over, and thought no suspicion would be attracted to this muddy, straggling town, that no Yankee would at that time have given a thousand dollars for. The law of this District requires that a will, to pass real property, must have three attesting witnesses. You had it recorded in Connecticut, with only two, and probated it here in the same way. Your plan was to impose, by this trick, on the devisee, who could not recover on such a title, appear to sell it for a song, or rather a psalm, and sing that yourself, and explain to the missionary board that nothing could be got for the land by reason of this defective title. You declined the trust as executor, so that you might purchase. Rube held the will, and was to share in the plunder. You did not account to him, and he moved the Withers heirs, and you had to buy them off. Rube went to Mississippi, and, as certainly as the world, left that will with the Brands."

"God forbid! That cannot be!" in the same solemn voice. "He went directly to New Orleans, and died of the cholera, and all his papers and baggage were lost. I followed him directly to New Orleans myself, and found it all out. Mr. Bardlaw told me that they could recover on this will with two witnesses, because I bought under it, and would be stopped from denying the sufficiency of it."

"Psh-h-aw! If you were d——d fool enough to go to him, he ought to tell you so, and you ought to believe it. I say to you that the trick of two witnesses was infernally shallow at the best, for, if the devisee under the will should exercise the least skill, she could undoubtedly prove that there was another, even in the absence of the will itself. But I'll wager a fig against your head, and so make an even bet of it, that Bardlaw now has that will, and, of course, he can prove its execution. That may be assumed. What more is there? What other points? Well, he must prove that this Alice is the daughter of Helen Craik, of course. You told me, when you found that she was in Washington, that you had yourself gone to Vicksburg, and that she was an only daughter; that her father and mother were dead, as were the parents of her step-mother, and that her step-mother's brother removed to Texas before the war; but that you found her nurse and her husband on the old estate. What has become of them? My agent at Vicksburg has instructions, if any thing happens, to take them to Memphis. That was two years ago, and I've not heard from him for a long time."

"Well, there is no time to be lost. Means must be found to approach La Belle Brand, and get from her where

3

these witnesses are, now. Why in thunder, when you found this young lady was here, didn't you buy out her claim, and so end it at once?"

"Well, I was sure she knew nothing about it, and when, as time passed, she made no claim, I was confirmed in it."

"There is something in that," reflectingly. "Bardlaw has got the will, but, if he cannot find the witnesses to prove her birth, we'll sweat him awfully, and make terms perhaps. What do you know of this Miss Brand?"

"Oh, she's a young woman—was in the Treasury."

"In the Treasury? I don't understand. There is some devilish mystery about it. So she's in the Treasury, eh?"

"She has resigned," with a groan and upward roll of the eyes.

"The devil!"

"There's a providence in it," solemnly. "God have mercy!"

"Because you cheated the heathen that perish, out of the Word?" with mock severity; "you let 'em slide."

"No, Teed. I gave of the proceeds and profits of that venture into the treasury of the Lord—yea, interests and profits, into the treasury of the Lord," unctuously.

"And, what is more, you looked in person to the application of the fund, as the rule sometimes is. I think He ought to be satisfied. It must be the other one who is getting up this providence. Well, who else is about this young lady?"

"A young sneak by the name of Warbel, as near as I can find out. He must have put her up to it."

"I hope he is a sneak. You love him like a Christian, and probably overstate his virtues. Anybody else?"

"Yes, an aunt by the name of Thompson, a widow."

"Bully! Why, Rymer, it brightens. You've been busy to some purpose. What'll you give to have this title made perfect?"

" Twenty-five thousand dollars ! "

" Twenty-five thousand fiddlesticks ! Quadruple it, with an additional fifty thousand dollars for fees contingent."

" Oh, God save my sinful soul ! " in despair.

" Can't do it. You mortgaged it to the devil as soon as you were of age, and any little equity of redemption, under any scheme of atonement, was foreclosed long ago."

" Oh-h-h-h ! " whether at the spiritual or financial prospect, was the only response to this cheerful view.

" Come, ten thousand as a retainer, ten thousand to begin on—and mum—mum as the grave—and eighty thousand when wanted to complete the purchase, and fifty thousand for fees. Is it a bargain, old Shadrach, Meshach, and Abednego, frying in one ? "

" Oh-h-h-h ! " with closed eyes, when, without a word, Rymer turned, and, with protesting hands to heaven, strode gloomily out.

After he went, a long, emphatic whistle conveyed off the surplus vim, still unexpended, which the interview had generated in Teed; and, taking out his watch—
" Thunder ! it is almost two—when I am to meet Ward, and perhaps Le Grand. Well, the old muff, doubtless, thought he was telling me a good deal of news; and it was a wonderful intellectual feat for him to pick up. Twenty thousand will do to begin with; and we want it badly."

CHAPTER ·IX.

THE HEART OF MIDLOTHIAN.

It was in the block on the avenue, between Thirteenth and Fourteenth; and, like many another heart, beat high at times, or ran low; was lonely, or tumultuously thronged, up on the second floors of many and divers buildings, with many open and covered approaches to it, while the mingled world of craft and intrigue, of plotters and politicians, of fashion and folly, sent its unconscious meeting, eddying and hurrying tides along the lower walks—innocent of its existence. Jewelers and cigar-shops, wine-saloons and milliners, picture-dealers and bazaars of fashion, received, and gave forth. Customers came, and priced, and gossiped; and went, and came again with more gossip; and men loafed and lounged; and young dandies, with red kids and small canes, posed and stared at ladies who fluttered and flirted with, and flattered the thoroughfare of lovely afternoons. And doctors, and dentists, and lawyers, and agents, had offices; and artists had studios; and all pushed their callings as elsewhere; and, amid them all, the unknown, mysterious heart beat on.

Here was an elegantly-fitted saloon, in quiet tones and colors, with roulette and faro, card-tables, and all the nameless appliances for chance and art. But the brindled lord of the jungle is not fought with here. Such contests were carried on behind green doors, up near Fourteenth, with his fashionables; or down below Seventh, with his roughs. These were for pastime, seemingly. Adjoining it was a spacious dining-room, where tables were constantly spread with choicest viands; and gentlemen came and went, ate and drank at pleasure, lounged into a reading-room, and smoked, or read, or talked, without question or price. All the appointments were in exquisite taste; many fine pictures hung on the walls, and busts and statuettes on mantels and brackets. The attendance was in keeping; and usually an air of well-bred quiet—not American—pervaded the whole. Many gentlemen, when about to leave the place, signaled their exit by losing a ten or twenty on the red or black—the only money return ever permitted. There were other rooms, seemingly connected with these by labyrinthine passageways, in some of which many clerks wrote, figured, and posted books, and to whom came messengers through still other entrances. There were other apartments, voluptuous and warm, with color and art, rich carpets and luxurious sofas, couches, mirrors, curtains, rare plants, and flowers, with nude female figures, rich in tint, or sensuous in marble.

At about the centre of the block, a broad, open stairway led up to the second floor, on the right of which was a large room occupied with desks; at these desks were busy clerks, in the rear of this two more, sumptuously furnished, with entrances leading to the net-work of veins and channels which connected the many rooms already referred to. In the last of these two was Ward, with whom, as we remember, Teed had an engagement. A handsome man, and a gentlemanly as Americans use the term, something there was in his air, not stopping at self-assertion, but just a tinge of the aggressive: the faintest shadow of a challenge, as if, " Try me if you doubt who I am," well dressed, or rather well clothed—the American barbarian taste for clothes—and there was a diamond cluster on the shirt-front, and a slightly-exaggerated ring on the left little-finger, and a chain whose weight was a little emphatic, almost loud, and the toes of his boots were narrow, almost pointed. His stride about the room was nearly with a suspicion of a swagger, and in speech his voice just out-topped the well-bred tone. His statements were usually reliable, with a margin for exaggeration. Few common things ever happened to him, and he was not always happy in his information; confidential he often was, and his confidence was impressive. Every thing he did was just the least overdone, and the breath of a breeze always waited on his movements. He came from the West: no region of the world could have produced him but the West of the

United States, so large is she; although her growth is so rapid, she must long remain young, and her men will long retain some of the gushes, the tastes, ways, and habits of the quite young man of ardent impulses, self-assertive, free, fearless, a little aggressive, and loud. Her travelers have made the American name abroad; her writers give a tone and spirit to literature, just discovered to be American; her sons can arise to a real refinement. They become raiders, masters of the plains, river-gamblers, desperadoes, as their paths lead them; and in each and all there is just a tone of exaggeration, when measured by the accepted standard of the world.

Ward had antecedents, plenty of them; had been tumbled and knocked about the world, till he was truly, for his sort, many-sided; not polished by books and colleges, not starting on or seeking high ground, but content in the common ways, in which he was thoroughly educated, and in which he was among the first—not self-sacrificing, and not given to postponing his interests to others, but coolly calculating all: his word once given, it could be relied upon. He was always in at the organization of new Territories: quite a calling, and in skillful hands it pays. Had been a delegate from one or two, where every election was always contested, and the case never ended until the end of Congress, when both parties drew pay and mileage all comfortably; and this was also a calling. He understood the laws of preëmption, squatter sovereignty; was profound in the lighter science of jumping claims; had been head man to discover and bring forward new Indian delegations; knew, as well as any one man can, the depths—the depths which lie below all other depths in the Indian Bureau; had speculated largely in Western mail contracts; knew all the prominent public men, all their ways and weaknesses; understood the whole process of running a Secretary of the Treasury without his suspecting it; was familiar with Washington life, and all the back stairways of approach and retreat; was master of the lobby, and knew the full force and scope of the indirect means of reaching members of the two Houses, and seldom used any other. No exposure ever followed any of his enterprises: everybody felt safe, and, in all the indirect ways of doing good things, he had the confidence of all who sometimes walked therein. He enjoyed a certain open consideration, could always gain access to the President and Secretaries, and was trusted by some of them; could always approach senators, and was on intimate terms with many prominent members of the House; could be silent, was discreet and prudent, with all his little, breezy ways; even his silence was emphasized, and his confidence exaggerated to darkness.

There was just an air of disquietude in the open brow of Ward as he paused and almost jerked out his watch. "Two," and the door opened to the senior Teed. At once confronting him—" See here, now, Teed, I don't like this colored bounty business at all. I never did, and the more I look at it the less I like it."

" Can't you trust Leibenthal? "

" Trust the devil! The man is a renegade Jew: I wouldn't trust any man in this. I wouldn't do it myself."

" What's up now? Le Grand—"

" I know; he'd light his cigar in a powder-house! I understand Baker is snuffing about something already."

" Buy him."

" Buy him! That's your one way unless a man is to be got rid of, and then it's ' Knock 'im.' Of course, you can buy him, and sell yourself, in the same trade. Just when every thing is ripe, in he'd come and arrest the whole of us; and then he'd go to Stanton and make his report, and lay down the money paid him, all marked with some of your T's."

" Did a people ever groan under such an intolerable

despotism? Shall we never be rid of this Baker?" exclaimed Teed.

"'Tis too bad," said Ward, ironically; "a free people, with a speculative turn of mind, ought to be left at liberty to cheat and defraud a few hundred thousands of colored soldiers, by the innocent pastimes of perjury and forgery, certainly."

"It pays, or will. Just think, we shall soon have forty-five thousand names, each entitled to one hundred dollars bounty, which is four million five hundred thousand dollars; and the costs of getting up the papers and all expenses are less than fifteen dollars in each case. Why, Leibenthal works off over one hundred a day in New Orleans alone, and don't use more than a dozen niggers for them all! The risk is next to none, even for him, while we can never be connected with it."

"I don't like it. The first you'll know, one of Baker's men will appear and personate some of the claimants, and then go and wash off. It will be the raid on the bounty-jumpers over again. It will blow up, and I ain't ready to go up. What's new in La Belle Brand's case? I confess that don't look much better."

"What the devil's in you to-day, Ward?" and, ringing a bell, Teed ordered the servant to bring a bottle of Hume's best Stag, which was soon before them, contributing its inspiration to their deliberations.

"Old Rymer-whiner-gospel-whanger-banger has just left me, and will pay fifty thousand; ten thousand dollars in hand, and—"

"Only fifty thousand dollars! I won't touch him; every thing about it and him is ugly and mean. Fifty thousand, indeed!"

"Well, as it has to be fought out in court, I'm to have fifty thousand dollars at the end, for my fee, under stipulations," responded Teed.

"Take the whole, and have the whole. Turn the whole in; make it one hundred thousand dollars, and I'm with you. We may be able to appropriate half or two-thirds of the claims, someway," said Ward.

"What does Le Grand say?" asked Teed.

"Oh! he's seen La Belle, and is in raptures. Poor thing! I'm sorry for her. He'll have her heart out of her bosom in a week."

"He may play to keep, and so take land and swag," answered Teed.

"Not as long as Marie is here. He may take—others may keep."

"Something hangs somewhere, with Madam Marie. Senator Joseph, whom you canonized Saint Joseph, don't come to time. He's never made that report yet."

"Never mind, madam's all right and so's the saint; a vast gain on the first gentleman of that name; but, as I understand this thing of the Brands, what are we to do for the one hundred thousand?"

"We are to get the money, for the principal thing; and I've promised to secure the title for it. Of course, we'll do this if we can; and do Rymer, any way. The principal thing will be to secure from Miss Brand a quit-claim of her rights. The will is undoubtedly in existence, and must be got from her, or this young Warbel, or Wobble. This will be our work here."

"Yes. Le Grand and I went over with this. Croly is to take Warbel in hand, with other help—madam, for instance—and he is to be disposed of, out of the case, anyway. Kramer is white-mad with him, and would have him, in some dark alley on the Island, run his head against a slung-shot."

"Why not?" asked Teed.

"Well, he's more useful alive; besides, it's an ugly thing, and the time is coming when such a thing would be looked into. He has friends—now. I am sorry for him. There ain't a finer fellow in Washington, and he may die hard; but must go. There's another thing: we are to take possession of Belle Alice and all her surroundings; and there's a weak-eyed, stringy, middle-aged aunt, some sort of a widow, vain and silly, whom some one must win; and I've thought of you, Mr. Teazer. Now, you're not a beauty; but you have 'winning ways,' as you say."

"Court your own widows, Mr. Wheezer!" dryly.

"I've two or three wives now—I don't know exactly the number," was the rueful answer.

"Good God! not all here, I hope?"

"None of them here," with an air of satisfaction.

"Then Croly is to go for the colonel," said Teed, musingly. "She'll have him in a week; and I'll have that will in a month, or you may call me any thing that begins with a T. I rather envy him, too," appreciatively. "How goes the pardon-business; is Tredgar through?"

"Tredgar hangs fire; but the President has promised Croly that, as soon as the parties pay her the stipulated price for the Chicago whiskey case, he will order the pardon to be made out. She claims seventy-five thousand dollars, one-half of the whole fee. It was an outside arrangement with her, though we helped it on; and, as some of the same parties who carried that were in this, Tredgar must wait. We sent off by express, the other day, one hundred —C. O. D.—at from one hundred to five hundred dollars each. Just now, we do every thing in this line through the Croly. The President is fascinated with her—virtuous Executive of a pure people—it was only two days ago that he debarred Mr. Corwin from all the executive departments, because the old man received five hundred dollars for procuring a pardon that he took proof in, and worked at a month. This thing won't last always, Mr. Tweed, nor will the Croly always be in feather—more's the pity!"

"Somebody said that the he-Croly had come on to look after his mate," remarked Teed.

"Well, he's only a brevet, to give her a name, and account for any thing that may happen," replied Ward. "She has her office, a suite of rooms in the Avenue, while he's quartered elsewhere. You see, as soon as old Gordon finds our gay young colonel snuffing about, something will be said—you'll see; and then, as the devil will have it, there is a sort of broken-down lieutenant, a dealer for McCarty, who once served with Warbel: and every thing will work to a charm. Poor, innocent-looking devil! it would be a great deal pleasanter for him, no doubt, to win these cases—for he's created attorney in fact, for Miss Brand—and thus win the heiress. But other and paramount interests and claims intervene, and it can't be helped. She'll be ready for any thing and anybody in a few months. But these color-bounties, and everybody and thing connected with them—"

A servant brought in a card, and Teed took himself and a full glass of whiskey off together.

CHAPTER X.

ST. ARNAUD HEARS MR. DRYBOW.

SARDOU'S, on Fifteenth, above New-York Avenue, was then, as now, a famous resort. A dinner at Sardou's, at his best, was an event in a common life, and a lunch an unusual occasion to many.

His ordinary dispensations were luxuries, and the low in finances sought him not out, while his higher productions were to ordinary mortals those special providences, to be followed, if not with fasting, coarser prog, and humiliation.

On this same afternoon, posed against a mantel, at Sardou's, in that case of Nature the result of long-studied art, was a male figure, that many women and some men would spontaneously turn to for another glance.

Slightly above the ordinary height, moulded within the easy lines of manly grace; with one of those poetic faces, irregularly-regular features, of striking contour; dark, wavy hair, with large, dreamy eyes as they looked now, but which had the power of falling like a weight on one; the whole arranged with negligent faultlessness, in the prevailing style, save the lower limbs, which had too many reasons to avoid the abominable baggy peg-top pantaloons of that day, and which threaten us again. Rather English, in its severe simplicity, was his dress; no rings, chains, or anything metallic, save the diminutive studs. At first, you would call him young; on a close study would only say that he was not old. He stood alone, in the dreamy, contemplative manner of an Oriental, when possibly every faculty, trained to its utmost power, was only in ambush, awaiting an approach.

It was St. Arnaud, the reigning sensation of the more exclusive official Washington circles. He came very quietly in advance of Congress, and took possession by right. He brought no credentials or letters, and nobody thought of asking him for any. President, secretaries, senators, and the nigher magnates, found him on seemingly easy terms with the foreign legations, and deemed his acquaintance a valuable acquisition; and the legations, seeing him received by the highest officials, regarded his status as fixed; and so it was. Is there another capital in the world where a man can so invariably pass at his assumed value? His air and manner warranted his acceptance, and so admirable were they, that a wooing solicitation seemed to make approaches to his almost coy diffidence. He spoke all the languages, and English with just a shade of Continental accent, at times.

Little whispers were running in the air about him; he was with Bazaine and Maximilian in Mexico; had had adventures with the bandits in Greece; had served in the army of the Viceroy of Egypt; had been with Garibaldi; had wandered with the Bedouins; had rescued the passengers from a burning steamer on the Danube; had witched the Austrian emperor with his matchless horsemanship; had, finally, come to turn the heads and hearts of all the women at the court of the great and still unhappy republic. Young ladies would see a new style; young America, a better bearing and manner; new and charming dances, brought from nobody knew where, would become all the rage; and yet, although the holidays were passed, and the season well opened, and the flower-strewn ways invited him, with houries beckoning, and allurement and opportunity waiting on him, the chevalier had hardly met his destiny.

He tarried and lingered, mused and dreamed. It was said he was on a secret mission; was composing a poem; was merely observing the Americans; that he was so immeasurably above them, that he refused to mingle with them; that he had a heart-history, and ladies could see dim shadows of a tragedy in his dreamy eyes, and dark hints of a nameless crime, which was no crime save to tender souls, which chained him within the shadow of its memory; and much more.

"Ah, chevalier—glad to meet you!" in the cheery voice of a gentleman who approached him.

"Colonel Gordon!" as if starting from a dream, or reverie, with a half drawl. "It gives me pleasure."

"What do you say, chevalier—it's latish for lunch, and early for dinner—will you join me in a compromise? Sardou can do something for us."

"Ah! I understand that, when an American gentleman proposes a dinner, or that sort of a thing, he assumes the place and responsibilities of a host. Permit it to be the other way, or in English fashion, and nothing would give me more pleasure," graciously.

"I am the elder, and resident of Washington; I really must claim to dispense its hospitalities." The chevalier bowed. As the colonel was about to summon a servant, another, a tallish, saturnine man, sauntered in with the sort of interrogating air and look of one inquiring for something, and which was usual with him. "Ah, here comes Drybow, one of the real Washington characters, rude and cynical. You will hardly know the capital, without his acquaintance," said Gordon.

"It will give me much pleasure, I'm sure."

"Hallo! Æsop!" exclaimed Gordon, approaching Drybow, " how are you? What are you looking for?"

"Not for a man certainly, here," running his eye over the two gentlemen, and continuing in a low, rather irritating voice; "and I don't see what I was not looking for, either."

"Ha—ha—ha! Not bad. Let me introduce you to the Chevalier St. Arnaud," and, turning to that gentleman, he presented them. Drybow advanced without bowing, and, looking St. Arnaud a little sharply in the eye, gave him his hand, which the latter took cordially. "Perhaps I ought to apologize for my last remark," said Drybow, "but I won't till I'm certain."

"Don't—don't—my dear sir," said the chevalier, with a little laugh, "and by that time we shall both have forgotten it." The manner of this little speech was quite charming.

"We were about to order dinner," remarked the colonel; "and I'm sure we should both be pleased if you would join us."

"Most assuredly," graciously from the chevalier.

"Well, gentlemen, I seldom or ever eat any thing; but, if I do, it is just at this time of day," was the assenting response.

"Your usual answer," laughingly replied the colonel.

On taking their seats in the room assigned them, and having settled the bills-of-fare—"Drybow," remarked the colonel to St. Arnaud, much as if that gentleman were absent, "is the most useful and valuable man in Washington. There is nothing he can't do, or help you to do, from getting up a speech for a non-fertile member of Congress, writing a state paper or report, to getting at a state secret, and writing up or down an administration measure." Drybow—or, as he would naturally be called, Dry, Old Dry, or Long Drought, as was sometimes the case—though a man of real and varied ability, and who had, without special effort, always managed to miss the position where his talents would be most available to himself, was nevertheless quite aware of his powers, and not averse to hearing them extolled, even in the exaggerated form of Colonel Gordon. Indeed, the colonel's statement was about his own estimate of his capacity. The compliment, conveyed in badinage, was so much of course, that he neither acknowledged it, nor did he make any remark in response to it.

"I have observed," said St. Arnaud, "that a few heads contain all the brains. Possibly, there were not enough for all, and so Providence placed them in nuggets, as in this instance," with a bland smile to Dry. "I am fortunate in meeting him, and hope, ere we part, to learn something of your capital, its real life and ways, which a long and close observer only knows, and which rarely find a place in books, even."

During this little speech, Dry regarded the chevalier with an earnestness that might have annoyed a less-collected man, and, at its close, dropped his head about a hair's-breadth, in token of entire approval of its justice, and not without the idea that its author would not be wholly disappointed.

"By-the-way, Dry—about that awkward little matter in the House. How happened it? I believe you're the only one who can explain it," and turning to the chevalier. "Two gentlemen of the House, and both from the same State, within four weeks of each other, delivered identically, *ver-batim*, the same speech—ha, ha, ha!" in which even the Drought joined.[1]

"Do you state that seriously, though?" asked St. Arnaud.

"It actually occurred," asserted the colonel.

"Impossible!" was the response.

"Nothing is easier in the world," remarked Dry. "The only wonder is, that it ever was detected. It must have been by the proof-reader of the *Globe*. You see, Chevalier, that every American-born can edit a newspaper and make a speech. And in the House, every man must, at the least, make or deliver one for the honor of his district, and secure his reëlection. Days are set apart for buncombe, as it is called, when the members who must speak are accommodated, and as nobody hears them, and few read them, so nobody could tell whether a given speech was made or not."

"I see how that might occur. But I don't quite see how two very honorable men could hit upon identity of matter and words, for a whole speech."

"Not unless both were inspired by the same oracle—bought of the same shop," added the colonel.

"And the stock was low, or a mistake made in the goods. It didn't matter much in this instance," said Dry. "The gentlemen were both Democrats."

"Mr. Drybow is a radical," remarked the colonel, "and

---

[1] This occurred in the Thirty-seventh Congress.

this speech was about as odious to the Republicans as it could well be."

"It undoubtedly did good," was Drybow's cloudy response.

"I thought I should meet Colonel Warbel here," remarked Gordon, "and he may yet come—you would both like to make his acquaintance."

"I've seen him," replied Dry; "and was much pleased with his appearance. I believe he led the charge when Hancock gobbled up Bradley Johnson's whole division in the Wilderness. Have you adopted him, colonel?"

"Not quite that; but I never met a young man who interests me so much," said the colonel.

"What is it about the newly-discovered heiress that I hear so much of everywhere?" asked Drybow.

"That she's an heiress; very rich and more beautiful and more good than beautiful," cried the colonel, with enthusiasm.

"'*More* good' is rather good," remarked Dry; "of course it will end with a wedding."

"I hope so;" and then fish and soup; and then substantials; then dessert, wine, and Havanas; and then more talk.

The chevalier asked Dry, "What would be the come-out of the threatened war between the President and the radical Republicans?"

"The colonel here is a great admirer of the President," he answered, "and can tell more of his intentions. The fact is, he was the Vice-President, and it is a law of human conduct that, when one leaps by indirection to the high seat of another, who reached it by the course of Nature, he is, really and essentially, a usurper, and falls under the law of usurpation, and as much so as if he achieved it by conspiracy; and when did a usurper ever take up the policy and keep about him the adherents and friends of the dethroned monarch? It is not in nature. A Vice-President is apt to think that it was a blunder that he was not elected President, and only exposes the blunder of electing him a Vice. Of course, war must ensue, and, as the President is a determined, obstinate man, the war will go on until he is crushed out. With power to change the Constitution, there is nothing on earth that can withstand the Republicans but their own feuds and follies. Of course, leaders are always enemies, and the Republican chiefs are no exception."

"There is another strong, perhaps controlling influence with the President. He was of low birth, in a slave country. Now, chevalier, all aristocracies originated in a savage or barbarous state, and they are never plucked up until the people among whom they grew are rooted out. Of all the aristocracies, slaveholders are the meanest and most proscriptive. With them, Andrew Johnson never obtained any recognition, personally and socially. It was the one ambition of his heart to be received as their equal. He hated with the hatred of an underling, and longed with the despairing aspiration of a servile. When they revolted, his hatred stood him in stead of patriotism; when the dagger opened the way to the throne, came his great opportunity. He is not without magnanimity, generosity, and much tenderness and humanity of feeling, and he is now laboring for that old dream—the recognition of personal equality by the slaveholders. To secure this he will give them back dominion if in his power; will even forgive them. Poor, infatuated man! they use and scorn him."

"I don't concur in this estimate of the President's character at all," said Colonel Gordon, emphatically.

"Of course not," was the answer.

"A very intelligent gentleman remarked to me the other day," said the chevalier, "that your Congress does not occupy the same place that it formerly did in the eyes of the American people. If so, is it due to the personal character of its members, or to what? are they to be charged with venality, or are they inferior men?"

After a pause—"Undoubtedly it is true that our Congress does not hold the same place in public estimation as formerly. When we had five, ten, or thirteen millions, Congress was the one important and conspicuous body of men. It was the first place of self-seeking ambition and talent. But now, with thirty or forty millions, with all the arts, colleges, and literature; with the developments of commerce, and the whole new field of railroads; with the upheaval of journalism, when a great editor or a railroad king is of vastly more importance than a senator or a Secretary of State; with all these avenues, and with the overgrown cities and conspicuous places withdrawing attention from Congress, that has become one of many important objects, instead of the sole, as in former times. There may be no man now in Congress the equal of two or three in the time of General Jackson, but the average is much higher, both in talents and morality. The American Congress never was a corrupt body. Venal men get into both Houses; and while in ability no one is the equal of Mr. Webster, perhaps, so now no conspicuous man of his practices would be tolerated in public life. He was always under a retainer — a stipendiary; while the very walls of the houses where he lived here are stained with the scandals of his profligacy, too gross to find a place in print, or gain credence out of the capital, and yet too true to leave room for reverence for him as a man. Nor could he ever have been sustained, if his course had not found countenance in the lives of other great men of his day. You could no more buy a bill through the House then, than you could rent a groggery in the New Jerusalem. There never was but one important measure that bought its own way through Congress, and that was the Texas Ten-million Bill. Single men may be corrupted—are, sometimes, I've no doubt. A turning vote in a committee may determine a report, and indirectly a measure; but I'd sooner undertake that sort of thing in the Senate than the House. Senators are here longer, are less under the eyes of their constituents, have more personal freedom, larger circles, and it must be conceded, I think, that there is just a little something in the atmosphere here a trifle depressing to rigid morality, something that corrodes and wears away the sharp edges and angles of severe virtue, and men, and women too, grow personally not less pure, but more tolerant."

The chevalier seemed immensely amused, while the colonel laughed or frowned as he approved or condemned.

"I told you he was a cynic, and you must remember that he preferred another great man to Webster," he observed to the chevalier.

"We are approaching a perilous period," Drybow resumed. "The public business rapidly increases, while the facilities for doing it rather diminish, so far as Congress is concerned; and every thing is more and more conclusively remitted to the moulding and controlling hand of a standing committee, until now several committees are potentially the House, and, by controlling a majority—and that can often be done by controlling one man—you control the House; for it becomes more and more rare to overrule the voice of a committee. When this has reached a point to which things now tend, venality and corruption may become the rule instead of the very rare exception. Our politicians, and possibly our country, labor under one great disadvantage, compared with England, and compared with the South before the war. In England, as it seems to me, the personal interests of those who govern lie in the same lines with the supposed interests of the country.

As at the South the paramount interest was slavery, and all members of Congress were slaveholders, and personal and national interests were identical—and that is a problem which the North has not solved, and for her it is insoluble—to make the personal interests of her members of Congress identical with an acknowledged paramount interest of the whole; so that personal ambition will tug strongest at the public burden. We have no paramount interest."

"And, if we had, the members of Congress would never see it," added the colonel.

"Who's the cynic, now?" asked Drybow.

Drybow hoped the chevalier had found Washington society pleasant. It was certainly accessible. The chevalier was not a society-man. His friend the colonel had kindly introduced him, as had others, and he remarked upon what seemed the unrestrained freedom of what he had heard called official society.

"Washington society is not what it was. There can now hardly be said to be any thing called society. We are overrun now with a scrambling herd of nobody knows who or what, and one is compelled to get away to two or three little circles beyond, if not above. It was bad enough in Buchanan's time, but Lincoln brought the very buffaloes from the plains," was the plaintive comment of the now pensive colonel on the social status of the capital.

"It is all rude enough, undoubtedly," replied the radical. "My friend always mentally compares every thing with the Tyler era, when a cabinet council, after much debate, settled that every lady or gentleman who said 'I done,' or ate peas with a knife, should be excluded from the real White-House society. State dinners were excepted, and so were the President and members of the cabinet, of course; and that was said to have continued the rule down to Buchanan's time, when the use of the knife was restored. With Mr. Lincoln came the deluge, and the colonel was driven to more private circles—one quite exclusive set, as I'm told, made up of the families of naval and army officers and their associates; for I will admit that, whatever is said of the commanders turned out at West Point and Annapolis, they usually produce gentlemen. Then there is the more exclusive foreign colony, formerly a little Europe, mostly on Georgetown Heights."

The chevalier wanted to know what influence the legations exercised at the capital, socially or politically.

"None whatever, politically; and, whatever they may have done in the olden time, they never will again. Perhaps I will except the English embassy; but, here is a little knot of common people, not speaking our language, not mingling with our people, not understanding them, unknown to more than two dozen of both Houses of Congress, and seldom meeting those they do know, and the idea that they did or could exercise any influence was an idea not entertained out of Europe. The queen usually sends us a man of brains, whom many of our people know and generally respect; but, save a little snobbish set, who cares for the rest?"

"And yet," said the colonel, "how every thing foreign, with a title, at any rate, is toadied to! Why, a prince or grand-duke can't enter a church on the Sabbath without breaking up the service."

"Well," rejoined Drybow, "we are about like the rest of the world. Were you ever in London, where princes, dukes, and duchesses, are the commonest; where everybody has seen them for all the days of their lives, and without much occasion to love them, and yet, at a royal procession, a ducal reception, or a public meeting, with the Prince of Wales or a duke to preside, the whole world is out, wild with snobbish wonder and admiration! When have we been more foolish?"

"I'm a little afraid," said the chevalier to the colonel,

"that on this point Mr. Drybow has the argument, decidedly."

"As for our official society, in which our high functionaries are the deities, what can it be better than it is?"

"A President is President because he happens to be, God only knows why. Certainly never because he has even high social distinction. Nominating a man for Congress because he was graceful and accomplished, would be new to caucuses and bar-room wire-pullers. He often succeeds because he has the antipodes of what makes up the gentleman, and his wife is such as happens, and his daughters such as happens again. A new President comes in with a new cabinet and a new Congress and new heads of bureaus, and nearly all as new to each other as to the *beau monde*. They must meet, receive, and tolerate each other and each other's friends. Little peculiarities of dress and eccentricities in manners must be tolerated. Even were one to come without dress or manners, he could hardly be turned away. Think of a Secretary's wife, with her two or three hundred cards, without a name among them known to her! When her afternoon comes, she receives them. When the evening reception of herself and husband comes, she sends her cards to these; and whom she receives all receive, and nobody asks questions—nobody can. Each must take the other on trust. It don't make any difference where a man lives, what he does or says, whether he is anybody or nobody; he goes where he pleases, and passes for what he assumes to be worth, and, if he can bring some sounding title, with some mystery about him, the chance is that he will be a sensation for a day. Things don't last long in Washington life."

These last sentences were said directly to the chevalier, who received them with the dreamy nonchalance which he maintained through most of the conversation.

"Of course," Drybow went on to say, "among the new

men and women will be many refined and accomplished, who soon find out and appreciate each other, and who attract and are attracted by the same resident elements; and among these are made the most charming, unrestrained, and delightful circles in all American life." And rising and walking across the room, and, turning back, with his asking eye fully on the chevalier—" What an opening, now, is here for a man of real genius, who has a turn for speculating in the finances! The United States owes everybody. Money is now plenty. We are accustomed to immense sums, and to irresponsible accountings. The air is thick with frauds and alleged corruptions. Every man's confidence is shaken. The great convulsion has disturbed the foundations of mind and morals both. The capital is full of desperate, sinister spirits, and further experiments in legislation must be tried. Let a genius appear, who can organize and manage with address and skill; who will encircle and swallow up all rings; make arrangements with subordinates in the bureaus, buy up claimants as well as claims, and turn all other claim-agents into his clerks; who shall find nothing too vast for his strength, or too small for his vision; make himself useful to senators and secretaries, and manage—not bribe; buy up now and then a seat, perhaps, in the Senate, and trade on the needs of the chairmen of leading committees, and do the whole without suspicion, and seemingly do nothing all the time;" and, fixing his asking look barely for a silent moment on the seemingly-dreaming orbs of the attentive, impassive chevalier, he turned away.

"What a Napoleonic campaign against the exchequer you have sketched!" cried the colonel, as they all arose.

"Colonel Gordon," said St. Arnaud, "I am under many obligations to you, and chiefly for the valuable acquaintance of Mr. Drybow.—Mr. Drybow, I must express my gratification and profit at this meeting. I have rooms at the Willard, and trust I may see you there at an early day." His air was frank and sincere. Did he have a suspicion that he was talked at? Seemingly not.

"And so this is the chevalier," said Drybow, thoughtfully, as he walked away. "Where the devil did he get that title, and how? Lord, what a smothered fire burned in those slumberous, dreamy eyes as I sketched a possibility! And how alert he was when the new heiress and Warbel were named! I meant to return to them. This purring panther is not idling away his time here. What infernal eyes he has, though. He seems to have swallowed old Gordon!"

CHAPTER XI.

THE VANES.

On the corner of E and Twenty-first Streets, West, stands the old Commodore Vane mansion—an old-fashioned Washington residence, two or three years in building, in old, staid times. Two-story, with thick walls, dingy and moss-grown, with small doors and windows; but such a cozy old house; so full of soft, warm carpets, and light-tinted walls, with plenty of solid, old furniture, and huge old fireplaces and firedogs, and ever and ever so many quiet little nooks and corners, where one could hide away with a dear, gossiping girl friend, and talk up all the delicious girl nothings, that Adolphus would give part of his ears to hear, and improve them by the loss; places to be found in by a lover, and who would compel you to remain, the dear rudeness; with old paintings on the walls, good paintings, bad pictures, pictures softened by time, and some immensely improved from having entirely faded out; and charts, and a model of the old Constitution, and lots of nautical things; a place of quiet and shadow—of rest and peace; of low voices and murmurous talks; of old memories, and all pleasant surroundings; where every lady went, and exclaimed, "Oh, how charming!" The outside wall inclosed quite a fourth of the square, and the whole devoted to flowers and shrubs, and walks, winding, crooked, and straight, and those that were neither; and there were large trees with seats, and seats without trees; and climbing vines and arbors, summer-houses and bowers—just such a place as old Commodore Vane, with abundant means, a love of his profession, and with no highly-cultivated taste in landscape-gardening, would build, construct, lay out, mingle, and snarl up, and then, in due time, die out of. He was married late—rather in the afternoon of his day, and left a young and interesting widow, a daughter, and younger son; and for years there had been with them the daughter of Mrs. Vane's older sister, and who used to be not much younger than Mrs. Vane. But, somehow, as the years wore on, and Mrs. Vane went on with them, the niece seemed to stand still—till, now, she was nearer the age of the cousin, as she should be. What young lady would not prefer to be nearer the age of a young lady cousin than an old lady aunt, especially when she could have her choice?

Strangers, who first met Mrs. Vane, were apt to say of her face, "How plain she is!" To which her acquaintance always answered, "How can you say so? she is just lovely!" and, when the first ceased to be strangers, they said so, too. A good face, fine eyes, and pleasing, womanly form—almost noble in contour; she was just lovely, with a loveliness that ripened, and softened, and deepened with years. Time had never quite finished her face; he was always in love with it, and as constantly adding delicate lights and touches; and, finally, when his loving pencil began to trace in it the faint lines of years, they were all lines of beauty. Not a wit, or brilliant—rather silent; not learned or original, and yet what a charm of ripe sense, and wise, prudent thought in what she said, and what womanly grace in what she did!

She was not the head or centre of a set. She was one of the many similar ladies, of the more permanent Washington, who, with their husbands, sons, and daughters, without formality or ceremony, enjoyed each other's society; and, wherever they went, carried with them that tone and flavor of unconscious refinement that instinctively comprehends the proprieties of all occasions, and never is at fault in any presence.

Margaret Marston, the niece, usually called Marge or Margie by young lady friends, was slight, but finely formed, lithe and graceful; dark, with lustrous eyes—just the tinge of a shade at the corners of the upper lip; and, withal, a beauty—a confirmed beauty—a thing acknowledged and conceded for a long, long time. She was full of unmixed Southern blood; and the feminine embodiment of its spirit, and the something common to the race. She still carried on the war; kept the field; had never surrendered, and held her forces, by no means slender, well in hand.

Lucy, the younger cousin, with her mother's form, not fully rounded; a face too fair for a brunette, and eyes and hair too dark for a blonde, had the wise thoughtfulness of her mother, which would have been precocious, were it not for the almost brilliant, girlish vivacity with which she carried it off; whose beauty was not thought of in the presence of her sweetness and winningness, and who was very apt to be a centre wherever she was.

Grayson, a manly lad of sixteen—that abominable age—neither boy nor man, when a youth so tries everybody, and most those nearest him; when a mother rests her irritated soul in the memory of the goodness of his babyhood, and hardly dares to look forward to the possibilities of coming years; when to his sisters he is a chronic tease and mimic, ere his nature has escaped from that barbarism which is the normal state of the young male, when he picks up only the semi-vices of men, and is loud and rude from irresistible impulse—Grayson had the normal share of these attractive virtues, supplemented with a pleasant spice of mischief—all his own. He did not, by any means, spare his mother; was usually at feud with his cousin, and sometimes had sharpish bouts with his sister. A fine, well-grown young male of the human species, fairer, if any thing, than his sister, he carried an enlarged baby face, soft and handsome, and relieved only by a strongly-marked brow; while his light, rather indolent-looking eyes usually had the good-natured expression of a rig, gibe, or joke, or mimicry, got off at the expense of somebody. At heart he was true and honest; no mean thought or really unmanly impulse ever invaded his mind or breast. Handsome, admired, and a tease, full of immature talent and possibilities, ready to do kindnesses, and quick in sympathy, he was, nevertheless, at times almost a burden in his mother's house.

He had just returned with his sister from a carriage-ride. It seems that their friend Colonel Gordon had taken Mrs. Vane and her niece to call on Miss Brand, at Borum's, to whom Alice had disclosed her present reduced condition more fully than had transpired to her counsel, Frank and the colonel, and that Mrs. Vane and Margaret were not quite in accord as to the propriety of asking her, with her aunt, who seemed not so objectionable to Margie, to become temporary inmates of the Vane mansion. Mrs. Vane had known Captain Brand, and was quite decided. The younger ones had just returned from a drive with Alice, and Lucy had fallen violently in love with her, and now expressed her passion with much warmth. Even Grayson, who could now see a difference in women, and had even noticed some young girls, admitted a qualified partiality for her, subject to the decided drawback of the aunt. And putting on a dolorous expression, in a thin, harsh voice: "'Ye see, Miss Vane, I'se a Biggs—one o' the Missouri Biggses; and I ain't used to the ways up here. I allus had plenty o' niggers; an' then I'm mostly narves, an' narves, ye know, is—' Confound her! she is a Biggs, and the biggest boress of her size that ever came from the South." And turning to his cousin, and letting his voice break into a treble: "She's one of the upper tones, from the very highest string, she is. She says 'clar' and 'do' and 'misto.' If she comes here, I'll have to dig a hole in the garden, and go in."

"I wish you would dig a hole," said Margie, sharply; "I'd have her come, and drive you into it."

"You'd cut the hole off tight to the ground, and keep me in," was the response. "I think I'd manage to stand it, with Alice here to take the taste of her out of my mouth;" and, going close to his cousin, "ain't she a beauty, though? We should look just a shade dark and thin, if she was here, wouldn't we? We should grow so wee in her presence that two gentlemen could not see us at the same time, and might not at all. I know why you don't want La Belle Alice here."

"What do you know about it, you overgrown baby?" a little snappy.

"Our goods have been a long time in the shop—are just a trifle stale—though they wear well," Grayson went on; "we came out before Miss Lane's time—I must read you up in Rollin's 'Ancient History'—and we don't like the effect—new goods, improved patterns, and freshest finish.—Mother," turning to Mrs. Vane, "it won't do. I am not certain but that Lucy would suffer some, also."

"Now Grasy," said Margie, recovering her forces, and

turning upon him, "suppose that, somewhere away down in that lazy body of yours, you should have just a faint stir of sense—not that you ever did or will, but suppose it—how do you think you'd feel?"

"Well, I s'pose I should feel strange. How do you s'pose you'd feel, if Count Renaud should fall on his knees before you, not that he ever has or will," and placing both hands on the left side of his vest, with an absurd bow and grimace—"*'Mam'selle pardonne mes,* my heart is all one, vat you calls him? bully for you!'—how do you suppose you'd feel?"

"Don't mind him," said Lucy, "he's improving. He got a swallow-tail coat the other day, and I found him up on a chair trying to see how it fitted in the back."

"O Lu! you got that from Thackeray. It's worse than Margie's stealing from 'Don Juan,' and calling me gracious, graceful, graceless, Grayson, grace."

"That," said Lucy, laughing, "was unjust. There ain't but one epithet of the whole applicable to you; and it shows you read a bad book, besides."

"Well, she read it before me, and I'm a man, you know; and you don't want that I should die young for my virtues, do you?"

"No danger of your being cut off for your saintliness, Grasy," answered the vivacious Lucy; "we should all see great amendment in you, without the smallest apprehension on that account."

Mrs. Vane, who had once or twice attempted to check Grayson, resumed the original subject: "We knew her father, Captain Brand, and common courtesy requires that I should give her what countenance I can—an orphan, a stranger, and overwhelmed with misfortune. These alone are sufficient claims."

"Why," rejoined the persistent Margie, "Lucy has just told us that an old friend of her father's had been there, and offered to advance her any amount of money on her claims; and then she has all her Vicksburg property. Why didn't she make herself known? What did she go into the Treasury for—and why has she left it, I would like to know? Then you'd have this Colonel Warbel, and his friend, that vulgar Western member of Congress—"

"That vulgar Western member of Congress, as you call him," fiercely broke in Grayson, "is General Mason, one of Sheridan's cavalry-generals, who sent the chivalry whirling through Winchester one day. You can go into the convent—I wish you would."

"I told Lucy to invite her," said Mrs. Vane, "to come and spend a few days with us, and she accepted, as of course she would. I know we shall all like her, and we can find a pleasant place for her in this neighborhood."

"And Margie will manage to endure the gentlemen who will call on her account. I never knew her to run away from one," put in Grasy.

"And I never knew you to say or do any but rude things," sharply rejoined Margie.

"Cousin Margie is truthful, after all, ain't she, Grasy?" quietly asked Lucy, with a manner that prevented reply.

The next day she came, Alice, Mrs. Thompson, and the girl Millie; and nothing could be pleasanter than her reception, especially by Margie; and, although none could better understand than Alice, that this kindness was in some part a grace to her position, so admirably did she bear herself under the sense, that even Margie forgot that she was the beneficiary, and looked upon her as somehow conferring a favor.

It was not in Mrs. Thompson's way to accept any thing, save as the delayed payment on overdue indebtedness, to be rendered with apology, also due; but, being at once placed in the easiest chair, with ottoman and cushions, she gave breath to her chronic complaints with an air of softened resignation, beautiful to see. "She made an especial effort," quietly explained Alice, so that no fears need be indulged in, "and obliged me by coming, under the arrangement that Millie will return her, before evening, to the quiet of her accustomed room."

"I'm hardly equal to any sudden change like this. My family, the Biggses, mostly staid in one place, and"— Grayson escaped while the pitiless monologue drizzled on through the vivacious conversation of the girls, addressed sometimes to Mrs. Vane, sometimes to Margie, and sometimes to an unheeding world generally, relieved with pious resignations that her misfortunes had been permitted, "though massy knows what she'd ever did."

Lucy stole Alice away to her own room, bright with color and warmth, and in an hour the quick currents between two rich, sweet natures made them the oldest of friends. How like heaven's grace, full of love and rest, it was to the lonely, thirsting heart of the orphaned child of the desolate South! The presence of Alice in the Vane mansion, with all her quietness and subdued manner, rendered even the mistress almost a second character; and the acutely-observing Margaret, with the seeds of rage and hate, remembered the prophecy of the rude Grayson. How thin, shrunken, and old, she felt in the presence of this Alice Brand, with the grace and dignity of a woman, and the spirit and vivacity of a girl!—and she disliked her all the more for her unconsciousness of her advantages, and she studied and cultivated her to find the clew to her weak point, and fancied that she found it.

In the evening Colonel Gordon brought in and introduced General Mason of the House, and Colonel Warbel; and the quick eyes of Magaret noticed a little flutter in the cheek of Alice as she managed to remain in the background till obliged to notice their presence, and something like being distrait for an instant in the air of Frank, as he approached her; and she noticed that he only approached and bowed, when he should have known that a little hand would willingly linger a moment in his. She could see it all, between these two, and for a moment its beauty came warmly to her woman's heart; and then a sigh that to her heart it had never been known. But what was it already between them, that just tinged the air of the youth, as if he had been repulsed? But some comfort it was, that this dangerous girl's fancy, at the least, was ensnared.

The gentlemen did not remain long—quite long enough to show Margaret that Mason was no vulgar Congressman; and after they left, and Alice had retired, she admitted that he was really quite charming.

"O Margie!" exclaimed the mocking Grayson, "he always went with a rebel's head lashed to his saddle, and now he sleeps with his spurs on, and you are just in love with him."

But, before they went, a few words were said between Alice and Frank. "For a few days I have accepted Mrs. Vane's invitation to remain her guest. I hope nothing may occur making it necessary "—she paused, and raised her eyes as if to convey the rest, or perhaps not knowing how to complete a sentence that might seem ungracious.

"I think," answered Frank, "I fully appreciate my position, one of pure business in your affairs, and I'm sure there will be no occasion for annoying you with it." His manner was cold, and there was just a little strain in his voice. Alice again raised her eyes, this time in surprise. Possibly he had understood more than she meant. With a bow he turned away to Grayson, who seemed to have taken his fancy, and paused for a moment's flashing boy-talk in which both laughed, and they went.

"And so this youth is your attorney?" said the pleasant voice of Mrs. Vane, as the door closed—turning to Alice. "How young men ripen in these fast years!"

"He's too young to be intrusted with any thing, unless it is a lady's shawl," said Margie, contemptuously.

"Cousin Margie," said Grayson, "thinks a man must be nearly as old as she is—five hundred at the least. He commanded a brigade." His manner was toned down, and his remarks less exaggerated than usual, in the presence of Alice, who rewarded him with a bright look for his vindication.

"He seemed on the heights," observed Lucy. "I wish he had come down just a little. He's one most people would be glad to like, if he'd let them."

"I've never met him in society," said Alice, quietly. "And the years in which young men may acquire ease and polish, he has devoted to other things, perhaps."

"How thoughtful you are!" rejoined Lucy; "I think he has fine manners, now. I'm sure anybody would trust him; only—pardon me—he seemed for some reason a little chilly."

Alice may have thought so, too. How quick both would have forgiven him had they known how surely he remembered that Alice had pronounced an expression of his feelings toward her "a foolish speech," and Alice would have understood his last remark which now surprised her!

On the day following, Colonel Gordon, with a little more ceremony, introduced the Chevalier St. Arnaud. None of the ladies had met him, and his presence was as near the approach of a sensation as any thing could produce in the Vane mansion. Mrs. Vane was dignified and gracious; Miss Marston, graceful and reverential; Lucy, flushed a little, and was impressed; Miss Brand's manner was that of one receiving an ordinary caller; and Grayson was stiff and frigid.

The alert Margie, whom nothing but her temper ever for an instant disconcerted, was fully herself. She thought that the chevalier approached Miss Brand with the air of a purchaser to whom the goods had been overpraised, but who saw that they had been decidedly underrated. He was evidently much struck. On the whole, she must give him credit for discrimination, for even in Alice's presence he was not unmindful of her claims, which were really very great. No woman in Washington better knew their exact value than did their beautiful and experienced owner, or better how to use them. At once a new passion, a new ambition seized her, imparting new interest to life. She was much mistaken if the chevalier had not formed the resolve to pay court to Alice, and she at the same moment formed the determination of winning him to herself; plucking this handsome, fascinating lion of European aristocracy from this girl-woman, whom no man would willingly leave. All the odds and all the counter-odds at once stood arrayed before her. Did she not know men? And the campaign and its vicissitudes, with all the opportunities of Washington social life, so free and careless, permitting such ample margin for skill and experience, flashed before her. And she opened it at once, with a reconnoitre in force. "He was," he said, "to idle the winter away, would observe and study the very interesting phenomena of the higher republican circles at the capital—not of the court alone, but something truer and really higher, a little outside of the court circle," with a marked inclination to Miss Marston. It was not lost, and now in a moment Washington life lit up under her graphic power — true enough for a portrait, and amusing enough for a caricature, and all within the lines of lady-like delineation. Her auditor—she addressed only St. Arnaud—evidently fully appreciated it.

When he was gone, the eyes of the ladies asked mental questions.

"I think he is just splendid," said Lucy, "a splendid

man for a capital—to be at levees and receptions, to open balls with, to head the procession to the supper-room, lead the German—oh, for a thousand, thousand things!"

"A grand-bashaw of fifty tails! and all tales, I'll bet!" declared Grayson, off-hand.

"How do you think you will like him?" asked Margie of Lucy.

"Like him? Oh, I should never come to that," laughing; "he ain't a man to like."

"What do you say, Miss Brand?"

"Me—I?" exclaimed that young lady, starting from a reverie—"I really beg pardon," coloring.

"She asked you how you liked the chevalier," said Mrs. Vane.

"Oh, he's well enough, I presume; a little dreamy and affected, perhaps."

"I don't see how you can say that," said Margie, pleased with her indifference. "I think his manner the perfection of that high-bred air that can only be acquired in Europe," with a fine enthusiasm.

"It may be. I really can have no opinion. To me he appeared a little like one playing a part."

"Cousin Margie puts a low estimate on every person young enough to be born in America," declared Grayson, a little sharply.

"And my cousin Grayson will soon give you to understand that few things of mine find distinguished consideration with him," very pleasantly.

"I suppose that is a young man's way to cousins," said Alice. "I'm sure he is really too generous to wound; and I mean that he and I shall be very good friends, indeed," with an ingenuous smile upon the youth that added force to the remark.

"Grayson often speaks with a young man's haste, and with much of the thoughtlessness of all young persons, and I hope you do not over-estimate him, Miss Brand," said his mother.

How the young man's generous nature opened to the kind speech of Alice! She called him " a young man, and could make allowances for a fellow; while Margie, if she ever was young, had forgotten it, it was so long ago," was his mental remark; and the youth relapsed into a train of valuable thought, quite new to him.

CHAPTER XII.

MRS. CROLY OPENS THE CAMPAIGN.

ON the day following the call at the Vanes', by Frank and his friends, he was surprised by receiving the card of Mrs. Croly, and much more when he received the lady. Her name, as bearing upon himself, was little less than a terror, and brought the vision of a large, dark, imperious Meg Merrilies woman, with a mustache, which was only dissipated by a light step, and a graceful, symmetrical form, round but lithe, with an almost classic beauty of face, straight brows over wide, deep, serious gray eyes of ever-varying shade, finely-cast mouth and chin, relieved by the fullness of the latter. She came in with the ease and assurance of a woman not unaccustomed to going to a gentleman's room, with the possible flavor of little suppers of five or six gentlemen and one or two ladies. Neatly dressed in sober tints for the street, and faultless in movement, she was new to the Washington public, which had rarely seen a more striking face, and men were very apt to turn and look after her, on the street. There was just an air about her, nameless and undefinable, and a little siss of whispers, that said—nobody knew what. There were marvelous tales of her influence in high quarters, and a great curiosity to see her; and she always brought a hush with her as she came, and left a whisper as she went. And some men looked at her, and then at each other, as she passed, saying nothing. Frank had never seen her, and when she entered his room his first expression was mingled amazement and admiration. He drew two long breaths ere he recovered. The effect produced by her on him was perhaps apparent, and, as her unshrinking glance rested steadily on his face and form, it may have occurred to her that she had rarely seen a more pleasing union of both than stood before her. A faint perfume of violets pervaded the room with her.

"Colonel Warbel, I presume," taking an offered seat.

"My name is Warbel. I was a colonel."

"Do you know Lieutenant Corflint?"

"I remember him."

A little pause. "Perhaps I had better say a word of myself first," hesitatingly. "President Johnson is very willing to oblige me when he can, for services rendered him years ago by another, and he permits me to come to him on proper occasions, and it has usually been my fortune to ask him for things that he saw good reasons to grant—for I'm obliged not only to provide for myself, but also for another. Well, I have been asked to see the President for Corflint, who, it seems, was dismissed for absence without leave, and Stanton is cruel and rude, and the President is afraid to have the order modified, so as to permit pay, etc. I know little of the merits of the case; poor Corflint is here, and says that a word from you would make it all right, as of course it will," with a smile of great sweetness. "He says that he can explain every thing to you, showing that, while he violated orders, he had good reasons for it, which any young and generous man will see the force of." With another smile: "Now, he dares not come to you.

Indeed, he is afraid to have it known where he is, for I think that, under the order in his case, he is afraid of being arrested, and I only came to ask if you will see him—meet him somewhere where he will feel safe. I'm sure you will," ending in a plaintive tone. And all the time her great eyes were full upon his, softening and deepening, as he looked into them.

"I really know no good reason," said Frank, after a moment's pause, "why I should not see him. My impressions were much against him. I certainly think he's in no danger of arrest."

"A man in his position is apt to be fearful, though you may not know it; and I will communicate your kindness to him, and find where he can see you, at some pleasant place for you. May it be soon—some evening?"

"At any time," still drinking from her eyes.

"Thank you. He understands that you are settling the accounts of your officers and soldiers, and, should you want any thing of the President, I wish you would permit me to do it for you; any matter in which you or your friends are interested. I know Senator Josephs, and Senator Pangborn, and many leading men of both Houses." For which offer Frank thanked her; and then she rippled off pleasantly into little topics with a woman's tact and skill; and then she went, leaving the faint violet perfume; and, perhaps, another stronger impression with Frank. As she went, she took with her not only a decided fancy for the young colonel, but a clear idea of the locality, surroundings, and approaches to his room. Not that this last was with any motive, but then she had an observing and retentive mind, and, had she thought of the matter, she may have seen how open and easy of access were the approaches to his confidence, his imagination, his heart.

CHAPTER XIII.

THE KING OF THE LOBBY.

This was an eventful day for Frank. In the after-part of the same day, while busy in his room, he was surprised to find a man quietly standing near him. Where, or how, or why he came in, Frank could not tell. The face and air of the man were those of one who was on a secret mission of the most confidential nature, and of such moment and delicacy as demanded stealth and silence. He stood, when observed, with his finger on his lip, as if forbidding speech or sound, and as if his presence would announce his mission, and render explanation, dangerous in itself, unnecessary.

The person and figure were not without interest, and seemed to have been designed on a general system of secrecy and entire confidence. The very eyes appeared to refuse to see or the mind to notice, and he may have found himself very unexpectedly in the room of a stranger with as much surprise as its occupant. "Gloster" finally came from him, and the aroused Frank recognized the name and form of the man who had been pointed out to him as the King of the Lobby. A public personage, better known and more observed on the streets than the President, there was an impression, which in the mass was a faith, that there was really nothing that he could not do, and which attributed to him every thing extraordinary which had been recently done. When the Chawpening claim passed Congress, men merely said "Gloss," and the Tonto Indian fraud found the same happy solution; and so of every thing else, "Gloss," or "old Gloss," was the glossary that explained the unusual. He was the wizard who could ar-range majorities, and twist and worm any thing through the two Houses; secure the allowance of a claim—a name and fame achieved in some of the inexplicable ways in which fames and fortunes are sometimes won.

The very odor of his fame excluded him from the personal acquaintance of every prominent and honorable man of both Houses. To know him was a danger, an intimacy was ruin. With Congress, or in the departments, he was without interest or influence; almost unknown. On the streets, in drinking-houses, billiard-saloons, etc., he was a king. Every stranger whom he approached, or who approached him, came at once to understand his wonderful power, and his fame brought such to him. He understood every thing, took all the money that could be wormed out of them, and did nothing. Others did the work, if work was done; he secured the pay and fame. He approached every claimant, always assumed to be managing his claim, and none was allowed that he did not in some way assert as finally due to his exertion. How numerous the Glosters were at one time in the capital!

"Gloster, how are you? Glad to see you!" was the hearty response of the amused Frank, to the announcement of the king's name. The king jerked his thumb toward the door of another room, to indicate danger of his voice, and, carrying a seat to a remote corner of the apartment, beckoned Frank to him with another; and, as Frank sat down, he drew his chair close to him, and placing his mouth close to Frank's ear—in a stage-whisper—while his eyes rolled about the room for eavesdroppers—

"Know your men?" No response from the uncomprehending Frank. "Colonel, know your men?" he repeated, with some energy.

"Yes," said the smiling colonel, "I generally do."

"Certain?" with a piercing look.

"Pretty certain."

"Only pretty certain!" with disgust. "'Twon't do. Let me see your list."

Of course Frank, who in this instance, like young Juan,

> " . . . . had no more notion,
> Than he who never saw the sea of ocean,"

what he was driving at, assumed to be as profound and secret as his mysterious visitor.

"See my list!" closing down his eyelids, and glimmering at him from the little crevices, as much as to inquire, "Do you see any thing spring-like around here?" To which an appreciative wink was the response, with "You're all right. There are little things, you know—of course you do—committee on claims—report, you know—you understand. Little things, with a little turn—why, they turn a little, you know. And turn 'em a little more—why, you see they turn a little more, you know. D'ye understand?"

"I think I do," was the intelligent response. "For instance, bend a little thing—just a little, and it is a little crooked, you see. Bend it a little more, and it is crookeder yet. Give it another twist, and it is still less straight —do you see? Do you understand?"

"That's it, colonel," said the puzzled monarch, "that's exactly it. You see there are ropes, and those who know 'em, and know how to pull 'em," motioning with his hands as if hauling in a line. "A man, you know, carries the ends in his hands, and nobody knows when or where he pulls, you know."

"And little bell-handles with rust-eaten wires," said Frank, entering into the thing fully; "connecting with clapperless bells, that won't ring, you know, and to which no one would answer, if they did; and little dirt-holes that lead nowhere, you know, and yet we know men who pass through them, because the soil is on them, and the smell of the earth, you know, Gloster—ch? you know.".

Gloster was not a little puzzled, and, throwing his thumb over his shoulder as a warning of the danger of being more explicit, bent his keen glance again upon the amused and baffling face of the colonel, uttered the one syllable—"Brand!" It may be that the quick mind of Frank had come round to this name, which was now seldom out of it—as the object of this far-off approach—for he heard it with seeming indifference, and responded in the most natural way in the world:

"Brand, Brand, of course, just that—why not?"

"Yes, of course, as you say, why not?" concurred the baffled king. "Brand, as you say, colonel, of course; of course, you know."

"Of course 'tis, Mr. Gloster. I'm not a little surprised that a man of your astuteness had not seen it before. But I'm glad you mentioned it, come to think of it. And I'm really much obliged," rising, as if to put an end to the interview.

Gloster rose also, and spite of himself was more and more puzzled by this turning of his indirect metaphorical slang upon himself.

"It's all right, is it? Of course it is, if we understand one another," he ventured to say.

"Of course it is," was the cordial assurance of the colonel. "And we do understand each other—at least I understand you, and if, on two or three months' reflection, you doubt whether you understand me, why, call again, my good Gloster. Don't stand on ceremony, come right in"—all with a bright way and pleasant voice. As the King of the Lobby went out, he may have thought that the Brand claims would not yield large revenues to his exchequer.

CHAPTER XIV.

MR. RYMER'S CROWNING MERCY.

The evening of the same day saw a pleasant, almost an hilarious, scene in Teed's law-office, between that gentleman and the worthy Rymer, who, with mute interrogation in his lugubrious face, made silent by apprehension, and who came in answer to a message from Teed. He stalked into the room and came to a solemn pause in the middle of it.

"All that a man hath will he give for his soul!" in sepulchral voice, was the greeting of Teed; "and what do you hold yours at, old sanctimony, sanctification, crucifixion, and circumcision? How much?—say quick!"

"O man of the world, why vex the sorely tried? Thy hand is a heavy one," was the reply, with a groan.

"The devil! only so much? Listen!" and, taking up a telegraphic dispatch, he read:

"Vicksburg, *December* 23, 1865.
"T. T. Teed, *Washington, D. C.:*
"All right, old boy. Both off, all safe.
"Paul."

A pause, during which the amused and radiant Teed looked into the uncomprehending face of his visitor. "The first epistle of Paul to the old boy," explained Teed, "announcing that the only witnesses *vs.* you are sent to the oldest boy; and that *Doe ex dem. Brand* has gone to the devil. We've won at one throw."

"Were you quite sure?" with tremulous anxiety, and clasping his hands—"quite—quite certain?"

"Ward got the names of the nurse and her husband,

and where they were, and Mack—Paul, here—started the same night, and Jim Bardlaw twenty-four hours after. Mack was to take them to Memphis, and they are where—"

"A crowning mercy!" exclaimed Rymer, rolling up his eyes with fervor. "Let us return thanks to—"

"The devil!" rudely broke in Teed. "We are lying and stealing to cover old robberies and lies," he went on. "There may be a God, and I won't run the risk of having him approached in this way: as we cheat all the world, let us be honest here."

"You're facetious—ha-ha-ha!" weakly laughing and cackling for a moment, and his anxiety returning. "You say they are safe?—they are—are alive, I s'pose?"

"Alive! Good God! you don't suppose I'd have them murdered, do you, old redemption, foreordination, predestination, and damnation without end?"

"N-n-no, of course not; but I didn't know but that some accident—"

"Another crowning mercy! and we'd taken them to Memphis to bury, eh?"

"How you do misunderstand a weak and erring mortal—a weak, sinful man, I may say!"

"Yes, you're all of that. Now what'll the Lord's treasury receive in acknowledgment of this mercy?"

"You'll remit something from—"

"Not a red! not a red! and besides, the case ain't over—hasn't commenced. Suppose La Belle Brand has a Bible—you've heard of such a thing?—a family Bible, you know, with the family record all complete, and can prove it—then what—New-England Catechism?"

"You never mentioned that," said Rymer, with dismay.

"You'd steal that, too, I presume, and send it to the heathen if it didn't cost any thing. Don't be too much overcome: Bardlaw wouldn't go to Mississippi if he had evidence in Washington."

"True—true—that's true," said Rymer, recovering; "there's great comfort in ter-uth."

"Now," said Teed, "that's one thing I sent to you for; and won't I like to see Jim Bardlaw when he comes back! Of course he'll find out that his witnesses have been spirited away; but that won't comfort him, for he'll also be told that they were taken to New Orleans.—The other thing is the next ten thousand."

"What, so soon?" almost collapsing. "I thought—"

"Bring me ten thousand, to-morrow. That's the way you're punished, having your money pulled out—cut out of you. What an instrument I'll be in the hands of Providence; and how earnestly I labor to do his will in this matter!" He arose, and with somewhat mixed feelings Rymer left.

CHAPTER XV.

AN OLD FRIEND OF CAPTAIN BRAND.

The distinction conferred upon Frank by the calls with which he was honored, was enhanced by other similar incidents which speedily followed. On the next day, two or three persons, of such doubtful appearance as to leave no doubt of their characters, on various pretexts sought him, and in each instance called upon Colonel Gordon to inquire for him, giving him to understand that they had appointments to meet Colonel Warbel; and on an evening or two after, latish, and as Gordon was about to retire, the inquiry was repeated by a dashing young lady in evening dress, who, on being told by the amazed colonel that the young gentleman was out, was much disappointed, and showed him a card on which was written, "Colonel Warbel, this is Miss Ware," and signed with a well-known woman's name. Miss Ware moved away quite rapidly. The colonel was greatly disturbed by these incidents, especially the last, but prudently resolved not to say any thing for the present to Frank about them.

With the commencement of the suit, and the dispatching of Bardlaw, junior, to Mississippi, cut off as he was from the society of Miss Brand, and in a frame of mind not inclining him to any pursuit of business or pleasure, Frank strolled about for two or three days preoccupied, looking at things which he did not see; pulling out and returning his watch without looking at it; occasionally asking a question, and never knowing whether it was answered; and, on the whole, conducting himself, as Colonel Gordon thought, like a very ill-regulated young man; and once or twice he left a question of the colonel's unanswered, or replied with a meaningless smile or a dazed look. Some hazy misgivings about the youth finally began to gather in the frank, generous mind of the colonel. On the third day since he had seen Alice, the brilliant idea occurred to Frank to call on Mrs. Thompson, and he advanced upon the Borum fortress with great promptitude. Millie was there, bright, and very much pleased to see him. Her young mistress was still at Mrs. Vane's, well and happy. "A gentleman was with Mrs. Thompson," she said, with a grave face, " but she would announce him, and, if the first was a gentleman, he would leave." A few moments later, and a breezy, showy, rather good-looking man walked past the open parlor-door, with an air, as Frank thought.

He found Mrs. Thompson in state, pillowed and stayed up in her easy-chair. "O Colonel Warbel! why didn't you call sooner and meet Mr. Ward? He's such a gentleman, so sympathizin', an' then he knew so many of the Biggses, an' seems to be a rale godly man, though not a Babtist — the Biggses mostly was — and you'd been so glad to 'a' met 'im. He's an old friend of Captain Bran's, an' soon as he hearn she was here he come to see 'er, an' she was out. It would 'a' did you good to hear his inquiries 'bout 'er—every thing, an' all about the case, and the trial, her nurse, and every thing; seem's if he couldn't hear enough."

"You told him every thing, of course?" asked Frank, with no attempt to hide his disgust.

"Of course, an' then—but this you mustn't tell; we don't want it known, an' Alice didn't want you to know it—you mustn't let 'er know I told you, or, if you do, you must tell 'er not to tell it to anybody else, will you?"

"Of course not; what is it?"

"Well, Mr. Ward, you see, has heaps of money, and he offered to buy Alice's right to the property here, which you know can't amount to much. Well, he is willing to buy it, and pay more'n its worth; an' I think she'd better sell—the Biggses generally do sell for more'n things is worth. He made 'er an advance "—sinking her voice to a whisper, with a strength which sent it to the battlements of Borum castle—" of, I think, a thousand dollars."

"A thousand dollars!" exclaimed Frank, in amazement; "sold!—it must be an —— sell! And I was not to know!"

"You see, Mr. Ward was so sympathizin'—"

"When will Miss Brand return?"

"I don't know."

"Good-by, Mrs. Thompson."

"Why, goodness! ar' you goin'? The Biggses—"

But he had gone. Millie was below, seemingly waiting for him; and her face was so full of kindly sympathy that he paused.

"Is your mistress well, Millie?

"Very well. I saw her yesterday; and to-day they were going out to look at rooms near Mrs. Vane's, in a very pleasant house; and I'm so glad!" and she paused and looked up, and then looked down, and hesitated.

"What is it, Millie?"

"Do you know this Mr. Ward that Mrs. Thompson told you about—of course, she told you all about him?"

"No. Who is he?"

"No one knows. He come one day when Miss Alice was out, an' got every thing out o' Mrs. Thompson, an' of course, when miss come in, he was an old acquaintance." In answer to Frank, she told him every thing she knew or suspected.

"And so Miss Brand has sold her place here, and got part of the pay," said Frank, a little hardly.

"Did she tell you that?" in surprise. "Oh! Miss Alice—you, colonel"—looking down while the tears came in her bright eyes—"Miss Alice could not bear that you should know how poor she is. An offer of money from you would break her heart—poor thing! She has high, proud ways, Colonel Warbel."

"My poor child," said the now tender-voiced young man, "she and her secret are safe with me."

"I know they ar'; I know they ar'," warmly answered the impulsive girl, "an' I'm shore she knows they ar' too."

The entrance of others into the corridor induced Frank to depart, when he went straight to the office of the Bardlaws. He found that gentleman with a distracted look. "Read that," he said, handing Frank a telegram just received. Frank took, and read:

"VICKSBURG, *December* 25, 1865.

"J. BARDLAW, ETC.:

"Found they had suddenly disappeared night before last; supposed down. Man about there for a day or two. Return at once." J. B., JR."

Frank continued to look at it a moment in silence, and

his first utterance was a low, peculiar whistle. Raising his eyes, now flashing, to those of his companion—"We are sold! sold through the stupid innocence of ourselves;" and he related all that he had just learned. Bardlaw heard it thoughtfully, and went over with it.

"Teed is opposed to us, and is in alliance with Ward, a sort of claim-agent and lobby-master-general; has a place on the Avenue above Twelfth; there is said to be a large association, with lady-allies, and all that sort of thing." And then Frank told of the visit of Mrs. Croly and Gloster. "Yes," continued Bardlaw, "we are in the 'Heart of Midlothian,' as somebody has named that region. Mrs. Croly, eh?" with a quick, meaning glance at the fine person of the youth, who stood finely strung up, with his teeth set, as if to lead a charge. "Well, we must look about; I've no confidence in Baker; but he can find out any thing. Do you know him, colonel?" Frank did not, personally. "He's just now the most odious man in America. Do you know Mr. Drybow?"

"Drybow? I've met him several times, but didn't take much to him. He's a dry bone, drier than that valley where they used to dry them, after a long drought," Frank dryly answered.

"He's called 'Long Drought' himself, sometimes, I believe," remarked Bardlaw. "He knows every body and thing, in Washington; knows Baker thoroughly, and has some faith in him. I don't know Baker—can't approach him; but you can, you and Mason, with Drybow; we must know who these men are, and their means of work; and, another thing, colonel—we must keep our own counsel—we—you and I. Even Miss Brand must know nothing from this time on; all depends on finding these witnesses; we haven't a scrap of record or writing, so far."

The whole position flashed on the mind of Frank, as that of the experienced lawyer ran from point to point;

and, accustomed as he was to encounter enemies in field or ambush, whom he might meet with sabre and musket, his thoughts did not readily adapt themselves to this intangible mental contest, with sham and shadows.

"I think you had better change your quarters, colonel," said Bardlaw; "our friend Gordon will be an open avenue of approach, which we can't protect, and," turning full upon the young man, "a good deal will depend upon you, a new enemy in a new field, which you must not avoid, for we must now turn and spy the spies." With some consultation as to plans and details, the council broke up.

CHAPTER XVI.

THE DETECTIVE.

Frank went up the Avenue, looked into the Continental and Metropolitan Hotels, went into the book-stores along up, and so into the Willard, where he finally encountered the wandering, hungry eyes of Drybow, whose glances betrayed that they had not yet found the object they were searching for, and, though always engaged, he could attend to any call, however sudden. He had taken a great liking to Frank, and, in response to a request for a few moments of his time, answered, "A whole day;" and, placing his hand within the young man's arm, he drew him into the street. On reaching the Treasury Building, Frank had possessed him with the status of his case. "We will go to General Baker," was his comment; "could I have invented an excuse, I would have taken you there before. Ever since I met that blessed old stupid—our best friend, Colonel Gordon, with—well, I've wanted to make you acquainted with Baker. He is a detective by instinct and habit. The only distinction that he can perhaps recognize between criminals and others is, that the first may be hunted, and he is a born hunter as well. A kindly nature too, and as kind to the one sort as the other. There ain't a man in the world that sees quicker, and when he makes a hit, as he generally does, he makes a big one, and when he loses, it is hard to convince him that he has blundered. If he makes up his mind that a man is to be gone for, he is generally a goner. He won't use many words, won't want any money, unless a journey is to be made, or somebody bought." They went through the Treasury, and out past the presidential mansion, and so on through the War-Office, across Seventeenth Street to Eighteenth, on which between E and F was the office of the dreaded Provost of the War-Office, and Chief of the Secret Service.

Drybow was recognized as a friend, and they were shown into the retreat of the grim spider, who in that small and dimly-lit room wove the webs that ensnared so many, and at such distant points. It was here that, taking a map of Virginia, he placed one foot of a compass on Port Royal, on the Rappahannock, and, describing a small circle about it with the other, he told Colonel Conger and Lieutenant Baker that within that circle they would find Booth and Harrold, and within that circle Booth was killed and Harrold captured within the next thirty hours. Frank and Drybow found him alone, and he arose—a thin, spare man, above medium height, with a decided stoop in the broad, powerful shoulders, swarthy face, black brow, full black beard, with large, dark, melancholy eyes; a man of more physical power than at first appeared, strong, with a spirit that only knew danger to confront it. His manners were abrupt, voice low, and words the fewest. He partly arose, and indicated with his hand the presence of seats, and awaited their communication. With a word or two of introduction, Colonel Warbel, with whose name Baker seemed familiar, laid before him the facts known to the reader. This was followed with a few abrupt and seemingly disconnected questions, as if some of the mental relations and connections were not quite perfect; and then, casting his head down for a moment, he pulled a bell, with—" Call Jones." A few moments after a thinnish, light-complexioned, youngish, Down-Eastish-looking man, with marked features and the air of a dissolute divinity-student, stepped in and took a seat, when the chief went over with the points, and indicated what might further be undertaken on the other side, and to what they must direct their own attention, and assigned Jones to assist them. " Of course," he said, " they intend to gobble up not only this square of city property, but the claims, and very likely the owner of them." This last was evidently for the benefit of Colonel Warbel, upon whom it was impressed with the full force of the dark eyes of the speaker, that had a way of throwing themselves upon those of others sometimes with the effect of a blow.

On their way down the Avenue, Drybow took Frank to the house in Eleventh Street before mentioned, where he secured a pleasant furnished room, and ordered it made ready at once, but was at a loss for a pretext for leaving the luxurious quarters of his friend Colonel Gordon. On his return that evening, he found this awaiting him. He was rather coolly received by the disturbed colonel, who handed him Miss Ware's card, and said he regretted that Colonel Warbel was not there to keep the engagement, but really he would suggest that some more fitting and less public place for an arrangement of the sort had perhaps better be substituted for his house.

The hot blood of the colonel leaped into his face for a moment, and then retreated from the surface as was its wont in moments of sudden peril, and leaving him as usual only a better master of himself.

"I regret, exceedingly, Colonel Gordon, that you have been subjected to annoyance on my account," placing the card in his pocket. "What I may, I will promptly do to save you from any repetition of this in the future;" and, turning into his own room, he hastily plundered his drawers and wardrobe, and prepared to vacate. His anger disappeared with the flash; his pride was rapidly mounting. The colonel was only aware of his intended departure when a hackman called for his baggage.

"Why, how now? What! Good God, colonel! you are not going to leave me? Why, I really—I regret—"

"Not a word, my dear colonel. You owe me no explanation—certainly no apology. I've none to make. I've troubled you longer than I intended, and annoyed you I don't know how much. I've nothing but thanks for your kindness—good-by"—the last in the tone of final adieu. And he left the poor colonel in a confused amazement, and feeling somehow as if he had driven the youth into the street.

While he was yet bewildered, General Mason called to see Frank, and was much astonished to learn that he had left, and still more at the cause, and he looked very grave at it. He was certain that the colonel or Frank, or both, were the victims of some practical joker. He had never heard an imputation upon Frank. But when Gordon told him that the Croly and Gloster had both had interviews with him, and other items, which, in spite of the colonel's generous nature, floated into the atmosphere of Frank's person within a few days, Mason looked grave. Evidently Frank had taken final leave of the colonel, and gone off in a proud fit, had not even left his new address, and, when Mason failed to find it at any of the hotels, his gravity amounted to anxiety.

CHAPTER XVII.

THE NEW ALLY.

On the day following Frank's change of base, Mr. Ward had a visitor. There came peering into the clerk's room an odd-looking figure in worn black, glossy a little at the knees, sleeves, and front; a shrunken, misshaped, weaselly thing it was, with a prominent nose, wide mouth, and weak chin, supported by an ancient stock, over which rumpled a limp collar. The forehead was low and wrinkled, covered well down with a faded wig; a pair of large, brass-bound green glasses shaded or aided his small, restless gray eyes. He had his hat in one hand, and a bandanna handkerchief in the other, with which he mopped and sopped his little cliff of a forehead; while he supported an old cotton umbrella under one arm. His make-up and air did not indicate a stranger wholly, yet his cute, wary way would have betrayed him, which nevertheless had in it a tinge of the faded minister.

"'Pears to me I don't see nothing of no Ward round here nowhere—I don't, do I?" he said, looking keenly at each man, and behind the desks, as if he might be hidden away somewhere.

"Mr. Ward is in the next room," said a clerk, pointing to the door.

"How are you, jedge?" said the intruder, rushing up to that comely personage, as he entered his room, and who looked at him with an unusual and puzzled look—"how are you, jedge? You don't 'pear to know me—like."

"Well, not exactly. I think I've seen you somewhere."

"Of course, jedge, I'm always there; but, then, you

never did see me but once, to know me, for sartin, an' then you didn't know's I's there—you see, jedge."

"Exactly—I see. If I'd known you were there, I might have seen you, but as I wa'n't there at all myself, you only saw me. That's the way, was it?"

"Jes' so, an' very well put, too, for one 'oo never ocke-pied the pulpit."

"Oh! so then you're a sort of a minister cuss, eh? I wa'n't at your meeting, I s'pose?"

"Well, jedge, it ain't worth while to make light o' heavenly things, an'—"

"Pardon me, poor sinner that I am," said Ward, with mock gravity. "I've no doubt you're heavenly; but you're not quite glorified, I see. And so you're a minister?"

"Wal, not ezactly. I had a natural turn for preach-in', but never had much chance to improve my bent in that way. You—but, jedge, I came in on a little bizness, ruther pecoolar—and," observing a bottle with some glasses on a sideboard near by, "I don't care if I do, jedge, bein' it's you;" and without ceremony he drew the cork, applied his nose to the opening, and filling out a glass, he threw it down as only an American born could. "Jerusalem! but that's licker, jedge," inspecting the brand.

"Fairish," answered Ward. "You'd better finish it," a little ironically.

"Yis, after this little bizness. By-the-way, my name is Smithers. I allus drops the 'ers,'" and, seating himself without invitation, he took from an inside pocket a large bundle of papers. "Jedge, do you have any thing to do with Gloster?"

"Well, not much; why?"

"Why, he's like a spring bumble-bee, a hummin' and a buzzin' round, and never 'lightin' nowhere, an' never doin' nothin', but buz, buz, buz!"

"Ha! ha! ha! Smithers, that's good. I'll tell Gloster that."

"Do, with my respecs. Kramer told me fust to go to Tunzle, Teazle, Tweezer, or what's his name, that red-headed blasphemer."

"He did, eh? Well, why didn't you?"

"'Cause I wanted to come to you, an' Kramer said I better; an' he wrote this in pencil," showing it on the files, "Show these to Ward.—KRAMER." "When you're satisfied it's all right, the words had better be rubbed off, I guess," said Smithers.

The sight of Kramer's hand excited the attention of Ward, and he ran the papers rapidly over. "Why, Smithers, this is a thirty-five-thousand-dollar case. Seizure of the Concord. Your ownership and value proved up, but, I see, rejected for dealing with the rebs. What's the proof of that? You seem to be certified to as loyal."

"Wal, you see, jedge, after the river was clear, I was runnin' on 'er from St. Louis to New Orleans, or from Cairo. Wal, she stopped sometimes o' nights, an' surely as she did, she was regalerly robbed of bacon, flour—any thing she had, by rebs or land-pirates."

"And this was so sure to be done, that she was loaded with just such things, I s'pose?" remarked Ward.

"Wal, I shouldn't wonder. There may a' bin a tendency that way."

"You didn't lose much, Smith—or Smithers?"

"Ginerally not. You see, in one sense it weakened the enemy," suggested Smith.

"And in another, it toned 'em up. Nothing like your good bacon and bread for an empty stomach, eh, Smithers? You were finally suspected, arrested, and condemned, and sold. Served you right, Smithers. Well, what can be done?"

"That's what brings me to you. I could put in more

testimony, you know, but how to git some out already in is the thing. It's easy enough to put it in."

"Yes, when you have it, or can find the right kind of witnesses," rejoined Ward.

"I think it's easier to make 'em," said Smith.

"Yes, that's the old heavenly way, parson, but we can't quite come that."

"Jest you write me your name, jedge, on this sheet o' paper."

Ward, as bid, scrawled, in a bold hand, "J. W. Ward," when Smithers, taking the same pen, on another sheet made, without apparent effort, a fac-simile, and, picking them up, changed them two or three times.

"Which's your'n, jedge?"

Ward looked at them in blank amazement for a moment, unable to distinguish between them, and, turning almost in alarm to his visitor, he snatched off his old wig and glasses, and there stood before him a shrunken man, at least twenty years older than he appeared before, and whom Ward knew he had never seen, which only increased his amazement.

"The jedge is a leetle playful to-day," said the unmoved Smithers, with a cackling laugh.

"Pardon me, Mr. Smithers," for the first time with a real respect, restoring the wig and glasses, which Smithers resumed, working another metamorphosis, which only increased Ward's wonder—"pardon me, if I did not at first notice all your merits. Take some more old stag?"

"Don't care ef I do, jedge," said the composed Smithers, throwing down enough to start a Laplander. "You see, jedge, I took naterally to writin', and used to keep writin'-schools. I'm ruther out o' practice now, but I kin do somethin' with a pen yit, when my hand gits in."

"Let me see you make some of these," said Ward, showing him several signatures, all of which with much readiness he imitated, as closely as the writer of the signature would have done. Ward rung a bell and ordered a lunch to be brought in, with another bottle, to both of which Smithers did ample justice, eating and drinking and talking with unflagging industry, exhibiting a rare combination of simplicity and shrewdness, which, with his frankness, won strongly on the cool, wary, experienced Ward, who, when he thought he must be loosened a little by his huge draughts of the generous liquor, got some items of his history. Of course he came, as he said, from "Vairmount," and he mentioned, with much *naïveté*, a little thing of his early manhood: he had a promissory note for a hundred and fifty dollars, drawn without interest, payable six months after date, to which were added somehow the words "with interest;" "an' it was in ruther pale ink, too, yit jest for that leetle thing, jedge, I had to leave," with an injured air. "I was actilly cut off from the church, 'n' I've never went back; an' the fact is, jedge, it's no matter now—that's why I dropped the 'ers' off the eend of my name." Nothing could equal this candor; and the memory of his early and undeserved misfortune, or the liquor, or both, brought a moisture to his eyes, which he removed his glasses to wipe, and a tremor came into his voice.

"Well, Smithers, how long have you been round Washington, and whom do you know?"

He had been there "two year and 'levin days, off an' on," and mentioned as his acquaintances every well-known man at the capital. Among these, Baker, who, he said, "scairt folks more'n he hurt 'em, a pesky sight."

"Smithers, are you married?" asked Ward.

"None at all, jedge. You see, though I'm fond o' women, an' have a high respec' for 'em, I've been too busy, an' now, when I'm a *leetle* comfortable, they'd think I'm too old."

"Not a bit, not a bit, Smithers. Why, with that wig on, dress you up in clothes not more than a century old, and you'd be a real buck among the ladies, Smithers."

"He-he-he! per'aps I'd do, eh, jedge?"

"Come, now, what do you say? I'll introduce you to a young, middle-aged Southern lady, full of the South, a widow—aunt to a great heiress, whom we are to collect a million or two for. Just the opening, and I'd like to have a shrewd, trusty man near her, you know."

"Jest to keep the lay of the land, jedge, eh?"

"Yes; have somebody that they could send word by, you know, and do little pleasant errands.—What do you say? will you put on a swallow-tail, and, with a flower at your button-hole, let me introduce you? Take another drink, Mr. Smithers."

"Sartin — sartin, jedge!" not finding quite a full drink in the bottle. "Is she a God-fearin' woman, jedge?"

"Oh, yes, pious and plaintive, and given to psalms."

"I'm a bit of a poic, jedge: shall I recite some of my varses? I used to make 'em when I was young, darned if I didn't."

The judge declined to have any, but told him to keep them for the Biggses; and it was finally arranged that, on the day following, Mr. Smithers should be introduced to Mrs. Thompson. Separating his papers, so as to leave with Ward such as pertained to the Concord case, Smithers let fall a package of greenbacks, which with Ward's aid he recovered, exposing quite a number, and some of large denominations. These he carelessly disposed of about his person, and a little maudlin, and slightly oblivious, he took his leave.

After his departure, Ward took a turn or two about the room: "Good God! I thought the whiskey would never reach him; it was like turning it into a woodchuck's hole; what a wonder that fist of his is! and he'd never got drunk and made such a confession, if he was playing. Tweed and Tweezer will make a million with him alone."

On the following morning, Mr. Smith called again at the rooms of Mr. Ward, with much of the look and depressed manner of a man whose excess had humiliated him.

"Good-mornin', Jedge Ward," with much humility. "I come to beg parding for my little *foxpass*, yesterday. Your licker had such a way of slippin' out, and slippin' down, that I slipped up on it, an' no mistake, jedge."

"All right, all right, Parson Smith; the best of men mistake their capacity. You remember that the only excuse St. Peter gave for being sober once was, that it was so early in the morning."

"An' he didn't have your licker, I guess, .nuther," quietly suggested Smith, a little struck with Ward's idea of the Pentecostal narrative, and perhaps wondering how the story would have run under other circumstances.

"I say, jedge, I s'pose I must a' said some queer things about—wal, about myself, my name, how it lost the 'ers,' and all that—didn't I?"

"Well, you were quite explicit, but then it was the confidential communications of client to counsel, you know."

"Yes, so 'twas. Thank you, jedge," much relieved.

And then Ward offered him another glass, which was quite positively declined. Then followed more specimens of his hand, and Ward sent for Teed, and many things were talked over; both were surprised at the acuteness of his observations, and the facility with which he invented methods for the transaction of business. The interview was followed by his accompanying Ward to Borum's, where he was formally presented to the Biggses.

CHAPTER XVIII.

MRS. CROLY AT HOME.

On his return to his new room, toward evening of the first day of its occupation, Warbel was surprised, and something besides, at finding a note to him, addressed to his new quarters, showing that he was an object of watchful interest to some one, as, save Mr. Drybow, Baker, and Jones, he had communicated to no one the locality of his lodgings. Upon opening the note, he found it to read as follows:

"*Wednesday*, A. M.

"Colonel Warbel: Lieutenant Corflint will be at my rooms at the Avenue, at eight this evening. I venture to hope that you will meet him there. Pray let nothing prevent it.

"At the office, ask for Barber, and hand him the inclosed card. Valeria C."

On the inclosed card was "Mrs. Croly."

They were right, then, and had touched the electric circle. He was within it, if not its present centre.

Dressed with some care, at a moment past eight, he asked for Barber at the office of the Avenue House, and a dapper gentleman stepped forward, took the card, looked at the presenter, and then at the card, as if somehow the former did not fill the bill; but, wisely concluding to refer that matter to higher authority, he led off, evidently not the most direct route, up a back spiral way, with two or three turns at the top, and concluded with a low tap at a door, which immediately opened, and Frank entered. The room, neat, airy, brilliantly lighted, was unoccupied, save by the maid who opened the door, but whose presence almost filled the room. Of light, graceful figure, dressed in dark colors, with a neat white apron, and bare arms, and a face with great flashing eyes, and a world of night-black hair, which a little jaunty cap tried in vain to conceal.

As Frank passed in, he received one gleam of those eyes, that seemed to light up the shadow of a recollection. She took his cloak and hat, placed him a seat, and, as he turned again to her, she was the demure waiting-woman, whose eyes were not again raised to his. She stepped within an inner door, and partly closed it. A moment later, and, though Frank had once before lost his breath at meeting Mrs. Croly, and well prepared, he was scarcely less surprised now. A moment, like a vision, she stood on the threshold, and the next her warm, clinging hand seemed to melt within his, with an exquisite thrill.

"It is so kind of you, colonel, to come to me!" with a little, fluttering, flattering voice, low and sweet, with her exquisite person arrayed and disarrayed to its best. How fair the billowy, pillowy sea of shoulder and bosom, with its unsubsiding, foamy waves rising and ever rising, over its limits, and how innocently she placed herself almost at his feet, on a low seat, with the throbbing light falling warmly on her person, as she held up her face and liquid, changing eyes to his!

Frank recovered his self-possession, and answered that the kindness was entirely on her part, and that nothing gave him more pleasure than to meet her wish, and dashing on: "I am really at a loss, Mrs. Croly, to know how you so soon discovered my new quarters; for, really, I could hardly find them myself."

"Well, it was good enough for you, you naughty man; you should have known that you would not escape by running and hiding. That must be new to you."

"I was never in such peril before, I do believe," laughing.

"I declare, Colonel Warbel, you didn't learn that in the army; you were born to say exquisite things, and—"

"Do very foolish ones," he interrupted. She looked keenly at him, as there was just a ping in the tone of the interruption. But his face wore the same bright smile, and the eyes looked as softly into her all-absorbing orbs as before. Somehow this pleasant opening collapsed; the lady was not equal to an apt answer, and turned, a little vexed, from her lost opportunity to Frank's experience in the city, how he liked it, etc., and whether he did not find the residents a warm-hearted people. Frank thought them very kind and open; indeed, the city generally was open—very; the very sidewalks and crossings opened deeply to his foot-falls, and his boots, at every step, were the victims of unrequited attachments. Those were in the bad days before Governor Shepherd and the Board of Public Works.

The time ran on, but Corflint did not appear. Mrs. Croly watched the face of her visitor, and finally affected to be anxious, and consulted her watch, and said that she feared the lieutenant had been detained, and she did not know how she could excuse his not kee·ing the engagement; and, a moment later, she received a note from him, regretting, etc. Mrs. Croly was in a real distress, and looked very pleadingly into Frank's eyes, where she saw something that encouraged her to look again, and she finally trusted that he would really excuse the disappointment; and Frank fully pardoned her on the spot, and assured her that his fortitude was equal to the present demands on it; and then the lady arose and ventured to say that she had ordered a little supper for the expected two gentlemen, and she begged that it might be brought in—that she would esteem it a great honor; to all of which her guest graciously assented, and in the most obliging manner accepted her invitation.

The demure maid drew out and deftly spread a little

table. A servant brought up a tray of various delicacies, with tea; the lady and her guest took seats opposite each other, and the maid with the hair and eyes served them. The lady affected to eat; the gentleman gayly toyed with the viands, and, when gently chided by his hostess for his abstinence, he "wondered that she should try to remind him of more vulgar meats," while his eyes seemed to feast off her beauty; and, again, she lost her presence of mind, and was vexed. The viands were removed; two quaint bottles of wine, with glasses, were placed on the table, and two glasses filled, and the demure maid retired. The lady took hers, and, "Will you pledge me, colonel?" raised it to her lips. The eyes of her guest were drinking at hers, and his glass remained untouched. His eyes fell, and, in a voice low and plaintive, he said: "A man's eyes are drunk, his spirit floats and swims, and you would have him take wine!"

"And why not, colonel?" with a smile arrested.

"And so awaken the evil—the dregs of his coarse nature! I don't drink wine, Mrs. Croly."

"Not drink wine? I do," wholly off her guard, and she drank off her glass. "Don't drink wine? I never heard of such a thing. Colonel, does your mother know you're out? Ha, ha, ha!—ha, ha, ha!"

"My mother!" in a saddened voice, unheeding her levity; "oh, she died long, long ago, when I was a little boy," and there was just a tremor in his tone, that thrilled the thoughtless woman. For a moment the color left lip and cheek, and, going around to his side and seating herself on a low ottoman, she clasped one of his hands in both hers, and, looking up into his half-averted eyes, she said: "O Colonel Warbel, forgive me! it was a rude, thoughtless speech!" A mocking look came into his eyes, now fully bent down to hers. "Oh," she said, "and now you will never care for me! will never love me!"

"Love you! love you!" exclaimed he, with a wide-eyed stare of surprise. "Why should I? I should have never thought of that." And he looked steadily into the dark, deep, inviting orbs, now full of that strange, tawny light that sometimes burns in the eyes of women of certain temperaments.

"What do you see in my eyes?" dropping them, and almost breathless.

"Clouds and darkness, and mists, with only flashes of light, and that not clear or steady," withdrawing his hand from hers. "Love! Your lips a moment since seemed warm with the life of real womanhood—there's the odor of wine on them now—faugh!" with a look of disgust. "Why, you have a husband now. Love, indeed!"

"I have not! I have not!" said she, springing up and flashing like a tiger-cat. "I bear only the name of a wife; no man claims me, and no man shall! I am compelled to play a part, I am alone in the world—no, not alone; I have the burdens of others. I could not work a day, even here, in this rotting city, and a male permits me to bear his name—his name, for a consideration—and even that is a crushing burden!" Never before had such a beautiful and indignant protest against the pitiless wrongs of the world toward her sex flashed upon the eyes of Frank. As she closed, she dashed her face into her hands, and one convulsive sob shook her frame. A moment, and, rising, she stepped within the adjoining room, and returned with her beautiful bosom and shoulders under a light wrap. Her face was soft, and the dangerous voluptuous light had died out of her eyes, but there was firmness in the compressed mouth, and will and determination in every curve of the form.

Colonel Warbel had risen as if to take leave.

"Colonel Warbel, be seated," in a tone which was a command, an invitation, and an entreaty. Frank resumed his seat. "I have been surprised into weakness, and something worse, in your presence, and that gives me a claim upon you. I need not ask you not to mention what has occurred. I know you cannot. I am yet to see more of you, and am yet to win your regard. You are not to abandon poor Corflint, nor to say that you will not meet him here. You can come, and the outside world will be none the wiser."

Frank bowed, and again arose: "May I now take my leave?" with a tender respect in voice and manner. She advanced to him and gave him her hand. He bent over without raising it to his lips, and stepped into the corridor. At the first turn, a servant met and conducted him down and out, avoiding the public rooms of the house.

As the door closed on Frank, a ringing peal of laughter, and Mrs. Harbeck broke together from the inner room, with her unconfined hair in clouds of down-dropping night about her shoulders, and her eyes wild with mirth. "And so—ha, ha, ha!—and so—this was the way it came out—ha, ha, ha! We went a-wooing and got quite decidedly wooled—ha, ha, ha! The young mouse came in as proper and nice as could be, saw all the trap, sniffed the toasted cheese, and found it a little—well, not to his taste—kissed his little paw, and went—ha, ha, ha!"

The Croly, who had thrown herself on a sofa, with her face down, started up with her beauty at its severest.

"I won't be beaten this way. I'll have him yet, see if I don't!" with defiance and determination.

"Have him? Why, you forget that it was *it* that you were to get."

"Well, how can I get *it*, except from him, pray?"

"Sure enough; and, as surely, you never will get him, Valeria."

"I will—I will—I will! and so there—"

"Well, we'll see."

"Do you go back on me, Harbie?"

"Not at all. But I can't help you, if you go on in this way."

"What way? He's a man, ain't he, like other men?"

"Yes, a man; and not a mere he-animal. You were too fast on the start. The truth is, Valeria, you were just like a woman—all for the man. You were more than half in love with him when he came in; and how coolly he took you! Two or three little compliments—pretty things, some of them—and you lost your head. You began very well, with your demure way, but you risked all on your shoulders and bust, exposed so that the light shone down to your belt"—a groan from Croly—"and all the time his imagination was hovering about a veiled bosom, which the sun never saw, and of which he dares not think."

"Tell me of her," said the subdued Croly.

"She has no more physical beauty than have you, not so much, and of a different style; but she has what never can be yours, and yet you are unconscious of its absence."

"What is that?"

"The flavor of untouched womanhood. She who has it is unconscious of it. She who loses it is unaware of its loss, and may wonder—her eyes ever as bright, her face as fair, her form as beautiful—and she only sees or feels a change in the look or manner of men, and innocently wonders why. That's it, Valeria."

"What shall I do? I won't give him up."

"Of course not, you cannot give *it* up, and woman-like must pursue it by pursuing a man. You must begin anew. We know now something of what he is; he will not be loved and cheated through his senses, and must be reached through his heart and sympathies. He loves this beautiful Southern girl—"

"I could murder her—!"

"You must learn to love her, and so know how to talk

with him about her, and become his nearest, dearest friend, do for him what he wishes, help him if in your power, betray secrets to him if he wishes, become—"

"I'll do every thing, be every thing—I'll charm every thing out of this red-haired, hideous Teezle-Tweezle and his horrid partner, who when he takes my hand I cover it with my handkerchief till I can wash it, before I dare look at it —any thing!"

"Croly," said Harbeck, a little tenderly, "you are at heart a woman, after all; and if you are really capable of a true womanly passion for this young man, you may through it escape to a better plane of life, for he is on its upper heights. If through you he stumbles, you will certainly be lost; while he—a man—may escape."

"Oh! I've tried to be good. But the world has mocked and scorned, and would not let me be. And I'm but here to become a lure, a bait—'toasted cheese'—that's the true word—for mean and detestable men, and for vile things;" and she hid her face again among the cushions, and great dry sobs convulsed her.

When Frank went to his room, on his return, he passed an intersecting corridor, in which stood Kramer and another, whose face was from him. He caught the words in an unknown voice, as he approached, "She'll not return to-night"—a hush as he passed, in Kramer's "There goes the damned fool now!" and Kramer never knew how near he came to being thrashed that night.

CHAPTER XIX.

MRS. THOMPSON HAS A CALL.

On the Sunday evening following the incidents just narrated, an odd figure attracted the idlers at Borum's. There were the wig, stock, and glasses of Smith, with the "ers" omitted, arrayed in a high-collared blue coat, with brass buttons, short-waisted, the buttons behind, up between the shoulder-blades, from which the skirts went downward "long and narrow," like Barbara Allen's death-bed, flapping against old-fashioned brimstone-colored cassimere pantaloons, of a long-ago period, and the whole surmounted with a bell-crowned hat of the same geological age. Mr. Smith carried an immense bouquet in his hand, and sent up his card to Mrs. Thompson, with becoming formality, and a moment later the amused Millie showed him up. Mrs. Thompson received him with more than usual flabbiness, as the female Biggses do, when desirous of bringing all their advantages to bear. Mr. Smith bowed low and squarely over the toes of both boots, number tens.

"I hope Miss Tomsing is well to-day?"

To which the lady, without rising:

"No, I thank you; I'm enjoyin' miserable health to-day. How is Misto Smith?"

"'Bout midlin', under the care o' Providence." And, approaching the lady with his flowers in one hand, and another square-toed bow: "I thought I'd fetch ye a boukwet; it cost sixty-two 'n' a half cents."

"O Misto Smith! La sakes, you're very kind, I do declar'—they're beauties;" and, pressing the flowers to her face—"how they remind me of old times, when me 'n' my poor husband, who's dead an' gone—anyway gone—for I'm good's a widow—"

"How long since the dear relic has been heerd from?" a little anxiously, inquired Smith.

"Better'n nine year. Nine year I've been livin' alone," in a dolorous voice. "It's very sad, Misto Smith; the ladies of the Biggses mostly makes second marriages, with new pardners, before nine year; not but that I've been pressed to marry, many a time. These flowers is so comfortin', they bring up all my suff'rin's so delightfully."

"What says the Scripters to the wearyin' and overladin'? You sartinly remember all the soothin' and harrowin' promises."

"To be shore, Misto Smith, or I should 'a giv' all out. Now Alice, you know, has Northern blood, whar's very little nerves an' feelin's, an' she goes through it in a careless way like, that is almost shockin' to one o' Southern blood an' raisin'."

"Of course," responded the complaisant Smith, "and how is the young woman?"

"Very well, she mostly is."

"What was it about her sellin' out?" insinuatingly.

"Thar'! I shouldn't wonder if that young Colonel Warbel had up an' tole you all about it. Between you an' me, Misto Smith, though he's peart, I don't think much o' that grown-up boy."

"A good deal like a bumble-bee, biggest when fust born, eh, Miss Tomsing?" suggested Smith. "I think the young woman had better be keerful who she deals with, though."

"Why, Misto Smith, she talked of sellin' to Misto Ward."

"Well, now, do you know all about that are chap, Miss Tomsing? It's none o' my business, though; have you seen him lately?"

Mrs. Thompson, a little concerned, admitted that she had not, and thought it strange.

"Not at all," answered the confident Smith, "an' you never will see 'im agin. He had a purpose to come a-purrin' round an unprotected female. You'll see. Mark my word!"

"But 'e paid 'er a thousand dollars," said the unprotected one, not quite willing to give him up.

"Yis, an' whose money was it? More likely than not, it come from them Teed and Tweezer fellers, who are on 'tother side. They are thick as hasty-puddin'; I seen 'em together two or three times lately."

"Why, Misto Smith!" in amazement.

"An' he two or three wives; I don't know which," put in the relentless Smith.

"Oh—oh—oh!—Millie! Millie!" but Millie was out, and no appliances were at hand, and Smith might not take it kindly; and so, with the explanatory remark that the Biggses were often taken in that way, she subsided into calmness at once, and, turning again to her visitor: "Misto Smith, I think you promised to bring me some of your poetry; have you thought of it? It would be very comfortin' to me now."

"Yis; I have one or two Scriptoor-pieces, not inappropriate to the Sabbyday, that has given me great consolation. These," opening out a full sheet of cap, "is extracted—I may say, it is a double-compound extrac', from the most strikin' events in the Old Testament, an' soothin'. The lines are a little uneven, per'aps, but the sentiments is, I may say, heavenly." Mrs. Thompson composed herself with an air of resigned expectancy. Mr. Smith cleared his throat, adjusted his glasses, and in a nasal voice, and a moving, old, sing-song intonation, he trolled out:

"'The children of Israel had to run their faces,
    And Faro chased them through the Red Sea flood;
The Lord He come down, and cut off all their traces,
    And left all their old army-waggins stickin' in the mud.'"

"O, Misto Smith! how movin' that is, an' kind o' comfortin', too, I do declar'!"

"Yis, it shows how the Lord deals with sinners, cuttin' 'em off at a lick, as it were. I think the nex' varse will also please you:

"'There was Joner, a sinful man of sin,
    Who run away from Ninevah for to be a sailor;
But God sent a big fish who suckèd him in,
    And so Joner he become a whaler.'"

"Seems to me, Misto Smith, that that is more touchiner than the other stanzer," said Mrs. Thompson, with fine discrimination.

"It's more pusonal, you see; and so is the follerin', which is also quite pathetic, an' may harry your feelin's some; though I'll risk it:

> "'Daniel he was a profit, and a good man,
> Who into the den of hungry lions did fall;
> All for to make him the lions' food-man,
> But nary a one got any on him, at all.'"

The voice of the reader drawled out the last line with such prodigious effect, that the lady, burying her sympathizing face in her bouquet, threw up one hand imploringly: "O Misto Smith! I fear I can't stan' much more—the poor, hungry things!"

"Wal, I'll jest give one more; this one is a *leetle* more lively, and will take the taste o' Daniel out o' your mouth, mebby." The lady braced herself up, and the poet went on:

> "'Sampsing he was the most strongest man, and he loved Delila fair;
> And she told the wicked Filistins that his strength lay in his hair;
> And she wheedled him, and kissèd him, and got him fast asleep;
> And in come the Filistins, and sheered him like a sheep!'

"Ha-ha-ha!—and sarved him right. I think that very good; don't you?"

"Yis," laughing faintly; "but then, Misto Smith, don't you think it's makin' light of heavenly things?" a little doubtfully.

"Wal, mebby 'tis a *leetle* mite; but then the subjec' allus calls for it, in fact; a man to go a foolin' round a woman, as Jedge Samsing did, might expect it. I should."

"Why; Misto Smith! You should be ashamed to say that. Do I look like Delily?" and Mr. Smith had the candor and gallantry to admit that, in his opinion, she did not;

and he didn't think that she'd fool Samsing; though he didn't know what Mr. Ward might say.

"Misto Ward! Don't mention his name to me agin as long as you live! Ward, indeed! I'd like to ketch 'im at it. Misto Smith," holding out her hand for the paper, "will you give me that movin' piece? and when I'm stronger I'll read them as I can," in a very faint voice.

"Sartin, sartin; and you'd better take 'em as I do, when I'm down in the mouth a *leetle;* 'bout one varse'll bring me up, they's so bracin'."

"I think they must be bracin'," was the flattering answer. "Misto Smith, do you write poetry now; any little thing, such as young men send to girls sometimes, ye know?"

"Yis; when I was young I used to have quite a knack at little love-varses."

"Oh! I wish, you'd write me some, Misto Smith," with pleading voice and imploring look.

"Sartinly, sartinly; but then, you see, Miss Thomsing, that one can't do these things in the winter. It mostly depends on the season; ginerally, only in the spring, when the weather's warm, an' birds come back, an' are matin', and hens begin to lay; when the sap runs, and bark peels; then, you know, these funny notions run right off a feller. Wait till spring, and you'll have one for every beauty in you."

"O Misto Smith, how you do talk! you mustn't go on so. But there'll come a warm spell afore long, I hope, which'll be spring-like, and I shall expect something. Most of the Biggses would, you know."

"Wal, I'll try; but there's no sartinty what you'll get;" and Mr. Smith was permitted to put his thin lips, which he smacked, as he took them from the skinny Biggs's hand when he departed.

CHAPTER XX.

WHO WOULD BE A MEMBER OF CONGRESS?

IT was after the holidays, after the reassembling of the two Houses, and all the arrivals for the winter, and the restless world of Washington life was at full tide. All that had designs upon the executive departments, with their memorials and letters, were on hand: The seven or eight men, each of whom was the original discoverer of Andrew Johnson, and who brought him forward for Vice-President at the Baltimore Convention; several more who had stood by Grant and Sherman, severally, in the dark days of their and the country's fortunes—and it was astonishing, their number; the crowds for the post-offices and places in the civil service; the greater crowds for places under the revenue laws, in the land-offices, applicants for Indian agencies, and speculators for mail-lettings, for routes in the new Territories—there is nothing like them—for diplomatic posts in South America, for consulates everywhere; crowds who bought the Blue-Book, larger crowds who borrowed it, the multitudes who read it; men—seedy men—dependants of Senators and Congressmen, editors who had failed, broken merchants, broken-winded lawyers, clergymen with cracked reputations, with all the masses of broken failures of all sorts, seeking places in the departments as so many hospitals and lazar-houses; men who had failed everywhere and at every thing, and men who did not arise to the dignity of failure, forming knots and thickets about doors and entrances; men who speculated in legislation, who wanted to reduce the tax on whiskey, who wanted to reduce import duties, who wanted to increase them; men with claims, and the swarms of feeders on claims and claimants; impotent men in the war, who had been dismissed for incompetency, for absence, for cowardice, for peculation, and who wanted to be honorably discharged with pay, and who had innumerable papers and affidavits; whole hosts, just out of the army and idle; men who had just discovered new projectiles and breech-loading guns; men who had in some remote part of the republic just stumbled upon new discoveries in mechanics, of which models were already on deposit in the Patent-Office; men with new schemes of finance, projects to pay the national debt; men forming pools to run the Secretary of the Treasury; men with new plans, and men without any, new or old; men on the make, and men on the spend; men with their wives and daughters to visit the capital and spend the winter; persons of position and culture; persons with neither, but with money; the odds and ends of men and women, set afloat or run aground by the convulsions of the times; the sinister and dangerous elements liberated by the war, and liberated again by the disbanding of the army; roughs, gamblers, and bummers; men who lived by their wits, and men whose wits furnished scanty prog; the vagabonds and idlers of the armies disbanded about Washington; hundreds of army and navy officers; unprotected women, widows who never had husbands, women with antecedents and histories, women with careers, women with missions, real widows with genuine weeds, women who thronged nameless places south of the Avenue, and made little plague-spots all over the city; vagabonds, beggars, burglars, and thieves—all were there, and in unusual force, in that winter of 1865–'66.

And daily, from eleven to three, the huge tide of mingled life, rich and brilliant with the dresses, the furs, flowers, velvets, and heavy silks of resplendent ladies, flowed down the Avenue to the Capitol, where the two flags floated over the two Houses—moving in masses up the huge marble stairways, crowding the immense rotunda, where the new arrivals linger, admiring the wonderful complexions in Trumbull's pictures, and throwing skyward glances up to where the unhappy George Washington and other worthies of his day are performing their eccentric gallops with the goddesses on the underside of the great dome's roof.

They flood and flow through all the corridors and over all the galleries, wonder at the unseemly noises of the House and go to sleep in presence of the Senate, stare at the occupants of the diplomatic galleries, and then from four to six, with parting commiseration at poor Pa George on the roof, the human tide ebbs and pulsates away again.

The old members of Congress came back to their old haunts to have the old sick feeling when they cross the different currents of hot polluted air from the various passages and openings, meeting them like the breaths of so many sewers; to feel the old heart-sinkings, as different objects bring back associations and memories of old anxieties, defeats, and fruitless triumphs; and are prepared to settle down to the old work, on the old, ever-baffling and never-solved problems; and to face the new questions that now so threateningly faced them. There were the old personal rivalries, hatreds, and jealousies; the old remembered slights and insults from political friends, for which a day of payment could never come, because they were political friends. Of the leaders of the majority, some had received the coveted places on the committees, and many were disappointed and soured; while the leaders of the minority, at the tail of these organs, felt at least the relief of irresponsibility.

The former had the dread of the unknown peril, from the course of the executive, just making itself felt, and settled back to the innumerable calls from everybody, for every thing, to going everywhere on all errands, receiving all manner of letters that could not be answered, that needed no answers, and yet must be answered under peril of enmity; of weary wanderings all the mornings about the interminable departments; of hurryings to committee-rooms, and of finally sinking weak and exhausted into the representative chair, in the House, only to have little clouds of cards shot at them from outsiders: there to the work of watching all manner of questions in the din of the hall, answering letters, answering questions, struggling ineffectually for the floor, correcting the proofs of yesterday's speech, and franking it, with mail-bags full of public documents to be sent away; of being waylaid at the door, ambushed on the way home, to find men there awaiting them, to be hunted and haunted till midnight, and then sit down to finish a report; and all the time to watch the home newspapers and find themselves misunderstood and misrepresented, and denounced for their most meritorious acts; to be spurred with ambition, and feel insecure; to labor with a real zeal for the real good of the nation, and. to find the work ineffective; to be charged with fraud, voting to raise their own pay, with the certainty of being compelled to retire poor at middle life, with a ruined profession, a scrap-book full of small newspaper puffs, a volume of speeches; to be followed by an ineffectual attempt for an executive appointment, and the final consciousness of misdirected effort, misapplied talents, lost opportunity, and a wasted life; with the fear that they may finally be so bitten with Washington life as to feel compelled to remain and linger, and haunt its resorts, like so many of the faded great men whom they daily meet, compelled but unable to retire—old stars which, though long since shorn of light, persistently remain above the horizon in melancholy darkness.

One of the ablest, by far the most brilliant American, and, as I believe, the most eloquent speaker of the English tongue, and second to the utterer of none, in any time, after filling with success every place below that of President, spent his last days in rooms over a restaurant, on the Avenue, and rests without memoir or monument. Who would be a member of Congress?

CHAPTER XXI.

THE YOUNG REPRESENTATIVE.

In the third circle from the rear, and the second desk from the broad aisle, on the Speaker's left, sat Charles Mason, the youngest member in the House. Of average height, slight, firmly-knit frame, and a marked face, that looked better the more it was studied; modest, attentive, and courteous, he attracted and charmed all who came within his circle of acquaintance. He came with the reputation of an enterprising, intrepid officer of cavalry, one of the numerous new members promoted from the army to Congress.

A child of New-England parents, born and reared in the West, early left to the sole care of a mother, for whom in turn he cared for till her death, as he reached manhood, of ardent and impetuous temper, yet dreamy and imaginative, developing the elements of a profound and brilliant intellect, he had been a student of law, had practised with great success in his native town, now a city of fifteen or twenty thousand inhabitants, and had been one of the first to volunteer under the first call of the President. The fortunes of the war had placed and kept him at the front in active service, and in the more stirring events. Chivalrous, romantic, yet practical, he realized in his own person the daring and the achievements of an older age, and came out with a personal reputation equaled by few.

The year before, without his knowledge, a Republican convention of his district had nominated him for Congress, and he was elected while still in the field, and was only mustered out a few months before the assembling of the new House. That he was very much gratified with this mark of popular favor, was true; like many young lawyers of ardent temperament, whose fancy had been influenced by the great names of American oratory and statesmanship, he had dreamed of Congress as the goal of ambition; of some rare occasion when great destinies depended upon great creative words, that should give birth to great actions, with himself on the floor and the American people as auditors. As the heat and glow of his fervid imagination had sometimes for a moment transformed a red and torn battle-field into a listed course of old chivalry, and he had fought in an unreal world, so, as he journeyed toward the capital, something of his earlier dreams would haunt his imagination, spite of him.

What an effectual disenchantment the first week wrought, past dream-power ever to reconstruct! How ordinary and common the great men of the House whose names had been watchwords, and whose speeches had been read in tents, in hospitals, and on the march! Of all the men, Sumner, and Chase, and Stanton, in any way realized, and that faintly, his conception of them. Stevens was sharp, bitter, and pungent—not much more; and Bingham, and Dawes, Washburn, Schenk, Colfax, Kelly, Conkling, and even Garfield, talked and acted, laughed and lost temper, without any thing remarkable that he could see. Then, save a half-score more, how vulgar, rude, and common, the mass was—not above a fair average of an equal number of men who could be selected from any city of the second class in America! How did many of them ever escape from the mediocrity of home to the mediocrity of the House? What had they ever done, what could they ever do? Where was the lofty devotion that saw only the country, and that held party and self as mere means and helps?—the far-seeing sagacity that, enlightened by familiarity with all the past, caught from the light of the great present events something of prophetic power to provide for the future? Was this a fair specimen of an American House of Representatives? Surely, such men, selfish, time-serving—men so anxious to know what was said by the little newspapers of their districts, of them personally — such men could never have built up and fostered such a country; and he began to think that the country, the people, had grown— would grow—not through the providence of their wisdom, but in spite of their stupidity; that they were but an inconsiderable incident of the nation, one not important manifestation of its spirit and power. How turbulent and noisy the House was! How whimsical and unequal, with its days of wrangle and moments of serious work! As he went on, he came to have better views, some insight into the men about him. He found most of them shrewd, quick, matter-of-fact, and sagacious; many of them with something, trait or talent, a little more than the usual; something that made them marked—a badly-dressed set of easily-approached men, with no pretense to dignity, and almost without reserve. Yet the House, as a House, was an awful despot, the most relentless and exacting of all possible bodies of men in the enforcement of respect to it in its corporate dignity and majesty. And he found, too, that amid all the confusion and involved wrangling of the floor, the House always knew what it was about; that it never for a moment lost sight of it, and that all the innumerable episodes of inconclusive nothings were, after all, the indirect means, the roundabout agencies, of helping it on; that its storms and disorders, its days of doing nothing or worse, were really but the blind struggles of a huge unorganized giant, but half-seeing, attempting to wield his half-controlled strength for some great purpose, which he never fully comprehends. Finally, there began to dawn and grow in his mind the superior intelligence that usually presided over the House—emanations from the half-score of superior minds which united over the heads of the mass, and to which it unconsciously submitted. He looked with astonishment at the fourteen huge volumes of legislation, the direct product of congressional brains and hands, mined from the mountains and smelted and hammered as the fashioning needs of a new people demanded; and when he came to look below its surface, its short-sightedness, and often lack of real intelligence, he thought he discovered a wise adaptation of means to ends, an earnest and clear expression of a will and power to accomplish good ends by just means. How strong and alive with the fibre of a young, great people these inelegant and rude statutes and statues were, in which alone lies hidden the philosophy of our history.

He was not long in finding how insignificant a thing a young new member was, and how impossible it was for a man to make a reputation by a single speech, or win a position in one Congress, and, graduating his expectations to the lowest scale of personal achievements, he determined, if possible, to master the duties of his place, learn something of the House, and fit himself as well as he might for his position. He had received from the Speaker an honorable place on the military committee, and was also placed on one or two others of importance, and soon won from his associates confidence in his ability and usefulness. In nothing, perhaps, is there oftener a greater diversity of opinion than in the estimate of the House itself, and that of the outside world, as to the merits of its members.

Mason was always in his seat, always attentive to the business of the House, and hence was one of the few men in it who always knew exactly what it was doing. Of course, he soon became the source of information to the careless men about him, and he was as courteous as accurate in his replies to the numerous questions addressed to him. He was not without ambition as a speaker, but had already seen how difficult it was for new members to get the floor, and how very difficult it was for them to occupy it when it was awarded to them. He justly concluded that the American House was the worst and most trying place in which a mortal, with the organs of speech, ever attempted to exercise them. The House he saw was, in this, exacting beyond endurance, and, unless a speaker had the exact thing which it wanted, it wanted none of his wares, nor of him. If he failed to hit it, and at once, the chances were that it would never again listen, perhaps not tolerate him, and, in calculating his chances, he could forecast no state of things which would be his opportunity.

It came very unexpectedly.

A very innocent German—a Democrat—had been admitted to a seat in the Thirty-ninth Congress, as was claimed by his competitor, by mistake; or, rather, by two mistakes. The returning officer—it was one of the Philadelphia districts—footed up, and reported a small majority for the Republican. The Secretary of State found, on going over with the figures, that a correct footing showed an actual majority for the Democrat, and issued the certificate to him, on which he was admitted and sworn on the organization of the House. The real mistake was in supposing, on the day of election, by the friends of Morris, the Republican, that a sufficient number of repeaters had repeated to elect him, when they stopped, without having exhausted their supply of the elective franchise. This mistake was merely repeated in the returns, and corrected as above. When Morris was made aware that he was counted out, he undertook to avail himself of the votes which he did not have; and with the facilities for correcting such mistakes, after the actual poll, not limited to Philadelphia, a recount of the contents of two or three ballot-boxes revealed the fact that there were ample votes to elect Morris, who at once notified Bergen, the Democrat, for a contest, and proceeded to take up his proof, which he filed on the opening day of the House. Of course it was not for a moment to be endured that a Democrat should take a seat to which a Republican could show color of title. The case was at once taken up, and the Republican majority of the committee promptly reported a resolution to remove Bergen, and seat Morris. Of course the Democrats unanimously sustained Bergen, but, constituted as the House was, there could be little doubt of the action of the Republican majority. Immediately after the holidays, the case of Morris *vs.* Bergen was called up for final disposition. The chairman of the committee had intrusted the case to the hands of another gentleman, emulous of the honor of expelling from the House a man still so misguided as to be classed with the Democrats. It had long been the practice of the majority of the House to sustain the party report of a standing committee, on questions of this kind, and especially where an opponent was to receive justice thereby. The gentleman having the matter in charge stated the case, read from his report, and made a fair showing by reference to the testimony, very satisfactory to the majority in the House. Two or three Democrats of considerable ability presented the case on their side, quite sufficient, in an ordinary question, to have convinced an unprejudiced judge, that the claim of Morris had its foundation in fraud alone; but evidently without having reached the ear and aroused the sense of justice of the rulers of the House, which, when reached, seldom failed of a true response. The debate became general, languished, and the gentleman who opened it was about to reply to the Democrats, and move the previous question, when young Mason arose, and was recognized by the Speaker. He had never addressed the House; none of the members knew that he was a speaker, and few that he was a lawyer. Considerable curiosity was evinced when it was known that he was up, which rapidly gave place to surprise, and that soon deepened into decided astonishment at the positions he took, and the striking ability with which he sustained them. A colleague of his was on the committee of privileges and elections, who boarded at the same house, and who manifested much doubt as to the justice of the case, and stated his difficulties to Mason, who became much interested in the case, and examined and studied it with care, and was entirely convinced of the justice of Bergen's claim. He endeavored to persuade his colleague to unite with the minority in sustaining this view, but he was a weak and timid man, unequal to such a position, and, when the report was made, his name appeared with the majority. So fully was Mason convinced of the entire right of Bergen, that to unseat him appeared to him nothing less than an outrage upon the right of representation, and he at once resolved not to permit it to pass without an earnest word of protest. The idea of making a speech did not occur to him, but he studied the case thoroughly, and knew he could state it clearly, and beyond this he had no purpose.

He was at the first a little nervous, and would have been embarrassed had he meditated a set speech. His own voice somehow reassured him in a moment, and he felt that his intellect was as completely in his hand as a sabre when that hand was at its best. He cut at once to the real gist of the case, which he laid bare in a few words, and, stating what could alone be the conclusions from the evidence, he marshaled and arrayed that in such a masterly manner that no other was possible. At the end of thirty minutes he sat down, having finished as complete, logical, and satisfactory an argument, as perhaps the House had ever listened to. His voice and manner were admirable, his language and elocution quite perfect. He had not been up five minutes when the House knew that it had a new and valuable acquisition, a man who could tell it something; and when he sat down, he felt that he had somehow made the House his own. Members from all parts of the hall gathered about him, and did not disperse till he had finished. The Democrats were in ecstasies. The Republicans were charmed with a mingling of unpleasant surprise in their admiration. The idea that this young man should signalize the opening of his career by turning his guns against the camp of his friends was a little startling. The wiser and better were not disposed to censure him, and all parties gathered around and congratulated him with a warmth which greatly surprised him. One enemy he certainly made—the gentleman who had charge of the case for the committee; at first he was carried off his feet, but finally rallied and attempted to break the force of the argument by interrupting the speaker with questions; but, as is usually the case, the answers were so complete and satisfactory that the House was more than satisfied, especially when, toward the close, the purpose of the questioner was so obvious that the listeners enjoyed and fully justified the wit and sarcasm that marked some of the replies.

It was apparent that the case of the contestant had disappeared. The discomfited manager privately appealed to his chief, who declined to aid him, when the House indulged him with making the case the special order for three o'clock the next day; and the House adjourned. On the next day, the manager made his reply, marred by personal reflections upon "the young man who had so strangely appeared as the champion of a Copperhead." At the conclusion, he demanded the previous question, which the

House did not sustain, and Mason made a trenchant reply of ten minutes, demonstrating that he was not to be the object of personal attack or remark. On the question many Republicans did not vote; many voted for Bergen, and he retained his seat by a majority of one. Some of the consequences of this action of the House are to appear in the further progress of this narrative.

The immediate effect was, to place the young Western Republican in a most favorable position before the House. He had evinced ability, courage, intrepidity, and independence; had shown that he was an accomplished lawyer and orator; and discerning men could easily see that, if his independence did not render him impracticable, he could hardly fail of a brilliant and useful career.

CHAPTER XXII.

LOVE AND POLITICS.

On this day, when our attention was particularly called to Charles Mason, notwithstanding his placid and rather cold demeanor, he was not at ease. He sat with his face to the Speaker, most decorously, with attention fully to the business of the House, and yet he was several times at fault. His eyes would turn occasionally to the diplomatic gallery, and his mind and heart were there quite constantly. It was near four, and yet all the afternoon, from a little past one, there sat the radiant and beautiful Ellen Berwick, and with her, his heavy, dreamy eyes ever falling on her, sat the Chevalier St. Arnaud. It is true that just behind them sat her father and aunt; but what mattered that? The chevalier had introduced them into that gallery the day before, and now he seemed to have colonized it with them and two or three hangers-on of the legations. Mason had met the chevalier, and had not liked him. Yesterday he thought him odious; and to-day, with the same logic which is said to control women under similar circumstances, he detested if he did not hate him outright. How devoted he seemed to the fair Ellen, and how undisguisedly pleased she was at his admiration! Her father a millionaire, the principal owner of the immense iron-mills near Mason's native town, a thorough American, sharp, shrewd, intelligent, and usually on the make, Ellen had taken much of his ready shrewdness with the higher qualities, beauty, and form of a deceased mother. Whatever this country afforded had been employed for her education; and now, at twenty, she might well have been selected as a representative of the current American girl of the higher type, in person, manners, and mind, dashed and tinged just a little with the West—not fast, not unwomanly, in the American sense, but self-possessed, quite well-assured, and knowing and dreaming of no ill— fearless. Is it a wonder that a beautiful woman should finally become what in a man would be a trifle assuming, almost arrogant?—accustomed from childhood to find flower-strewed ways for her, and, as she approaches womanhood, to find all manhood bending and bowing to her, and all the world's avenues sloping downward, to make their passage easy to her? By royal right all is yielded and conceded that the worthier may never win. All this had been and was Nell's; and yet, as near as may be, she grew up unspoiled and gracious; did not presume; was liked by young girls and women, and went about with a modest graciousness; was not loud-mouthed nor pronounced; and yet she was not averse to the homage of men, nor was she over-grateful. Why should she be? It came spontaneously, and was pleasant; and yet she was twenty without any decided affair, except indeed in the instance of this young General Mason. That seemed to come in the natural order of events in the preordained life of a beautiful and somewhat romantic girl, as a matter of course; and to an observing world it seemed the most fitting thing in it.

When Charley went to the war, Ellen was a romping, hoidenish girl of sixteen, to whom he was a real young man, and very pleasant to romp with. He was at home but once, slightly wounded, with his left arm in a military sash; handsome and pale, when she was a dreaming maiden of eighteen, pensive as all high-hearted American girls were, in the shadow of the war, and he came now into the realm of her imagination. Finally, he came home a general of division, and hero. But she had seen a good many handsome heroes; still somehow this one seemed to be more particularly handsome. A good many of the young men of that town and vicinity had served with him; he was the product, pride, and hope of the region, already elected to Congress. If, indeed, the brave really and in honest truth did deserve the fair, as seemed just and right, she was not disposed wholly to deny his deservings.

Mason, as we have seen, was poetic, imaginative, ardent, and still at the youthful age, when coming from the rude isolation, from the society of women which war imposes, he was peculiarly susceptible to the influence of maidenly loveliness. It was said he fell in love at once with the beautiful Ellen, who was not inclined to reject his attentions, which, though marked, were manifested in almost the romantic way of an older time, of a returned knight, and in no way displeasing to the young maiden. Mason, in the ardor of a real first passion, was sure of his sentiments, and with the frank directness of his nature, in the golden holiday of the leisure of his return, he told her that he loved her, and told it well and manfully, and as a woman would be told that dearest tale to woman's ears, and the listening maiden heard it right well pleased. It seemed very natural, and she was a little flustered, and the coy maidenly spirits did not play her false, but she did not lean her head against his bosom, nor drop it on his shoulder, nor fall into his arms, nor commit any indiscretion, though she could feel how these might happen. Her face suffused; and a sweet little swimming moisture, half sensibility and half a tear, came into her eyes as she averted them; and then she turned toward him, and half raised her eyes, with her quick wits all in hand again: "General, you surprise me! I—I—had not thought of this."

"Do I offend you?" The voice was deep and sad. "My love will not be obtrusive. It would speak itself; but it can remain dumb," and he turned a little away from her. The young girl was really a woman, and now with all her womanly nature, in voice and manner which her lover never forgot, she made a little movement as if toward him —"I do not mean to repel"—and, collecting herself, "I—I must think of it all"—and with a look that seemed to finish out the words as if with—"you must see that this is reasonable;" and not much more was said. Mason was not elated. What more could he ask? or what, like a vain and conceited man, could he expect? What more womanly, or what more flattering and hopeful? There was a wondrous charm in her manner, and the little words that she did "not mean to repel." But somehow she had not realized his poetic dream of a coy maiden of the olden time, when her knight knelt and told his tale. But, then, she was not a maiden of the olden time, nor was he a knight, nor did he kneel. How wondrously well she managed it! Cool and as if experienced. Was it really so little to a woman to be loved? After all, what did he know of women anyway? He might have been disappointed. He was not vain; might not have thought it possible that she should love him. His notions were very romantic for 1865, and he thought that love would instinctively recognize love, and, as a matter of course, when it existed, would respond to love. Of course, she did not care for him, and he had foolishly, without the least assurance, cast his love at her feet; and though she did not repel, she could not accept it, which was its rejection, and he felt the mortification of a high, proud nature that had in a word given its all to one who left it to perish at her feet. All right. He knew he should not complain. He could only think how cool and prudent she was, and that first she "must think it over," weigh and calculate it all, this young girl! She did not love him, and never would. Faugh! and this a matter of the heart, of soul, and all that. Let her think. He would give her plenty of time. She needn't hurry a bit. But then was it not a matter of awfulest moment of life, death, and eternity, and why shouldn't she think? Well, he had not thought. He spoke as he felt and when he felt. On the whole he didn't like it, nor any part of it, save Nell's superb manner at one moment, and was humiliated at his own stupidity in the matter. So, now he was to be a dangler, a declared but not an accepted or rejected lover. But a non-accepted lover is a rejected man—especially while the lady thinks. Well, he would be cool and wary, and—not make a fool of himself again. And then, "I don't mean to repel" was in his ears, and on the whole he was well in the preliminary phases of a lover's perplexity, dissatisfaction, and uncertainty, which, after all, was quite certainly against him.

And she—she had heard the word which no woman ever heard with indifference, which avowed love, a man's love, a full-grown, heroic man, full of power and depth, with the tremor of suppressed passion in his voice, and had caught a gleam of his eyes and almost glorified face, as her eyes went down under his. Perhaps she had wondered if she would really hear such words. They came to many women —would they ever come to her? They had, and had just that ineffable thrill never dreamed of before. She was actually loved, and her first impulse was to abandon herself to a new strange gladness that so strongly drew her to her lover, and yet repelled her. Under the first she spoke, and under the last she suddenly stopped and changed. And then she regretted her first words. But were they not true? she did not mean to repel him. He was to her the most beautiful man in the world; and she was glad he loved her, and then, in a way, she was her cool, cruel, collected self, not her old self, would never be again. What she had heard had changed her. During the day the words kept coming to her, and she paused in her walk, in her woman's work, in her song—suddenly, to listen to them and feel them again, and a pleased, subdued joyousness lingered in her face all day. Her observant and considerate aunt knew that she had heard something, and was pleased. There was not another man in the world to whom she would so willingly have yielded her as to young Mason.

From that day on, Mason played admirably the *rôle* of the considerate, devoted, but rather proud and doubting lover. He made beautiful verses; had a rare knack, for a man, with flowers; turned the leaves of a music-book with grace; was a bold and skillful rider; and had that high and generous appreciation for women, and the quick perception of her varying shades of mood and temper, that fitted him for ladies' society, while the strong and manly lines of his character always kept before them the attractive image of a strong and heroic man, chivalrously devoting himself to their service from choice. Those beautiful summer days which followed were full of the romance and poetry of young life to Nell, of anxiety and growing doubt to her lover. Sweet, kind, and gracious, he could discover nothing that he felt would authorize an honorable man, of nice sensibility, in pressing his suit beyond such attentions as a spirited woman might accept from one whom she permitted to approach her as a suitor. He knew he had spoken too soon, and could not speak again without some warrant, and how he expected to receive that from a proud, sensitive, and womanly girl, he never troubled himself to work out. Under the high law of love it would be revealed.

In early August, Nell, her father, and aunt, hurried off for three months to Europe; and Nell's adieu was joyous and unconcerned as if she expected to meet her lover the next day, and if she did not it would make no difference in the world. When they returned, Mason was in Washington, where they arrived at the beginning of January, and took rooms at the National. When they met again, it was, on her side, as if they had parted the day before. Her head was in a whirl with Paris and Rome, and in her memory and thought Mason mixed and mingled very pleasantly with the broken recollection of pictures and music, as some part of a pleasant pageant, surrounded with romantic associations. She was glad to see him; she was very proud and glad of what was said of his speech, and did not at all share in her father's distrust of his political career; and she was proud and glad of his devotion to herself, and that her power over him remained unchanged—and that was all she wished, for the present. Like most American girls, she meant to have a good time in Washington. It was very pleasant to be on her present terms with her lover, and possibly her heart beat a little when she thought of a change in them; she did not mean that any present change should take place. Surely, he would not at all object to seeing her power over other men. He certainly would not insist on any claims upon her, and they would not be acknowledged if he did. If he really loved her, he would expect that she would put his love to some test, and she was so sure he did, that she would not fear the result

Mason was not very hopeful before she came, and he thought that he marked in her manner, at their first meeting, that she intended no nearer relations should subsist between them. He had no shade of misgiving as to the reality of his love for her, when he so precipitately declared it, and found, with concern, that it had immensely strengthened and deepened since, and both his love and self-love were deeply wounded by her seeming indifference to him. And when he saw her as now, in the face of the world, flirting with this unknown adventurer, as he was pleased to call him to himself, he had little doubt that his only course was to drift as rapidly as he might out of her train, and this he resolved to do. Curiously enough, as if to execute this masterly movement, when he observed Miss Nell and her party leave the gallery, she, with her aunt and father, found him in a corridor at the foot of the great Leutze stairway.

"General Mason," said the young lady, with a little pique in her tone, "I fear the public service has been a little overwhelming this afternoon; for two mortal hours, I sat nearly over you, and was not honored with even a glance, and doubt whether you saw me."

"Really, I beg your pardon; if I did not, I must have been the only gentleman in the House who did not; and you will overlook so trifling a matter."

She looked up quickly, but his voice and manner were gay as if uttering persiflage, notwithstanding its possible sarcasm; and he walked by her side toward the rotunda.

"The diplomatic gallery is so delightful!" she remarked, after a moment's pause; "we were so fortunate as to be invited there by the Chevalier St. Arnaud, who took us there yesterday and again to day, and introduced us to some of his foreign friends. Do you know him?" looking up with some interest.

"I have barely seen him," dryly.

"I think him just splendid! And then he seems so taken with papa."

"And papa's daughter," added Mason. "He has seen the daughter; can it be possible that he has heard of the father's wealth also?"

"Perhaps so! It seems that others have"—with a little spirit.

Mason felt the point of this remark, and moved on in silence, with a new smart.

"What do you know of the chevalier, Mr. Mason?" directly.

"Not a thing; nor does anybody. Frank Warbel calls him the Chevalier of Castle Como—"

"Frank Warbel had better attend to what is said of himself, I should think!" a little tartly.

Mason's only response was a quick, startled look at the lady's face. They gained the stone plateau, west of the Capitol, gilded with the warm rays of the setting sun. The lady was a little piqued, and saw a look in the face of her companion new to her. "Mr. Mason," she asked, "are you quite certain that there is not just the slightest tinge of spring in one of your eyes?" The voice, soft and low, had just a touch in it. If she wanted to have their relations redefined, or to give notice that they were but those of pleasant acquaintances, the stroke was not impolitic.

"I really do not know," was the frank answer, in his usual voice, and then, with cold gravity—"I think not. No man, I am sure, would presume to be jealous, unless his claims had in some way been admitted. He who has laid his homage at a lady's feet, and who only has not placed them on it, would hardly dare entertain that feeling, I think." Nothing could be more direct.

"The distinction is so apparent, general, that even I appreciate it," was the response of his companion, with a little laugh of seeming gayety. Both remained silent, as if looking over things in a new light. They walked down the broad, flagged way, where children were still lingering with their nurses, setting up pennies in the rapid little currents in the polished stone gutters, and watching their rapid course downward, sustained on their edges, and borne onward by the tide. Each found matter for thought in this subject so abruptly brought to the surface, and, notwithstanding the predetermination of Mason to push it to a point beyond misapprehension, he did not reply to the lady. Perhaps he shrank from the humiliation of any thing more definite; perhaps it seemed already clear. At the Avenue they paused a moment for a gay cavalcade of three or four ladies and gentlemen, who rode down the hill and dashed up the street.

"Oh, how beautiful!" exclaimed Nell, with animation. "Nothing would please me so much as a good gallop."

"A wish easily gratified," answered Mason; "I know of a pair of superb saddle-horses—"

"Oh! I should be delighted," broke in the girl, with rapture.

"Shall it be to-morrow, then, at ten? Nothing will please me more," said the delighted Mason.

"Thank you, I shall be glad to go; and we may have another of those delightful days, and one of those very, very pleasant old rides;" and, as she spoke, she turned her face, fully lit with sparkling animation, up to the eyes of her lover, who was powerless under it. The walk up to the National was very pleasant to both, and they talked of their impressions of Washington, and saw how much they thought and felt alike. Then they found that both were going to the reception of the Chief-Justice—his first for the season—which was to come off that evening. They had reached the ladies' entrance to the National, and Mason stepped up on to the stone step, where Nell paused, only to drop him a curt good-evening, and passed in. He had, of course, expected an invitation to enter, and stood in a moment's amaze, staring stupidly down at the broken limb of one of the couchant iron dogs which guard the entrance, and then, with a darkened face, he walked up the Avenue.

CHAPTER XXIII.

AT THE CHIEF-JUSTICE'S.

ALL that evening, from eight till eleven, just within the door of his spacious reception-room, stood the Chief-Justice, the one form whose personal advantages marked him out the most conspicuous man at the American capital; a noble, massive head and handsome, manly face, indicative of strength, power, and will, and which could, from dignified gravity, relapse to the most genial suavity, full of the pleasant graces of refined social wit and humor, which were constantly sparkling from his large, bland, and finely-formed mouth. Those who have conceived him as the stately, cold, dignified, unbending Chief-Justice of the Supreme Court of the United States, have greatly misconceived his nature and character. Nothing could be more attractive, pleasing, and inviting, than he in his hours of social relaxation.

Ambitious he was, but it was the ambition of a great, just, and pure soul, that would rule, from conscious power to rule, with sagacity and wisdom. On the bench of the Supreme Court he dwarfed the place, where he sat like the sitting idol of Buddha, which made his temples always seem small, and which, had he risen to his height, would have been shattered in fragments at his feet. And now, genial, yet stately, as becomes a host, he received and welcomed his guests with happy manner and words, and passed them to that rare combination of womanly grace and dignity with the supple, sylph-like, girlish winsomeness of form and freshness of manner of a young maiden, his eldest daughter, who with him did the honors. What was best and most gracious in her father, was in her united with what was good and gracious in women. No one ever thought of analyzing her face and form, to determine whether she were strictly beautiful. That with her was a matter of no consequence; all saw more than mere beauty of face and form. Was it mind and spirit, tact and talent, taught by Nature, and refined by study and social experience, until it came to be the highest art, or the spontaneous inspiration of womanly genius, that made her always so exactly equal to the varying demands and exigencies of the changing moments, and which enabled her to get from each person his best; that flattered with mere manner, which her words only did not belie; that enabled her, amid the incongruous elements that often mingled in her father's rooms, to bring out and give play only to the harmonious and concordant? And men hardly knew that the bending form of light and grace, that glided with a smile and paused with a word, was the genius of it all.

These two received the guests, who began to arrive at eight—the pleasantest though earliest hour, when the host and hostess were at leisure, and the rooms, with their attractions of pictures, sculpture, and flowers, were uncrowded. They came—the members of the Supreme Court and bar; of the Senate and House, Army and Navy, citizens and strangers, and finally the embassadors and legations, distinguished foreigners and leaders of fashion, with poets, painters, and literary celebrities.

How a crush belittles and reduces a man or woman from a dignitary of importance, or a personage of consequence, to an individual—a mere human unit, and sometimes to a fraction, and a vulgar one at that! How rapidly the supreme judges descended to common men, and the leaders of the Senate and House were reduced to their original insignificance! Here was a great admiral, one of the compressed mass; and there was General Sherman shut up in a corner, cut off from supplies; and General Grant, a mere unidentified item, whose only relief was, that he was not compelled to talk. And the wonderful toilets—well—

Mason and Frank came a little past nine, and were presented to his daughter by the Chief-Justice, with marked graciousness, as commending them to her special consideration. "General Mason," he said, "was the representative of the beautiful Miss Berwick," etc.

"I know then that there is one constituency who will be faithfully obeyed," remarked the lady, "and I've no doubt she will have her eyes on her representative. You will find her in the room toward the music, I think." And to Colonel Warbel, whose manly person and manners commended him to most women: "There is one Washington young lady whom I wish to introduce you to—Miss Vane."

"I have had the honor of being presented to her."

"Which you appreciated, and I will not keep you from her," as she turned to a new throng.

On their progress through the room, the young gentlemen encountered Colonel Gordon and Mr. Drybow; the latter with his usual dissatisfied eyes, rejecting all they saw, and still looking for something else. Frank had met the colonel once or twice, since his sudden departure from his house, and, like quite a young man, elected only to regard him as a mere acquaintance, whom he did not care to cultivate. He had a few hasty words with Drybow, who looked more than he said, and the two passed into the inner rooms, where they found Mrs. Vane, Lucy, Margie, and Grayson, surrounded with their friends, to whom Mrs. Vane introduced them. Frank, somehow, was conscious of undergoing a good deal of looking over by many of the group. It had, in a hazy way, come upon him that he was in some way under a cloud, or in the shadow of one. Some almost unpleasant words had passed between Mason and himself, that evening, the occasion for which he did not understand, and to which he replied in a way to repress inquiry or remark. Mrs. Vane was very gracious, and seemed to find, in the clear outlook of his open, honest eyes, much reassurance. She saw disappointment in them, and said to him: "Miss Brand did not come; she is not quite well—not well enough to come out; and," marking the quick anxiety that came into them, "not ill, or I should not have left her—only not quite well; and, colonel, though General Mason has permitted us to see him, we have not had the pleasure of a call from you?"

"Mrs. Vane," said the young man, "I really did not know; I am merely the business agent of Miss Brand, who is your guest, and, unless obliged to see her, I half fancied that I was without an excuse for calling—I felt that I could hardly have claims—" and he paused. It was a difficult thing to manage, as he looked at it.

"Then let me set you aright, Colonel Warbel; I do not speak for Miss Brand, and was quite in earnest in asking you to call on our account," with a look to Lucy.

"You are very kind, Mrs. Vane, and I hope to deserve it in the future," with a very graceful bow, and pleased expression of face. Miss Marston looked as if she were not to be included in this expression, and were not to be taken in by a handsome, clear face, although he was in some sort her ally *vs.* Alice, in her war with that belle for the homage of a certain chevalier. She would not only carry him off, but she had no doubt that Frank was utterly unworthy of Alice's confidence, and it would not be her fault if Alice was not herself made to see it. The motives that controlled this curiously-organized woman were not only involved, but difficult to comprehend. Lucy and Grayson received Frank very cordially, and when the full gush of the music came from the dancing-room, with its inviting appeal, Frank proposed to conduct Lucy and her party thither, which was acceded to; and when he led her on to the floor, with the dancers, Lucy was surprised as well as pleased with his grace and skill as a dancing-partner. On returning her to her mother, he could not forbear speaking to her of Alice, so gentle, sweet, and sympathetic was she, like a sister, and he had never uttered a word of her to mortal; and as he spoke, a subtile, sympathetic tremor was in his voice, that went at once to the heart of his listener. She told him how Alice was—that she was very quiet, and somewhat anxious; that she was the dearest, sweetest girl in the world, and that she loved her as a sister, she knew, though she never had a sister; and Frank never had a sister, and how precious it would be to have one, to whom a young man's foolish fancies could be told; and then—"Miss Brand is to me the most beautiful and interesting girl I have ever met or ever shall meet. Yet how strange, and weak, and foolish this must sound to you, Miss Vane; and what I would not dare to say to her, and which, for the world, you will not repeat. I am only her business agent, and never look for any other—" And then he relapsed into sudden silence, leaving the sentence unfinished. How did Lucy make answer? She did not think it strange he should feel thus toward Alice, and not at all that he should say it to her; and she was glad he had, for she should confide in him now. But she could not make any answer; for Alice had never said a word of Frank to her, and, if she had, Lucy would have kept it. But she thought it strange if this frank, handsome man should love any woman in vain; and she knew that the little things that had been said of him, and pointed with looks by Margie, and one or two, as coming from Colonel Gordon, or somebody, were untrue. She had gone over the floor under the experienced eyes of her mother, who was not indifferent to the flattering things said of the beautiful couple by many spectators who were decided in their admiration.

"Why, Colonel Warbel," said Mrs. Vane, "I believe we may congratulate ourselves on our valuable acquisition to the dancing society!" Bowing his acknowledgments, and laughing, with a little color: "I will forgive the irony of the words for their flattery, so unused am I to compliments!" and the ladies present thought he escaped quite well from the embarrassment of being openly praised.

"Mother is never ironical!" said Lucy very quickly, and in a way that showed that she concurred in her mother's judgment.

Mr. Mason did not offer to dance; whether he did not feel like it, or thought it beneath the dignity of the House, or, with Margie before him in an attitude of hopeful expectancy, he saw no attractive partner, may not be known. If the latter, the amiable lady referred to took, in her subtle way, ample compensation for his want of appreciation. She managed to monopolize him, and, having duly admired her cousin—"Poor innocent thing! how almost revolting to see a poor girl unconsciously whirling in the arms of a known *roué!*" with a sigh, whether of commiseration for herself or cousin was, perhaps, a matter of doubt. Mason did not take the application of her words, and made no answer. "They say," continued the artless woman, "that Colonel Gordon turned him away from his house, literally into the streets, for his misconduct."

"Who—what? Miss Marston, of whom do you speak?"

"Of Colonel Warbel, of course; why, everybody speaks of it."

"Then permit me to say, Miss Marston, that everybody is so foolishly mistaken, that to repeat it again would be more than a mistake!" There was a smile on his lip, but a little ping, like the sting of a Minié-bullet, in his voice.

"Oh, I beg your pardon, Mr. Mason, for my thoughtlessness! I really forgot that he is a friend of yours. I admire your defense of your friend, almost as much as your blindness to his faults. Both do honor to your heart. But then you know that he was in the Northern army, and you'll admit that the officers on that side were dreadful men," with an air of innocent earnestness.

"While the officers of the South monopolized all the known virtues, public and private," added the now amused Mason in mock earnestness; "you must admit, Miss Marston, that their patriotism was only equaled by their personal morals!"

"Oh, I beg your pardon again, Mr. Mason! I'm constantly putting my foot in it, as a Yankee woman would say. You must overlook the blunders of a little young thing!" (casting down her head with the utmost humility). "I think I've heard that you were yourself some sort of a general, or something, in the Northern army."

"I'm a 'sort of a general, or something,' I believe," good-naturedly; "and whatever I was, I assure you, I am too considerate to take offense at the innocent prattle of a young girl of Mrs. Polk's time," with a bow of mock reverence.

"Thank you, general, you are very considerate," fire flashing under her still drooping lids, and burning under her olive skin, of course in her usual unmoved voice. "You have met many of the gentlemen of the Southern army?"

"Occasionally, when we did not run away from them," laughing. "I became personally acquainted with a good many of them as prisoners of war; and I assure you, Miss Marston, on the honor of 'some sort of a general, or something,'" laughing, "I found them brave men in the field, and thorough gentlemen in private; and I assure you also that the best—the proudest of them—found his peer in Colonel Warbel. He may have been imprudent."

"Yes, General Mason," raising her fine eyes, still dark with spirit, that found no profit in further war, "you must admit that he is imprudent."

Just at this point Master Grayson, who was on duty in the full dignity of dress-coat, and, when Frank relieved him of Lucy, had started on a raid through the rooms, returned, full of a report of his observations.

"Young wonderful has returned," exclaimed Margie, "and would astonish his mamma. Attend!"

"Of course, I avoided Europe; though, as I passed, I thought I saw Count Renaud cutting the tassels off the curtains," Grayson replied.

"Well!" responded Margie.

"The first thing that I stopped at was Dorothea Dulcie Dilcie Dubois," he continued.

"Oh, where is she?" asked Margie. "What did she have on?"

"Nothing—to speak of," innocently.

"You deserve a good—"

"I only mentioned the bare facts without naming them," deprecatingly; "and they were nothing to the South-American ladies—those extensive daughters of the Peruvian minister. I doubt if there ever was so much undraped truth spread before the public before."

"Grayson," asked the dignified Margie, "if a contagious disease, mortal to fools, should break out, what would you do?"

"Go into mourning for Cousin Margie, I 'spose. How melancholy I'd be!" with gravity.

"Well, Mr. Vane," asked the amused Frank, between whom and Grayson quite a liking had sprung up, "what else did you encounter in your travels?"

"Well, not much that can interest you. Just opposite the grand mirror, I found Jim Worrel, petrified by the sight of himself—it was shocking—and a little beyond, Edward Lacy, still languid from leading the German night before last. He feebly quizzed me about my coat, and I told him I had observed that every young man of mighty intellect like him parted his hair in the middle—it is the only way of balancing the brain, which in his case was lucky, otherwise the universe might wabble and topple over. To that he said that I was a bore, I believe, and I bore away. Then across the corridor I came upon the most distressing spectacle—five girls, all dead or dying! Sallie Ward, in the pause of giggle, said, 'Oh, I shall die!' Miss Morris, 'Oh, I thought I should die!' Mary Webster, 'I shall have to give right up—I shall die!' Sue Clarkson was already dead; and little Slobbery Shorley laid out. Then I turned north, and reached a room of bald-heads. The place where they were presented one brilliant expanse of polished pate. I never saw such an outside show of shining intellect. When I recovered from the effects, I turned back."

"Prudent child," from Margie.

"On my way back, I encountered the ponderous bashaw of the many tails, rolling those eyes of his over that beautiful girl we saw with him in the diplomatic gallery this afternoon, and I hurried back to tell Cousin Margie of that. I knew she'd be interested. I don't wonder these chaps want to marry American girls, from the show they make of their own women. And then—" But the clamor of voices, with a movement toward the supper-room, cut him off.

Had the more penetrating Drybow speculated upon what met his famished eyes, he would have said he saw in the Chief-Justice the cherished hope of the presidency; that the smiles and graces of the daughter had that, as their ultimate great reward; that, among senators and members of the House, he heard incipient mutterings of impeachment, and anxious words about reconstruction. He would almost swear that he heard the closing of an arrangement for a transfer of Pacific Railroad bonds; heard Glozer, of Massachusetts, say to Senator Pangborn something about Credit Mobilier, and that Pangborn opened his eyes, blowed out his cheeks, and punched the punchy Glozer under the waistcoat; that he saw the dashing wife of Senator Wardlaw arm-in-arm with the embassadress of Gloomland, the two stars of the upper circles of the republican court, whose open admiration of each other was beautiful to see, estimating and computing the decay, wear and tear of time, and dissipation in the face, neck, shoulders, and arms of each other; while the wives of several millionaires were openly discussing the cost of the diamonds worn by the wife of a foreign minister; and much more ineffable stuff, to which no consideration whatever should be given.

The evening wore on, late arrivals ceased; and the departure of the early guests thinned out the crowded rooms, and remitted the host and hostess to more pleasing duties.

Ere the fashionable world retired, the chevalier, who had been received with a cold politeness, and was one of the observed and remarked-upon personages of the assembly, met Miss Marston with—"It has just come to me what special attraction it is, Miss Marston, that draws me so strongly to you, if you will permit an almost stranger to address such a remark to you. Anybody would see that there was abundant reason for it"—with a bow, and look of undisguised admiration, which the lady, though flattered, took as her usual due; "and it has just this evening come to me—it is your striking resemblance to the beautiful Princess of Sorrento."

"Really, and in truth?" with a lively sparkle in her manner.

"It is two years since I saw her, or I should have recalled it at once," continued the gentleman, observing her; "even to the shadow of a shade on the upper lip." She raised her eyes, with startled inquiry in them. No man had ever dared to seem to see that decided shadow before. He went coolly on: "When she was in Paris, the shadow became the rage, and the empress, the Princess Esterhazy, and all the ladies, patronized it. I've forgotten the expedients. At Turin King Victor went almost mad over it, and the ladies of his—whom he honored with his regards—adopted it at once. She was an English lady, daughter of the Dowager-Lady of Sark, in North England—a superb, dark, Lady-Macbeth woman—and, as I've been recalling about the Sark family, I remember to have heard of a younger branch who went to America, the West Indies, and thence to some of your Southern colonies; and of course you must have the blood, and all the personal traits. It is singular how these things are diffused, scattered, and yet remain the same. Miss Marston, you are a Sark, if there ever was one."

"Why, chevalier, how you astonish me!" cried the pleased and eager listener.

"I see it all now, and almost feel that I have a sort of claim of kinship, by right of discovery. I think I've understood that this younger branch, which had not the title, of course, went by an older family name, which they may have changed in this country; but you are a Sark"—decidedly; which kindly assurance was a solid gain to the young lady. "You are about the age of the young princess, who married an Italian prince—just your height, form, features, complexion, eyes, hair, and every thing. It is really quite wonderful. How I would like to take you to Turin, and introduce you! How stupid King Vic would stare!"

How the heart of the dark woman swelled, and tears came to her eyes, as the ecstatic vision of glory and triumph arose on her fancy! "The gods, you know," he went on, "sometimes clothed themselves in the lower world in mists and clouds. Some time they will be dashed away." Timidly and reverently she raised her moistened eyes to the lofty brow and wondrous eyes. Here, then, she thought, is indeed one of the sacred, real divinities of a mythology of which she had dreamed. She saw it now, as she had felt it before. She did not venture any question; the light vouchsafed was enough for her. The god, however, turned to less celestial subjects—remarked pleasantly of the distinguished people about him—even condescendingly—and then inquired after a young lady he had seen at her aunt's, and whose name had escaped him. He believed he had not met her in the rooms, and Miss Marston explained that she was not there; and then he remembered cloud and mist, and that, when he called the other day, she had said something about a young colonel, a *protégé* of his friend Colonel Gordon. He thought Colonel Gordon had not turned him away, but was about to, when the young man took the hint and left, and the colonel had been annoyed by the calls of the queer people who came to his house afterward to meet the young man; and he added some more lower-world talk. The lady remarked that the youth's friend General Mason, a representative in Congress, had said to her that very night that the young man was "very, very imprudent."

All this time, Grayson was hovering around, to catch her eye, and, as she knew, snatch her away from blissful cloud-land to her aunt and cousin in the robing-room, to which the chevalier graciously conducted her.

Frank, in a state of half blissfulness, left immediately after the Vanes. General Mason, who had strolled about, finally intercepted Miss Berwick for a moment, annoyed at her seeming avoidance of him, and still fresh from her abrupt dismissal of him at the National. For a moment only—it was to remind her of the proposed horseback-ride the next morning. She started, with a little color and surprise. "Why, general, really you must excuse me; I have made an engagement for that hour, *which I must keep!*" turning away, and then, in her best manner, back to him, "you won't mind to-morrow, and—I'll send you word when!" and dashed up the stairs after her aunt.

She had really forgotten—how comforting to the heart of a lover!—and had made an engagement which *she must keep!* "Indeed! Let her keep it, and—"

When Lucy got home from the party, she found Alice robed for the night, in their cozy room, who started from a sort of day-dream as she came in.

"O, Alice, you should have gone! We had a delightful time! The crush was horrid, but the music was just delicious, and there was a world of flowers, and no end of distinguished people;" and so she ran on—"and there was dancing, and who do you think I had for a partner?—somebody whom you know, though you never mention him. He wasn't on the heights, to-night. He was low down enough; and, if it was not for what he told me of a certain dear, dear friend of mine, I'd fall in love with him myself. He was as natural and graceful, and oh, such a delightful partner!—why, you indifferent thing, you don't know what I'm saying!—and then he inquired about a certain young lady, and somehow his voice was full of tenderness and tremor; and he said it was a queer thing for him to say to me, but that—but that this young lady was the one only, sole young lady to him in all the world. He couldn't help saying it, and it did him good, and me too. It was almost blessed to stand in the light of a man's love, even for another. Of course all the horrid things that Margie has picked up, and that Colonel Gordon has insinuated about him—I hate Colonel Gordon!—are all untrue; no young man with such a love for such a blessed angel was ever any thing but good!" And so she went on, and Alice sat with head a little averted, and a deepened color. "He somehow was surprised into saying this to me," she resumed, "but he couldn't help it. He told me I was not to say a word of it to you, but he must have known I would, though I'm half sorry I have, you cold-hearted thing! You may not love him, but a real man's love is not so common in this world that one should hear it so indifferently." The last was said with her lips to the kindling cheek of Alice, whose arms went up about her, and Lucy felt a tumultuous throb of her bosom against her own.

CHAPTER XXIV.

MASON SEES THE GODDESS OF LIBERTY.

VERY brightly came the sun and soft vapor of the next morning over the straggling city of the Great Republic, and the personages particularly brought to the notice of the reader arose to their various plots and pursuits, some of them under the influence of sun and vapor, and some of them even beyond the reach of light and soft air. Mrs. Thompson at Borum's reminded the calling Smith of the genial state of the weather, with a suggestive reminder. "Yis; but, then, Miss Thompsing, every thing's tighter than the bark on a beech—sap won't run yit," was the discouraging response. An hour later, and Alice and Lucy were at Borum's, to see to some final arrangements of the former, incident to her change of residence, where they cut off the rereat of Mr. Smith, who was introduced to the young ladies by Mrs. Thompson, in so marked a way that, after the escape of that worthy, Alice pleasantly congratulated her on her conquest of her hereditary enemy, and was reminded that, "when a Yankee was good, he was very good, but quar!"

"Almost good enough for one of my kind aunt's family," pleasantly remarked the young lady. "I believe Millie also has found good in him."

"Indeed I has, miss," was the response of the bright attendant.

The young ladies returned to Mrs. Vane's to find that Frank had called in their absence. "He came in brightly and pleasantly," Mrs. Vane said, "but did not remain long, and seemed a little depressed when he left. He inquired for the young ladies, and left his compliments for them."

Margie was not a little annoyed, not to say alarmed, on this same forenoon, by the funny, knowing look with which Grayson from time to time regarded her. She seemed aware of it, well knowing that, in his own time, good or bad, he would develop the evil that was in him. He finally came around where she was caring for some plants on their stand, and spoke out in the deep baritone of the chevalier:

"'You are a Sark—you are a Sark!' and permit me to add, in the language of the immortal Tam, 'a cutty-sark!'"

This imp of mischief, then, had overheard that! The tears of rage dried in her eyes, and the flash of anger from her face, and she turned in a helpless and hopeless mute appeal to the youth, than which in the world of inhumanity nothing is so pitiless in its unknowing cruelty. He waited with all the spirits of mischief playing on lip and eye, when something of his cousin's appeal reached the real generosity of his nature, and, with regret on his handsome face, he approached her with a kindness she never saw in him before.

"Forgive me, Margie; I don't mean to wound you."

Lucy, who had just returned, came into the little conservatory in time to hear Gray's speech, mark its effect, and hear his manly apology. Margie, touched by it, looked her gratitude, and passed out at the opposite door.

"Now you are my real, noble, manly brother, Gray, just beginning to grow into your true manliness," putting her arm about him and her warm lips to his peachy cheek. "Now you must begin to realize what a glorious thing it is to be a man, and what a sad and depressing thing it sometimes is to be a woman. No matter what the real mental strength or force of character a woman may have from Nature, our life and the structure of society, Grayson, put her, after all, on the losing side of almost every contest with a man, without reference to the right of it. Man decrees himself her absolute lord; and, however unjust, she must submit. There is no ground which she can call her own, no law on which she may rely, no power she may wield. She can only win by her weakness, make war with her helplessness, and conquer with submission." Her face was sad with its pleading earnestness.

The aroused boy looked at her, at first with wonder, and then with the startled expression of a new view of life. "Why, Lucy, is there really any thing in this, and do you and mother believe in it?"

"All thoughtful women think of it, but it has never come to us as to many women, and I only speak of it to you, that in your boy-contests with poor Margie, and in all your associations with women, you'll remember she is not a man or a boy, but only a woman, who can neither resist nor oppose, and that your rude man's strength, loud voice, persistency, and claim of superior sex—which, however founded, she and none of us can oppose—finally silence her. And, Grayson, do you know what it is to remain dumb under a sense of injustice? If you smite a woman, she must submit; if you trample on her, she must cry in silence. The real injury is beyond the reach of law," with a sob.

"Don't, Lucy, don't!" in real anguish. "I'm a ruffian and a brute!"

"No, Grayson, only thoughtless, and a little rude. You are strong and brave, will come to be a trusted and thoughtful man, and the protector of women, in time."

Mason had to meet the Committee on Military Affairs at half-past ten, and was on his way to the Capitol, thinking more of the events and words of the afternoon and evening before, than of the sun and day about him. Indeed, he saw little in passing. He paused a moment at the curbstone opposite the Capitol-grounds, to decide upon the best place of crossing the north arm of the street, when a splashing clatter of hoofs, with a little rush, made him suddenly lift his head, and there flashed by him the queenly form of Miss Berwick in her black riding-robes, with face and eyes lit up, mounted on the splendid cream-colored horse he had destined for her, and on her right the black charger, bearing the stately form of the chevalier in his riding-boots and velvet coat. The eyes of Nell fell full upon his, as the black spume of the gutter was dashed over him by the spurning feet of her horse. As the blasting vision passed, the fixed eyes of the young man met the pitiless back of the shapeless Goddess of Liberty on the Capitol-dome, where they traced a mental resolve.

Once, when a huge steamer, with hundreds of passengers, was about to be dashed by wind and wave on a rocky shore, with her head to the open sea, the engineer turned on the utmost power of steam, and, seating himself on the lever that closed the safety-valve, forced the groaning, struggling ship from destruction.

Some such process the young man now mentally performed. He quietly walked up the flagged Avenue between the trees and mounted to the hall of the House, where, in one of the cloak-rooms, Mr. Johnson, long the kindly genius of that pleasant retreat, removed the stains from his dress, when he proceeded to his committee-room, just as General Garfield, the chairman, called it to order. At twelve he went to his seat in the hall. Not on that, nor the next, nor yet the third day, did he raise his eyes to the ladies' gallery. At the adjournment of the third day one of the pages placed a note in his hands, which read thus:

"*Thursday* P. M.

"GENERAL MASON: Shall we let those horses go tomorrow morning at ten—or when?

"NELLIE B."

On the whole, Nell did not enjoy that ride. When Mason parted from her the night before, she wondered at her infatuation, and the next morning she wondered that she did not cancel her new engagement, and was almost astonished when she found herself by the side of her gallant cavalier, galloping down the Avenue. For a block or two, what with sun and air and admiring eyes, she triumphed. At the turn she met the eyes of her lover, and never before so realized his love as when the pain in them smote her heart. She saw his person soiled with the mud her horse dashed over him, and went away, swaying with the easy motion of her leaping charger, up the paved ascent of Capitol Hill. The programme of the chevalier, in the condition of the streets, was, at the top of the hill, to turn down New Jersey Avenue over the paved surface of F, dash up that to Fifteenth, and down the Avenue past Willard's, and all the gay throngs, with his latest conquest. The mind of the lady was different, and changed it. Instead of keeping on to F, she turned down Louisiana Avenue to Sixth, and, in twenty minutes from her gay departure from the National, she passed in at its ladies' entrance again.

Her aunt received her with speechless amazement. When she went out her aunt supposed that she had gone with Mason, and only learned of her mistake as from the parlor-windows she saw her return. "Aunt, aunt," said the a little-excited girl, "you never scold me, I wish you would now, it would relieve me much. I ain't a born coquette, aunt, and I'm not heartless. I've known for some time that I had a heart somewhere about me, aunt, but I didn't know just where till now. Why do you look so scared, aunt? was it so really awful? I did forget myself, and felt that I must do it, and I told General Mason that I must be excused to-day."

"Told him that you had forgotten your engagement to ride with him this morning? I think he will excuse you!"

"No not quite that. O aunt! if he loves me, he'll forgive me, don't you think he will—a silly girlish freak just to try his love, aunty dear?"

"There is not a man in the world that would forgive it," said her aunt, in her firm, quiet way.

"O aunty, you don't know men. Charlie is noble and generous. He don't pretend to have any claim upon me. We talked that over yesterday, and I purposely omitted to invite him in when we came home. He understood it. I will remain home all next summer, for him, if he has to stay there. And he'll know that I never would have acted so, if I didn't love him," the last words very low.

"Every man has a claim upon a woman to be treated as a man; to say nothing of your permitting him to address you as a suitor. Try to imagine how delicate his position is. He spoke six months ago, and, with no encouragement, it would take but little to drive him from you. Had you wished him to go, your own self-love would have devised a womanly excuse for it."

"Very well, aunty, let us consider him as gone, then," said the girl, with a proud toss of her head, as if that disposed of the matter. A moment later her aunt heard her fresh, clear voice, in her own room, swell out a strain of a favorite air and song, and she noticed that it stopped suddenly at the highest note. Somehow Ellen did not feel like going to the Capitol that day, nor out anywhere, and had her dinner in her room, which she did not eat; and the next, dressed with much tasteful care, she did go; and the next, and sat in the ladies' gallery, on the Speaker's left, where if Mason raised his eyes he must see her, and yet he never raised them; and she sent him the note, as in her last words to him, she had promised; and, when it went out of her hands, she would have had it back; but it was too late, and she hurried off out of the Capitol with her aunt and father. That evening, in her room, one of the hotel messengers brought her the answer.

"Thursday Evening

"MISS ELLEN BERWICK: By all means—let them go to-morrow, or whenever they feel like it. You will not expect my attendance at the spectacle.

"CHARLEY M."

CHAPTER XXV.

ROCKS AND PIG-IRON.

WHAT a wonderful field the future philosophical historian will find in the labors of the almost wonderful Thirty-ninth Congress! The principles of right and justice, upon which the structure of the government was built, had been so overgrown and overlaid with the excrement of slavery, and the rank growths which sprang from it; so incrusted with the exfoliations of dead parties, and their fossilized platforms; so widely gone away from in the lust and madness for power and dominion, that thoughtful men doubted their existence in modern politics, and partisans scoffed them as the dreams of speculation. Suddenly their inner throbbings broke up the incrustation, and crushed into ruin all the institutions and orders of men and things resting upon it. The Republican leaders blindly strove to raise a temporary, fragile political structure over the mighty pulsation, but it went to shivers in their paralyzed hands; and, in striking at the armed rebellion, they struck blind, unwilling blows at slavery, and when it perished, with the civilization and institutions to which it gave life and power, now with more or less clearness of vision men saw again the old principles of right and justice, and felt the necessity of so readjusting their political institutions that they should find their sole support on these foundations. And this first session was emphatically a session of declarations and platforms, of elementary truths and half-truths, all in some way efforts to give expression, predicated of the new conclusions of the old logic; efforts to realize the new fulfillments of old prophecy; numerous propositions to secure a fuller constitutional recognition of these principles by amendments of the organic law, by ever-varied declarations of a purpose to govern legislative enactments, intended for the reorganization of the States, by these principles. Indeed, never before in American history was there so unanimous a determination to compel and coerce the new political growths, which were to be cultivated on the fallow grounds of the South, to take root in these elementary truths, and grow up in their forms, as during that Congress. There was every shade of opinion and view, from the shallow idea of huddling together the broken fragments of the rebellion, with whatever of *débris* the waste of war and destruction had left on the ground, into the forms of States, without growth, crystallization, root, or even seminal principle, and which would be animated only with the venomous hatred of the conquered but not subdued rebellion, and recommit the whole South to them; to the clearer and more intelligent idea of regarding that whole region as without recognized political forms, and proceed with care to lead the people through the pupilage of new and arbitrarily-formed Territorial governments, to the final realization of the prevailing idea of American States. And all the capital, even to its social centres, and all the States and Territories to their remotest bounds, were agitated by, and profoundly sympathized with, the debates on the questions involved, which often arose to the level of the great argument. On these propositions Congress and Executive divided, and that contest more sorely tried the civil institutions of the land, of which the Constitution is but one form of expression, and not its highest, than the great physical rebellion which Stanton and Grant and Sherman and Sheridan had just crushed under the relentless heel of war.

My tale only touches the fringe upon the margin of this contest, and deals with a few of its less obvious elements, and only hovers modestly around some of the combatants in it, rather than employs them in its humble and modest course. I shall have to do with the House only as its dealings with one or two minor matters may bear upon the fortunes of the personages of my sketches of life at the capital.

It was on none of these old adamantine rocks that the bark of the young representative was wrecked, fatal though they were, notably, to two or three of the tall senatorial ships. He ran upon and was battered on some of a much later formation, laid down among the difficult waters of tariffs and internal revenues. The long war, inflation and depreciation of paper-money, with the duty on importations, had wonderfully stimulated many domestic products, and especially all varieties and forms of iron fabrics and their germane industries. It could hardly be said that the war majority had any definite policy upon the antagonistic dogmas of free trade and protection, and every shade of individual opinion was tolerated by them. Many leading men, away from the great mining and iron regions, felt the justice and necessity of a change in reference to these interests, such as would reduce them from monopolies to the level of other industrial enterprises; and quite early in the session the Committee of Ways and Means, or one branch of it, had reported a bill for an important reduction of the duties on iron, etc. This sounded the signal-note of alarm, and at once deputations from all the powerful iron and coal regions concentrated at the capital, armed with all the inducements that are supposed to be influential with public men, whether addressed to their ambition, understanding, or other motives.

This was one of the reasons which brought the strong, bold, and enterprising Berwick to Washington. As has been intimated, he was a powerful iron-producer, and no district in the West was more immediately interested in the proposition before the House than Mason's; nor, perhaps, was there one more within the control of any single class or set of men. Though not a majority, their numbers, concentration, and the wealth and intelligence which controlled them, made them a power which no aspiring man would willingly array against himself, whatever might be his ability and nerve; and, when it is remembered that the question, as ordinarily viewed, was quite one of expediency, in which a superficial observer would discern no abstract principle of right or wrong, the average mind which felt its interests to gravitate in the same line would easily find abundant arguments for continuing the present monopoly.

Mason had been nominated and elected without the slightest reference to any opinion of his on any subject whatever. When Mr. Berwick reached Washington, he supposed, as a matter of course, that Mason was in accord with the governing sentiment of his district. Berwick liked the young man very much; true, he had no particular family, but then, people were only beginning to have family interests in the West. He had a brilliant reputation as an officer, was very able, and personally popular, and Mr. Berwick liked him. He was well aware of Mason's devotion to the beautiful Ellen, and was very much inclined to have him favored. When he approached Mr. Mason, he was not a little astonished at the seeming difficulties which the young man fancied were in the way. A clear-headed protectionist of the Greeley school, Berwick undertook to argue the question, and was not a little annoyed to find that his representative did not regard it as involving the question of protection—unless, indeed, that consisted in equalizing the burdens of taxation and the distribution of favor. In fact, Mason went beyond, and showed that he was none too well-grounded in the fundamental doctrines of the Greeley school, evincing a very dangerous familiarity with the whole subject. Mr. Berwick was more than uneasy, he was anxious; he had not only pledged the vote of his representative, but thought that he could count on his advocacy on the floor, and he remembered with dismay that Mason had been the means of retaining a free-trader in the place of a high-tariff man, and had thus increased the danger by at least one vote; which, taken from one side and added to the other, was really a gain of two. Though wealthy, he had recently extended his enterprises, and it needed a year or two more, of enormous profits, to make himself wholly safe. In his anxiety, and without any thought, he made known his fears to Ellen, and, in a roundabout way, shrewdly intimated that she might aid him. He explained the danger of Mason's course, and the almost certainty that it would ruin him and greatly embarrass himself. He was not long in discovering his mistake. The quick girl comprehended the position of things, and could not wholly conceal her surprise at her father's request.

"Why, father! I'm sure I should have no influence with Mr. Mason whatever; and, if I had, I should urge him to do what he thought was right, without the slightest reference to consequences, as I know he will." In vain he strove to show to her that there was no right or wrong in the matter. A woman sees right and wrong in every thing. As the question developed, the peril to "pig-iron" and all its metallic progeny thickened, and it was whispered quite audibly that Berwick's man was more than doubtful, and he sought another interview with him. From argument he proceeded almost to entreaty, and from that he spoke of personal consequences to the representative, and finally threatened him. It pained Mason beyond measure to find himself unable to meet the wishes of Berwick, whom he liked both on his own account, and most abundantly as the father of Ellen, and he managed his side with coolness, tact, and forbearance. When, however, he heard himself threatened, he replied with spirit and warmth. They parted, with anger on the side of Berwick, and almost defiance on that of Mason. This was only the day after Miss Nell received the answer to her note; and, on his return to their rooms from his last fruitless interview with the inflexible Congressman, Mr. Berwick indulged in some quite unguarded and pointed reflections upon the young man, in Ellen's presence.

"Father," very mildly, "pray do not speak with severity of Mr. Mason; he has suffered quite enough at our hands," a little sadly.

8

"How—what? You've rejected him; and I'm glad of it—I'm glad of it! I'll sweep him off the face of—"

"Father," with the emphasis of her hand on his arm, "I pray you, be your own good, just self."

"And this, then, is the reason of his course," with the air of a man getting new light; "why, Ellen, you—"

"One moment, father dear. Don't think so meanly of Mr. Mason as to suppose he would act in his office from such ignoble impulse. This thing only happened four or five days ago. I did not reject him, though he may well have supposed I would. I conducted myself so toward him as to wound and injure him beyond endurance."

"I'm glad of it, I'm glad of it—the ingrate! Let him find out who and what he is. I don't care what you did to him."

"Father, may I say how much you pain me?"

"The wretch, to almost defy me to my teeth! We'll see now who is the strongest in the Berwick district," exultingly.

Ellen walked away to the window, by her aunt, and made no further attempt to stay her father's wrath, which in all passionate natures soon subsides in the absence of opposition. When he had fallen to the level of his ordinary frame of mind, ere the depression which would be likely to follow his excitement, she approached him again.

"Father, I feel that Mr. Mason has now a sort of claim to forbearance and generous treatment."

"My dear child, I can't see that his constituents should forgive him for his treason because my daughter jilted him. It may be logical to women, but the world of men will hardly be governed by such sentimental nonsense; and I could not put that forth as a ground for overlooking his infidelity. But what is this mighty matter—this lovers' quarrel? I thought there was something unusual in your manner, for two or three days."

"Wait till some other time, papa. I can't quite tell it to you to-night."

"Is it something really serious?" noticing, beneath her seeming manner, a shade of depression.

"Aunt may tell you—good-night," and, with her kiss left on his lips, she went to her own room.

Strange, that while there were few or no petitions in reference to the recognition of the foundations of the government, yet the matter of two or three per cent. duty on iron not only agitated many sections profoundly, and produced numerous petitions, but strong delegations, of which a full share fell to our young representative! He was waited on, argued and expostulated with, and told that the people were misled; and it was in vain that he reminded them that his opinion was not asked, nor had any question arisen, etc. He was answered that he could see what the interests of the district were, and that impliedly, in accepting the trust of his position, he had pledged himself to their faithful support; and his response, that no man could by implication be pledged to do injustice to others, was not admitted. The bill came up in Committee of the Whole, in presence of the strong lobby on both sides, and under a ten-minute rule, which often produces the best debating the American House ever hears, and which at times equals the best witnessed anywhere. Mason expressed his views in a clear, terse, forcible way, more than satisfactory to his side. The clause in the bill which reduced the duty was carried; and, when it was reported back to the House, the yeas and nays were taken on this distinct proposition, when it was carried by a majority of one, Mason and his *protégé* both voting in the affirmative. The result was really a surprise to both sides, and was received with bitter denunciation in all regions more immediately interested, and Mason came in for more than his share of denunciation. His was the only instance of a representative with independence and firmness enough to disregard the special interest of his constituents for what he regarded the broad interests of the whole. Then it was remembered that he secured the seat and vote of Bergen; and it was charged upon him that he was bribed from the beginning, and one went so far as to say that he had received fifteen thousand dollars of British gold, sent over as a missionary fund from the English free-traders.

In his own district the excitement was extreme, and at Berwick Falls he was publicly hanged, burned, and drowned in effigy—the fathers and brothers of some of the boys whom he had led and fed and fought with during the war, participating in the indignity. Every paper in the district denounced him but one, and that was an obscure Democratic journal, without influence, whose commendation only injured him with his former friends. From the most popular man ever known in his district, he passed in a single night to the most odious. So effective were the means employed for his instantaneous and utter extinction, that those who had become his enemies were surprised at their success. All the more offensive newspaper paragraphs were cut out and forwarded to him, by scores of copies; personally abusive letters, with real names, fictitious names, and with none, showered upon him. Cold, haughty, and proud, with no word of reply, none of excuse or complaint, no seeking of sympathy, and no thought of evading responsibility, he sent a resignation of his seat to the Speaker of the House, to take effect on the first day of August, and a bold and manly card for publication to his district; and then, with heart and head full, he went steadily about his duties in the House, and prepared for the life-struggle that awaited him, in which he would single-handed battle against the fearful odds of his adversaries. The hope was the most forlorn, but he was one to lead a forlorn hope—nay, to constitute the whole of it himself.

CHAPTER XXVI.

IN A MIST.

TIME wore on. Frank had pushed forward his cases of settlement as rapidly as possible, and finally became aware that he was isolated from most of the few already mentioned who were his friends. It must be admitted that, under pretense of meeting Corflint, he was several times seen at the resort on the Avenue, where that gentleman officiated as "dealer," or filled some equally creditable position. I am afraid, also, that he many times visited the Croly, with or without any pretense, and that some people not weighted with much reputation were often about him, and sometimes at his room. Had the war depraved him? Had he regarded himself at the capital as remitted to a lower standard, as so many do? Did he despair of Alice's love, thinking himself rebuffed, and recklessly not caring? Was he incapable of a noble and pure passion, and under its guardianship to walk unharmed amid the allurements about him? Had he really fallen into the siren snare so artfully prepared, in the passionate way of his hasty young manhood? He certainly was not very prudent, or else the most extraordinary means were employed to betray to the public, or a private part of the public, his lapses and indiscretions, where a most damaging impression was finally made against him.

Margie seemed to be the first to hear of them, and usually referred to Colonel Gordon, who from becoming cold had become contemptuous when Frank's name was mentioned, and was the usual authority for the rumors. Alice, if present, remained silent, and Mrs. Vane and Lucy seldom undertook to venture a word for him; and Gray, ardent and impetuous, was the only friend who defiantly stood by him; and, although he in the main kept his truce with Margie, yet any remark of hers about Colonel Warbel was usually successfully met with "Cutty sark! You are a Sark."

Alice, with Mrs. Thompson and Millie, were pleasantly established in their new residence, near the Vanes, and the ladies were as inseparable as ever. Frank had called there once, and did not see Alice, under circumstances which led him to think that she intentionally denied herself to him. A day or two later, when they were in the Crystal Conservatory of the Botanic Garden, where the fiery heart of the tropics faintly pulsates in its own flowers and perfumes, Alice was suddenly met by the young gentleman. Both were a little surprised, and the young lady not a little embarrassed; the gentleman not at all, but, as if aware of the cloud that enveloped him, he said, "Miss Brand, I hope you will try not to—to think illy of me;" the voice was low and very earnest. The reply was, "Colonel Warbel, I hope you will not compel me to think illy of you." The manner was cold and the voice not sympathetic, and, as Frank thought, accompanied with a scornful or contemptuous toss of the head. It certainly was acknowledged with a very haughty bow, and he passed Lucy with a mere military salute, as if on dress-parade. Whatever he may have thought, Alice condemned her own words and manner to him, and wanted to explain why she had not seen him when he called at her boarding-house; but he was gone.

Frank called upon Alice, really with the intention of trying to relieve himself of the imputations which he felt rested upon him, however difficult he may have found the undertaking; and, when he met her in the conservatory, the impulse to do so was yielded to, and in a way repulsed, as we have seen. On his way to the Capitol he overtook Mason, who had once or twice pointedly spoken to him of the rumors concerning him. The young men had seen little of each other since the reception at the Chief-Justice's, and possibly Frank had fancied a coldness on the part of Mason, who certainly was preoccupied, and had very coolly taken Mason's reference to himself and affairs. He made no denial, and offered no explanation, and said little about it; and to-day, when Mason, who had a very great liking for him, again referred to the matter, he quite distinctly intimated to him that, while he was very grateful for his kindness, he felt quite equal to caring for his own reputation; and that, if General Mason was apprehensive of suffering in his own person for his friendship for him, he (Frank) must make up his mind to forego it. Mason was piqued and irritated, but managed to make no reply; and the young men parted at that time, without an open quarrel. And yet while one of them, perhaps, would have been most glad of the confidence and solace of the other's friendship, he felt now how utterly impossible that was.

CHAPTER XXVII.

MRS. LOZIER'S PARTY.

THE Loziers were among the prominent of the old residents of the West End. The old general found easy repose on "temporary duty" at the capital, for twenty-odd years, incapacitated for service in the field. One son had been slain in the war, and another was a promising young officer of artillery, now on leave. Mrs. Lozier was a woman of the world in the true sense; as often thought and spoken of, in a large circle of friends, as any lady of the city; a daughter of about the age of Lucy Vane, and the youngest son, a chum of Grayson, made the present family. Mrs. Lozier usually opened her house once each season, and the occasion was always an event. Those who were honored with her cards seldom had their social status afterward questioned. Alice had become a great favorite with the Loziers; and, although she had met many of the Lozier and Vane circles, she had never been formally presented to society—whatever that may be—and, in the opinion of her elderly lady friends, was fully entitled to that consideration; and it may also have been thought that society would also be enriched by her acknowledged reception by it. Mrs. Vane had revolved the subject of making a party herself for the occasion, when Mrs. Lozier proposed one of her affairs, and kindly offered to bring the young lady out under her own auspices. The thing was settled, time fixed, and a new card specially devised for the occasion, followed in the young-lady circles with a world of fluttering, anxious preparation. Lucy and Kate Lozier were in a state of semi-angelic efflorescence, and even the dignified and usually subdued Alice was not wholly without a pleasant and somewhat anxious perturbation.

Mrs. Vane suggested only two new candidates for cards, Colonel Frank Warbel and General Charles Mason, the latter as the friend of Frank. Margie managed to get the name of the Chevalier St. Arnaud on to the list, which was revised by the Lozier council of war, comprised, as usual, entirely of Mrs. Lozier, who unhesitatingly struck the chevalier out, as unknown and unvouched for. In young and other ladydom, next to Alice, the personage of most interest was Colonel Warbel. Many had seen and most had heard of him; and there was just that haze of rumor, of that vague glamour of gallantry, and young-man imprudence, that made him specially interesting to a woman's imagination. He was handsome, and gallant in battle; and the hinted-at irregularities, so far from excluding him wholly from favor, rendered him an object of rather dangerous attractions, and then it was understood that in some way he had taken Alice out of the Treasury, and was her chosen champion, and undoubtedly her lover. Of course Mrs. Vane, while she may have feared, yet did not believe the grosser charges against him, and had no hesitation in placing his name among those whom she wished to be present at Alice's formal introduction to the fashionable world. She thought he would be present, and hoped on his own account that he would, while Margie darkly doubted it, and hinted that his audacity was not equal to it, and his possible engagements elsewhere might prevent; and a world of uncomfortable insinuations, which, with Mrs. Vane's full knowledge of the infirmities of her character, after all, made her feel anxious.

The evening came, and found the Lozier house rich with light, color, flowers, and music. The guests came very quietly, without dash or ostentation. That breezy air of consequence, and slightly aggressive self-assertion—the rather loud-voiced and red-faced swell of importance, which many foreigners find ingrained in the American nature—came not. We are a young people, and the older nations still judge of us by our failures. The world's wise equity transfers the shortcomings of one of us to the whole, a rule which time will do more to change than any needed improvement of our manners, much as that is desired. A foreigner, less acquainted with American society than the half-dozen representatives from the legations present at Mrs. Lozier's, would have doubted that the company was so entirely American. Of course the army and navy were well represented, with a fine sprinkling from the professions, as well as literature, art, and journalism; also several from the two Houses, while the larger number were of their friends and neighbors. Very quietly they came and found their way to the dressing, and thence to the assembly rooms. No crowd of awkward, half-dressed ushers and servants. No presence of management or giving of orders; every thing knew its place, and everybody fell as naturally into his and hers, with that easy, noiseless grace, never achieved by study and painful rehearsal, but is the delicious outcome of the culture of mind, heart, and soul, under the control of that instinctive sense of propriety, and the fitness of things, that is never at fault in its perceptions, and whose pose nothing disturbs. Nobody thought of inspecting, praising, criticising, or congratulating. Nor did anybody say 'How exquisite it is!' or 'How delightful!' or 'What a pleasant party!' or 'What a good time we are having!' Every thing was faultless and in keeping, and everybody harmonized with it; yet all was bright and gay and joyous. Eyes flashed, mirth rippled, words sparkled, some funny things were said, some witty, some stupid, and many that were neither. The finest music, a corps of handsome and faultless gentlemen dancers, several flirtations, and that "conquest of arts and arms," peculiar to such occasions—

". . . . When youth and beauty meet,
To chase the dying hours with flying feet;"

whether they parted ere the morn or not.

Alice, the particular star, more than realized the expectations of her friends. How proud Lucy was of her; and even Mrs. Lozier could not but feel that she was an added charm to her chaplet. She entered, moved, stood, sat, arose, spoke, listened, and danced, with the unconscious ease and grace of one born, and all her life practised, for such occasions. Lucy, who kept near her, once or twice caught her eye wandering just a little, and thought she knew why; and a few of the younger ladies asked if he was not coming; and wondered a little, and ran their eyes over the persons of the gentlemen they did not know, but knew that he was not there. Finally, Mason was shown in—

> "The knight rode late,
> And he rode all alone."

Mrs. Vane was a little disturbed. He had sent no regrets, but Colonel Warbel did not come. Lucy fancied she saw a little tremor at the corners of a beautiful mouth, when the eyes of Alice fell upon the solitary form of Mason entering the room—nothing more. Soon after, she observed him and her mother in earnest conversation, with significant glances toward Alice. The brow of Mason was a little clouded, and her own wore a rather severe look for a few minutes, and she felt indignant in her gentle heart against the worthless recreant, which she recalled once, months afterward.

The party had its commencement, its progress, its deepening to its zenith, and then its waning, fading beauty, and dying moments. Its roses were plucked, its wine drunk, its music hushed, its glad joyance stilled, and its lights extinguished, and it lived only as an exquisite and long-cherished memory.

CHAPTER XXVIII.

WHERE FRANK WAS.

FRANK and Mason met once or twice with coolness since the somewhat decided words of the former, which may be remembered; and now, on his way to the party,

Mason called at Frank's room, expecting to accompany him there. He found him taciturn, indifferent, and repellant. Frank had intended to go, but had given it up. Had he sent a note? He had not. What would they think? He didn't care; he was not expected—would not have been asked, had it been thought he would go. His presence would only annoy. He was a fool for having intended to go. Mason looked at him in surprise, and, burdened as he was, he was greatly moved at Frank's words and manner. "Frank, my dear fellow, what is the matter?"

"Nothing. You are only beginning to find me out. I am only just beginning to find myself out. Let me alone, Mason; I'm just where I must work out—or in—alone. Don't ask me any thing; and, when you hear any thing, believe it, as all do. And I may as well tell you all the reasons why I don't darken the Lozier glory of this evening. I leave this delectable capital at eleven this night, for—no matter where, and will come back some time—must; and, before I go, I have an engagement which I will keep. I am to meet Mrs. Croly. Well! it is not the first, and may not be the last time. If any inquire why I did not accompany you, tell them the frank truth. Whatever I do, I don't lie—much. If you don't care to tell Mrs. Vane, mention it to my latest benefactor, Colonel Gordon, or Miss Marston, and all the West End, from Seventeenth Street to sundown, will hear of it before midnight." His face was hard and old, and his voice sharp and bitter. Mason lingered a moment, and went his way in silence.

All the evening, in her warm, bright room, attended by the dark-eyed waiting-woman, sat, or walked, or fidgeted, the restless, anxious Croly, a little coquettishly arrayed, with bosom and shoulders draped, but with arms bared from the shoulder; and, if arms ever had the right to be thus arrayed against the senses of men, the claims of hers would not be disputed. She sighed and laughed, and said petulant things, and looked in her glass, and waltzed and sang, and thrummed a guitar, while the patient waiting-woman, with her hands in the pockets of her white apron, sat contemplating her, with a long, unwinking stare of something like incredulity, or relapsed into a dreamy reverie. A step approached, and with a motion to the maid, who reluctantly retired to the inner room, Mrs. Croly answered to the tap on her door herself, when Frank stepped in.

"Oh, it's you!" with pleasant vivacity.

"Unless I've been exchanged on the way. It was I when I started," with a little sarcasm. He declined to remove his outside coat, declined the offered easy-chair, and sat on a camp-stool.

"Why, Frank—may I call you Frank?"

"Any thing, any thing; it can make no difference."

"Why, what is the matter? What has happened?" with alarm.

"One of the iron dogs at the National broke off a foot about ten years ago, I'm told; and Beau Hickman lost a battered hat about the same time—are the latest things," with affected gayety.

"Ha! ha! ha! You've been studying things for me, I see; but I don't care. I was really frightened when you came in."

"Mrs. Croly," said Frank, gravely taking from an inside front-pocket a large-paper envelope, from which he drew a worn paper, folded, of some thickness, which he extended to her, "there is the paper."

"And do you give it to me to keep? Are you satisfied?" eagerly.

"Perfectly, and I give it to you to keep; and I don't expect that you will not tell who gave it to you."

"And is this the very paper you showed me?"

"The very paper. Examine it."

She opened it and read, " In the name of the Father of All, I, Rachel Withers, of Windham, in the State of Connecticut," and ran her eye down and over the two or three folios. "Yes, this is the same, the will of Rachel Withers, and here are the Connecticut seals, and here is the little notch I snipped in the ribbon;" and, springing toward him, as if to throw her arms about him, "what will I not do—"

"Not now," coldly rising from his seat and repelling her. "If my honor is betrayed, it shall not be for a kiss, even from your lips."

"Why, Colonel Warbel!" in real alarm, "what has happened? What am I? Are you a man?"

"I'm nothing just now, Mrs. Croly. Permit me to say good-evening."

"Oh—why—now? You shall not go now—now, of all times in the world!"

"Now, good-night, Mrs. Croly." She felt the impotence of attempting to keep him, and with disappointment in her voice, "When you come again—" and her looks completed the sentence.

"When I come again—" was the response from the door as he departed.

"Harbeck!" and, as she appeared, "here is the will; but he is gone," despondingly.

Mrs. Harbeck coldly took and examined the document. "Yes, this is indeed the will. I will never believe in mortal, never again." And, throwing herself down beside her companion, and seizing her with a real and little-suppressed rage, "You good-for-nothing ——, what have you done to this proud and handsome youth? I know he is wretched, by his voice and abrupt departure. I could tear your treacherous eyes out of your good-for-nothing, silly head—there! I believed in this man, I believed in his honor, I believed in his love and devotion for that beautiful girl, who loves him. Ah! what is this?" as she detected tears from the eyes of the unresisting, silent Croly; "are you sorry? You're full of your—your passion, which you think is love, and cry from disappointment. Croly! Croly! look up here. How is it, after all? Did we buy—or are we sold?"

"Is not that the will?"

"Yes, that's the will! What did we give for it? Are not part of the goods still spoiling on our hands?"

"You mean, malicious thing!" and she sprang to the inner room and slammed the door.

CHAPTER XXIX.

ANOTHER CROWN.

Joy in Washington, exceeding joy at Teed & Tazewell's—one great point won. The devout Rymer, on being shown the recovered paper, clasped his hands and raised his eyes to heaven, when, suddenly seizing the document, he opened it with an eager, trembling hand, and turned to the authenticating great seal of Connecticut. He scanned it a moment, and exclaimed, in his sepulchral tones, most unearthly when gladdest, "It is here, the cross, the cross!" and, pointing to a faint and faded tracery of that emblem just above the seal, "I made it myself. Let us return thanks. Our—"

"Hold on! shut your old, hypocritical trap! Jemini! Crucifix! We can't stand this! I'm infidel enough now," exclaimed Teed. "This comes from bribery, by ———. Ha! ha! ha! Thank the devil—devoutly."

"Old Rymer," said Mr. Tazewell, who was present,

"the daintiest morsel in Washington got this—and how do you suppose? Just think, you sanctimonious old rat, try to think of the particulars."

"It was a crowning mercy," moistening and licking his chops, said that worthy, mixing the mental pictures thus conjured up, at which both the lawyers laughed.

"And now, gentlemen, it's about over, ain't it?" a little anxiously, asked Rymer.

"About over!" from Teed, contemptuously. "It's about begun, and very well, too.—Teazle, what's the latest from St. Louis?"

"Old mammy couldn't hold out more'n a day or two, and that Rymer may thank God for when she dies, for he had some hand in that," was the answer.

"Blessings multiply. We read how Job—"

"Job and you be d—d! If she dies, there'll still be the old man to be kept out o' the way.—Now, Teazle, about this paper—of course, Bardlaw will miss it; if he can trace it into our hands, we'll have a notice and an order to produce it—then, what?"

"He can't do it; who'll tell him? This d—d puppy, Warbel, went off last night—the devil knows where! He'll never let out. Croly never will. How'll it get out?"

"Well, s'pose we get a notice, as we shall, for you forget that it's part of the grand scheme, and Kramer insists on't, that every thing that can be put on Warbel shall be told in the First Ward; and this'll be all over Washington before night, and from whom would it get out but from us? And we'll have a notice—then, what?"

"We won't produce it."

"He'll prove the contents—use the copy on record in the City Hall."

"That has only two subscribing witnesses."

"I know; but, then, he probably can prove that the

original had three, unless Rymer is the heavenly heir to more mercies—'The righteous shall never be forsaken,' eh, Rymer?" After a pause, "I wonder if this third signature can be removed?"

"Well, s'pose it can, what then?" asked Tazewell.

"Well, there would be but two left." The men looked at each other.

"Rymer! Remer! Rammer! Go round to Ward's, and tell him to send Smith here—if he can find 'im. Let us see—it will then bear two, which will agree with the recorded copy here and in Connecticut—if the thing can be done."

"It won't work," said Tazewell, decidedly.

"It will work; we can swear it came to us in this condition. You're more timid than old Ward."

"If it was to be used in any of the departments, or before a committee of Congress—but before our judges, with Bardlaw, who, of course, has seen this, and nobody knows how many more—it would be the foolishest thing ever heard of," said Tazewell.

"Well, let us see what Smith, with the 'ers' omitted, says about it. He will find some way out of it."

"It's my idea, Mr. Teed," said his partner, "decidedly, that if we can get this thing closed out for fifty thousand, it had better be done at once; and without his witnesses, and with the loss of his will—Bardlaw will agree to it."

Smith came in.

"Good-mornin'—good-mornin', Tweed. How are ye, Tweezer?"

"Good-morning, Smithers. Good-morning, Smith without the 'ers'—

'General Jackson are a hoss,
And so are Sally Thompson!'"

"How is Mrs. Thompson? How goes courtin'?" This from Teed.

"Wal, she's all right, a *leetle* mite tame, perhaps; widders is apt to be. She says she hain't any thing agin Yankees, they's only a leetle quare. He! he! he!"

"Oh, you wicked Smith—ers! your 'compound extract' must have worked like a good rule," remarked Teed.

"I wish he'd give a dose to Rymer," said Tazewell.

"It is jest a mite strong," said Smith; "but then she took it in small doses. I'd have to try fire'n brimstone on Rymer. Nothin' but Soddum and Gomorry'd hit his case. He! he! he!"

"Did you ever see that before?" asked Teed, thrusting the will suddenly into Smith's face, who took and looked it over with care.

"'Pears to me I hain't. Oh! this's that will! Poor, poor thing; I declare, boys, it's too bad. How one of them wimen will take a thing right out of a feller. What says the Samist?—'So she caught 'im, and kissed 'im, and said to 'im, I've perfumed my bed.'"

"Solomon," broke in the awful voice of Rymer.

"The Samist," persisted Smith.

"Solomon," responded Rymer.

"Bully for Smith!" said Teed.

"I'll go Rymer," put in Tazewell; "an oyster-supper on Rymer."

"'Tain't no consequence, gentlemen. He'll say Solomon writ Ruth, next. About this bisness. I'm sorry about the gal. I fear she'd eny most sot her heart on this 'ere young feller, an' it's too darnation bad—darned ef 'tain't."

"Yes, 'tis; but, then, it can't be helped," said Teed. "Now, see here, Smith, can this last name," with his finger on the third subscribing witness, "be removed from this paper, slick and smooth, without a trace?"

"Le'me see," said Smith, his face brightening. "Le'me

see—yis. This ole ink is easily taken out; but it'll leave a stain. It was tried by Munroe Edwards, you know; but it left a stain; he 'counted for that by sayin' the paper had ben in the Misysipy. I'll tell ye what, though, this leaf can be removed—ontie the ribin, and we take it out, that's easy enough; an' put in a new one," examining the paper with care. " This is like the bond-paper now used. I kin git plenty jist like it, an' I'll bet half a dozen dried herrin' that I'll put a leaf in there, an' not one o' you can tell which 'tis."

" Smith, can't you make a whole paper, seals and all ?" asked Teed.

" No trouble about the seals," answered Smith; " not a bit. The paper, you see, is in a 'grossed hand, and easy enough, an' these names I can make with my eyes shet."

" How long will it take to get up the whole document?" asked Teed.

" 'Bout a week; yis, easy in a week."

" Do it," said Teed.

" But no trickery with the original," said Tazewell.

CHAPTER XXX.

HARBECK'S LITTLE SUPPER.

On that night, came off Mrs. Harbeck's promised supper. The innermost penetralia of Midlothian received her and her guests, of whom she was only nominal hostess, to do the honors and grace the occasion. It was given in honor of Mrs. Croly, and several very distinguished persons were to attend. In a room just a trifle gorgeous, for Midlothian, sat Mrs. Harbeck with Mrs. Croly—both becomingly arrayed, and the latter just a little languid. There were already present Senator Josephs, canonized for his virtues by Ward, as may be remembered, spread lazily over a sofa and chair or two, and giving out a strong odor of fresh spirits—"liable to indictment, for retailing alcohol without license," as the same high authority said of his emitting alcoholic vapors and odors. There was George Kramer, ineffectually attempting to attract the Croly. The red, stubbly-faced Teed and his cadaverous, slimy-handed partner, and the lugubrious Rymer, whose woe-begone look indicated that he had triumphantly passed death, and was only awaiting beatitude beyond. His countenance always fell in proportion as his spirits rose, and he now seemed nearly dissolved in silent thanksgiving. Ward, breezy and overdone as usual, was of course there. Soon, the Hon. Mr. Brasson, Mason's opponent of the election committee, and the Hon. Mr. Pympton, also of the House, were announced, and received with great cordiality, and were apparently known to all but Rymer, whom Mr. Teed introduced to them. And still the hostess seemed in expectancy. The attempt at conversation failed, and the ladies sat passive. At length, a little commotion, and a sort of flourish at which all arose, and Senator Pangborn and the Chevalier St. Arnaud were announced. The ponderous senator, with a puff and blow, swaggered forward, and with loud pomp introduced the stately chevalier to Mrs. Harbeck, who presented him to Mrs. Croly, and in turn to the two or three who had not the honor of his acquaintance. Soon after, the hostess touched a silken cord; a side-door was thrown open, disclosing a supper-table, resplendent with silver and crystal, flooded with light, near which stood as many neatly-arrayed servants as there were guests. With two or three blows, the Pangborn conducted Mrs. Harbeck to her place, while the chevalier escorted Mrs. Croly, who sat at the lady's right, while he was seated at her left. The funereal Rymer was the last to be seated, and ere he was he paused, raised his hands, and turned up his eyes in mute grace, unobserved by all but Ward. The ordering had been done by Ward, and a little overdone. Every thing was complete and the service perfect, and nothing more so than the royal, gracious presiding of the dark-eyed hostess. The guests lingered long, and St. Joseph came wellnigh remaining. The hours ran late, and, soon after the return to the drawing-room, the gentlemen took leave of the ladies, whom Kramer attended in their carriage to their homes. Mrs. Croly was the last whom he left, and he went from her door with a smart sting on his cheek and a ring in his head from her small hand. When Mrs. Harbeck's guests left her, by a roundabout passage, they were conducted to the supper-room, from which the tables had been removed, and in which two or three changes had been made. St. Joseph was placed on a large sofa, many of which, couch-like, had been added to the room; and a few bottles of champagne and brandy were placed on a sideboard, with cigars, glasses, etc.

"And so Glozier did not come," remarked Pangborn to Brasson.

"No; I didn't much expect him. He would only have been frightened, and gone away. The fact is, he will place the Credit Mobilier himself, and, under one pious pretense or other, it will be found in the hands of Christian statesmen."

"What's the difference anyway?" remarked Pympton. "There's only a few hundreds to be made; let's have something worth being sent to the devil for, if we must go."

"Two or three Indian reservations, for instance—eh, Pimp?" said Pangborn. Pimp was on the Indian committee, with a thrifty turn of mind.

"Yes—that might do," was Pimp's drawling answer; "or one's wife, or brother's wife, or somebody's wife, might come by fifty thousand in railroad bonds, you know, which a grant of public lands would not hurt much—eh, Pang?"

A little silver tinkle of a bell was heard, and a curtain at the other end of the room vanished, disclosing a small dais in an alcove, flooded with light, and discovering the voluptuous forms of four beautiful girls in ballet-costume, of the least superfluous drapery. The room was flooded with soft music, when the girls, holding long garlands, flowers, and gossamer silken scarfs, came with easy, swaying motions forward to the front of a little stage, when the music died away, and they sang:

> "We are children of light
> Though born of the night,
> The souls of its sweetest hours;
> We come from their homes,
> And we bring from their thrones,
> For our loves, these garlands of flowers."

A swell of music and a *grand pas*, and coming forward again, while the music sank to sighs:

> "O lords of the night,
> Ope your hearts to the light,
> Lay your heads on these bosoms of ours;
> Drink the breath of our sighs,
> Drink light from our eyes—
> We come with our garlands of flowers."

With a loud flourish of the music, a wilder flourish of rounded limbs, a heaving sea of bosoms and shoulders, with flashes of dark eyes and ripples of rhythmic laughter, the girls came forward, and with deft fingers entwined each wondering head with a crown of flowers, and at the same time filling the room with perfume. Poor St. Joseph rolled his too heavy head, and leered out of his swimming, half-open eyes, like a drunken Silenus crowned by wood-nymphs.

The swollen Pangborn; from whose bald head a playful nymph had snatched the wig, with his red, burning cheeks and unsteady, twinkling eyes, and bald pate shining up through his crown, came wellnigh losing the severe dignity of a great senator, and reminded one of Friar Tuck. Poor Rymer, who had, under the influence of thick potations thickly taken, descended from one downward stage of death and darkness to a lower, until there was none below, threw up his arms and rolled up his eyes until the whites alone remained, but whether in thanks or deprecation, in ecstasy or despair, was quite uncertain. He, too, was crowned, presenting the appearance of a melancholy satyr on a gala-day. As each guest was garlanded, he received a kiss from the nymph, and was pulled and pushed upon the floor, and compelled, as he best could, to join in a wild bacchanal dance—pulled and pushed, pinched and escaped from, by the laughing, supple sirens. Even the stately St. Arnaud was not exempted from the saltatory exercise; while the red-haired and bearded Teed leaped and streamed through the room like a drunken comet at a revel of the stars in the milky-way.

CHAPTER XXXI.

ALICE SERVES A NOTICE TO QUIT.

THREE or four days after Mrs. Lozier's party, Alice, accompanied by Millie, called on Mr. Bardlaw, Sen., at his office, and was at once shown to his private consultation-room. Something in her air and manner advertised the wary and practical counsel, as well versed in feminine traits as in Tidd and Chitty, that the cool, collected young woman was really under a high strain. He was not one to keep a lady long in waiting, and when he approached her, with a woman's directness, she said, at once:

"Mr. Bardlaw, I want to see that will—or, rather, I want to know if you really have it, or know where it is."

"Of course, I have, or had it," and going to the office-room, where stood a large safe, he returned with a bundle of papers, carefully tied, labelled "Miss Brand," from which he took a large envelope, on which was written "Will," from which he drew a document of about the thickness of the papers sought, but which did not much resemble it, and opened it with surprise. Of course, it was not the will, nor did nor could he find it. In astonishment, he looked at the observant young lady. "I cannot explain it," he said.

"I can, Mr. Bardlaw," with a cold and distant voice. "on Tuesday night, Colonel War—bel," with a little effort, "delivered that will to—to a woman."

"How?—what! It cannot be!" in surprise.

"It was, and is. Do you know where the gentleman is?"

"I do not," still regarding her with surprise.

"He left the city on that night. I've no doubt I surprise you, Mr. Bardlaw," now wholly herself. "Friends of mine have from the first had suspicions of the person named, and have found means to be advised of his movements?" her voice and face fell as she said this, and a little color came into the latter, "and this will is now in the hands of the other side; and I suppose this case is all over. I don't so much care for the case—I never did—but—" She did not finish the sentence, but compressed her lips, and there was just a tremor of the muscles of the throat, as if she swallowed something, or tried to.

"Miss Brand, I am very sorry that any thing has occurred to so disturb you. So far as the case is concerned, there is no legal significance in the matter—none whatever. If they have the will, they will be compelled at once to produce it. If they don't, I can prove its contents by a dozen. Colonel Warbel—"

"I pray you don't mention that name again," in the cold, far-off voice. "Here is a paper I wish him to receive," handing the lawyer a folded paper, which, opened, read as follows:

"SIR: It is my wish that you at once withdraw from all and every thing connected in any way with any of my affairs.

"All charges and expenses will be paid at the first moment I can command the means.

"ALICE BRAND."

At first, the paleness of anger spread over the fine face of Bardlaw, and its fire just lit up his eyes. He arose, walked once or twice across the room and returned, with his old, bland manner, and a little sadness in his voice.

"Are you quite decided in this matter, Miss Brand?"

"Fully," in the firmest of voices.

"I do not know where—the person is. He will return to Washington, however, and will receive this paper," and, with a tinge of spirit almost sharp, "I think I can assure you that you will never be troubled again by Colonel Warbel." It touched his listener.

"I would not, for the world, offend you, Mr. Bardlaw," said the girl, with womanly sincerity.

"You cannot offend me," with softness, almost tenderness; "I'm only disappointed a little. I thought that where you gave your confidence—"

"Mr. Bardlaw," with a quiet dignity, "I only called upon a small matter of business, which, I believe, is accomplished."

"Pardon me, Miss Brand," with a lofty humility, "if, in my momentary feeling, as a man, I forgot that I could be any thing but an old edition of an almost laid-by lawyer—

in soiled sheep; and I am grateful for being recalled to my true position."

"I believe I am in fault, Mr. Bardlaw," with a sweet frankness, coming forward and giving him her hand, " and I will beg your pardon, and say good-morning." Yet she lingered a moment, with a warm little hand still imprisoned in that of her counsel. "I believe in you, and I know I can trust you," raising her eyes with innocent confidence to his.

"Thank you, thank you," with real gratitude in his tone. "I—I wish you could shut your eyes and ears; but no matter now—no more mischief can be done."

She waited a moment, as if for an explanation, but none was offered; and, lingering an instant longer, she went out, drew her veil over her face, and, sitting well back in her carriage, drove straight home, and remained very silent and quiet for the rest of the day, as one who had, in some sort, severed a bond, and entered upon the task of forgetfulness.

CHAPTER XXXII.

THE CROLY'S GRIEF.

WASHINGTON could still have a twinge of surprise and feel a shade of passing interest. Richmond had fallen, the President had been assassinated, Booth shot, Mrs. Surratt and the rest hanged; events great and small were daily occurrences—great crimes and great escapades were merely mentioned; and yet one fine morning Washington mildly stared from its languid eyes. Mrs. Croly had been arrested by General Baker, and the great detective was charged with the compound crimes of robbery, assault and battery, malicious arrest, etc. The traffic in executive pardons had become not only enormous, but a national scandal. Thousands of packages, containing each a pardon, addressed and marked on the outside, from "one hundred dollars" to "one thousand dollars," " C. O. D.," were shipped by Adams's Express all over the South. The most active agent in this trade was the Croly, as the feminine Mercury to whom the gods were at all times accessible. Her exact relation to any ring of brokers was never known, and she was often employed directly by parties whose conduct required to have the presidential sponge passed over the black-board containing their record — among others, one Captain Bassett, Company K, Ninety-third Illinois, who had been summarily dismissed for the trifling offense of repeated absence at his own discretion. It was important that the pardon be procured, so that he could, if possible, receive it the next day at evening after the employment of Croly, and for that he would pay one thousand dollars. Mrs. Croly doubted her ability to secure this, but would try, and had no doubt of procuring it by the evening of the second day, for which she would ask five hundred dollars. To this Bassett assented, but preferred to pay the one thousand dollars on the evening of the ensuing day. He delivered to her a memorial, and paid to her five fifty-dollar bills. The Croly applied herself with alacrity to this quest, the whole profits of which would be her own; and the thought of a beautiful gift for her young colonel, who still lingered unaccountably away, had its stimulating effect upon her. The executive approaches were opened to the sweet solicitor for mercy, and the President with his own hand referred the memorial to the Judge Advocate-General for immediate report, and by the fair hand of the Croly, who at once went to the heavy-browed, iron-gray-haired General Holt, whose face never relaxed, even when his great melancholy eyes fell upon her face. An immediate search of rolls and records, and a sending across from the Windsor to the War-Office, to General Townsend; and time passed, and the little lady fidgeted and became restless. Finally, the official envelope addressed to the President was placed in her hands, and she flitted back. The face of the President grew blank as he read the report:

"No such officer known to the War Department.
"JOHN HOLT, etc."

What was to be done; surely there was some mistake. The grave and kindly-hearted President, with a look at the anxious face, now sharp in its lines of severe beauty, seized his pen and wrote a direction to the Attorney-General to prepare a general pardon for Captain Franklin P. Bassett, etc., saying he had no doubt he needed it. "Oh, you blessed old dear, how can I ever thank—?" as she dashed off ere he could tell her. She reached Mr. Pleasants, the pardon-clerk, in the Attorney-General's office, who contemplated the order at first with a rueful and then with an amazed look, and leisurely proceeded to have the pardon drawn out. But alas! it had then to go to the Secretary of State, and the official day had lapsed, and, as Frank had said, nothing was ever done in one day in Washington. Five hundred dollars was annihilated, as the hand of Time struck the magic three, and the saddened lady turned back to her rooms. Her client called, and was told to call the next evening, and did, and received a full pardon for all infractions of the Constitution, and fourteen volumes of statutes of the United States, Story's edition, with the great seal appended, and the signatures of the President and Secretary of State at the bottom; and, paying the remaining two hundred and fifty dollars, departed with this clarifying paper.

Shortly after, two gentlemen requested to see Mrs. Croly, and were admitted. One, a dark, heavy-whiskered, black-eyed man, announced his name as L. C. Baker. The lady's breath and pulse stopped. "General Baker, the—the detective?" with frightened utterance.

"Baker, the detective, madam;" with a glance of those eyes, one flash of which was arrest, and a full look, imprisonment. Booth, Mrs. Surratt, the Old Capitol, and a whole horrid troop of ghastly phantoms, thronged in the startled imagination of the trembling woman.

Baker produced the Bassett pardon, saying that she had no occasion for alarm, and asked her if she procured it. She did. He paid five hundred dollars, two hundred and fifty that evening, and in two one-hundred-dollar bills and one fifty? He did. Baker would like to see the notes. She produced and handed them to him. He immediately pointed out to her the letters "L. C. B." in small characters, written on the back of each of them. The lady drew her breath hard, and saw the Old Capitol for a moment. "Mrs. Croly, I must ask you to accompany me to my office. If your husband is here, or any friend, gentleman or lady, whom you wish to accompany you, they are at liberty to do so." A bell brought a servant, and a note a gentleman, whom she named as Mr. Croly, upon whom Baker did not bestow a second glance, and no thought. The lady was soon ready, and a carriage took them to the general's quarters on Eighteenth Street. The male Croly, with the attendant, remained in an anteroom, while the lady was shown in with her captor to the adjoining room. Mrs. Croly had now recovered her poise and spirits. It was a blunder on the part of Baker to give her this intervening time. Had he questioned her in the moments of her first terror, in his dreaded presence, any secret of hers would have ceased to remain such. When she had time to reflect, she knew that in no event would the President permit her to be injured, and she sat down, collected, cool, and a little saucy, as the general soon discovered. He asked a good many questions, and received the smallest amount of information. As observed by the younger Weller, "it was a pursuit of knowledge under difficulties." Did she know Le Grand? What would he give to know? he must make it an object. Who were her employers? What about the place on the avenue, and innumerable others; and so of a little supper, a week or ten days ago, at which, to the lady's surprise, Baker named the guests; and still more was she surprised when he mentioned some of the incidents of the after-piece. At the end of nearly an hour, the baffled detective arose, threw open the door, and called Jones, who stepped in. "Mr. Jones—or, rather, Captain Bassett, Mrs. Croly. You know him already; he's a man who plays many parts. You must excuse me for a time," and to Jones, "I will send in Mr. Croly," who also came. The lady opened her wide, gray eyes with surprise and alarm as Jones-Bassett entered, and turned herself from him, who, taking a seat near the door, was compelled to remain silent, when he would willingly have given his guests the luxury of his conversation.

The detective found the President still in his office, whose reception of him was usually without recognition; and Baker, as was his custom, proceeded without an introductory word to the object of his visit.

"Mr. President, I bring back to you your pardon of F. P. Bassett, captain of Company K, Ninety-third Illinois Infantry. There is no such man. One of my men, John Jones, under the name of Bassett, at my direction, procured Mrs. Croly to obtain this, and paid her five hundred dollars, two hundred and fifty in these bills with my marks on them."

"With your marks on them? Your marks are on the whole case! Why do you come with this stuff to me?" in a deep but disturbed voice.

"Mr. President, parties are trading in your pardons, buying and selling them for—"

"What!" in a voice of thunder, and starting to his feet, "what's that?"

"Buying and selling your pardons," without flinching.

"Who says this? who dares to say it?"

"I say it."

"You say it? On what authority?"

"On my own authority," in a voice deeper and firmer than that of the President. "I tested it, and have the proofs," holding the pardon up to the President's face. "I bought this pardon of unknown crimes for an impossible man, for five hundred dollars, and here is the money. I wanted to see if this could be done, and how it is done. These pardons have been sold by those who procured them, all the way to ten thousand dollars apiece. You don't know this, and I thought it my duty to acquaint you with it, and that is why I am here."

"Who made this your duty, you intermeddling jackanapes?"

"I am the provost of the War Department, and this thing is a public scandal under my eyes, and it was my duty to investigate it."

"And I am the President of the United States," in a loud voice, "and it is my duty to investigate you, and I'll dismiss you!"

"You'll do no such thing, Mr. President," quietly turning to go.

"And what is more," the President went on, "I'll see that you are prosecuted for robbery. You took this money from this woman, you never owned it, money which she honestly earned, and I'll appear as a witness in court against you;" and, pausing, "this is a trap, a treacherous trap set for me, and Stanton is at the bottom of it. Who set you to this precious job of deceiving this little girl, and then of deceiving me? Come, out with it!"

"Nobody. The Secretary of War knows nothing of it."

"I don't believe it. These men in Congress are in the plot, and you're a mere dirty tool, an—" What else the incensed President added was cut off by the door which the detective closed, as he walked coolly from the presence.

On his return to his quarters he conducted the Crolys to the carriage very courteously, and, lifting his hat to bow, said that Captain Bassett would attend them home, and bade them good-night.

At the earliest hour of admission, on the next morning, Mrs. Croly presented herself at the front entrance of the Executive mansion, and to her amazement was refused admission. Flying to the southern entrance, which was opened to her, she rushed to the President's presence.

"Mr. President," with flashing eyes, "I demand to know why I am denied admission at the front-door."

No less astonished, the President rang a bell, motioned her to a sofa, and sent for the man who had repulsed her, and who falteringly came forward.

"Who are you?" demanded the incensed President; "what is your name, and what business have you about this house?"

"My name is Wynn. I was placed at your door by General Baker."

"By Baker! For what? How dared he?"

"To protect the President."

"Protect the President! Did you forbid this lady entering this house?"

"I did."

"How dared you? What right had you?"

"I was ordered to."

"By whom?"

"General Baker."

"When?"

"This morning."

"You may go, but don't leave the premises. Send for Baker."

Another bell brought a domestic from the family part of the mansion, to whom Mrs. Croly was committed, and conducted to a room below. The strongly-marked face of the President worked for a moment in the grasp of the emotions that almost shook his compact person. Strong in temper, inflexible in will, quickly aroused, the jealousies and suspicions of the President of the feelings and views of those about him were on the alert, excited by the irregular chasm which, tearing its jagged lips apart, was separating him from the mass of the Republicans, as well as from many to whom he was personally strongly attached—who were bound to him by personal association and mutual benefits, and whose incipient defection filled him with sorrow, half indignation, and half self-pity. He was personally attached to the suave Secretary of State, and felt that upon him he could rely. The quiet, contained Secretary of War was to him inscrutable. He was never at ease in his presence, and, while he had the utmost confidence in his ability and sagacity, he had none in his devotion to himself personally. Already the mutterings and whisperings of the storm gathering on the Capitoline Hill had reached the President, and he found that most of the Republican members of the Houses were less frequent in their calls, and less cordial in their manner. The days of delegations from the different States, headed by the war governors, or great senators, or leading representatives, were over; and the cold, thin atmosphere was rife with distrust and suspicion. The incidents of the last night had intensified and deepened the impressions produced by all these things, into a defined feeling that he was sought to be victimized by the unscrupulous Baker, through his easy nature, and the innocent favor which he had in his kindness extended to the Croly, of whom he really knew little, and of whose reputation he was ignorant. But no matter; he was a man of nerve, and never went back: and here this miserable, meddling Baker had set his tool at his door, the residence of the President, and undertaken to say who might or who might not see him; and he remembered at the same time that he had been betrayed by the man's cool insolence into undignified wrath the night before, and he felt, too, that this was the commencement of an open rupture with his opponents and possible enemies. And when, in obedience to his summons, Baker entered, dark, cool, and self-possessed, as usual, he met him with a look as cool and dark.

"And so, Baker, it seems that the President is not master of his own house?" And, getting no answer— "May I know by whose orders this Wynn, or Grinn, or Shinn, or something, was placed at my door?"

"By mine, sir."

"And how long, pray, has he been on duty at my door by your orders?"

"He and another have been at or near your door since about the first of last June."

"Indeed! And may I know for what purpose you have had me under this surveillance?"

"I have had no watch on you, Mr. President. It reached me about the last of May that a well-organized conspiracy was on foot to assassinate the President of the United States. I collected the information and reported to the Secretary of War, who laid it before the Secretary of State. They advised that, without alarming the President, extra means should be employed to protect his life, which was thought to be an object of some interest then. On consultation with Major Richards, chief of the Metropolitan Police, it was decided that he and myself should detail each a reliable man to this duty, which was done. Ney Wynn, a brave and faithful man, is in my employment. I am answerable for any misconduct of his. I am sorry if his presence has given annoyance."

The frank, manly way of this communication a little touched the President, who was aware of his threatened danger.

"Did Wynn have orders to exclude Mrs. Croly?"

"He was ordered to see that no person whom he regarded as dangerous to the President was permitted to approach him," with the ghost of a smile about his lips.

"Dangerous to the President! Good, Mr. Baker! Ha, ha, ha! This would exclude Mrs. Croly, of course. Ha, ha, ha!"

"Mr. President," said Baker, "I this morning directed Wynn, if Mrs. Croly came to your door, to prevent her entering it."

"You—you, Lafayette C. Baker, dare to tell me to my face that you ordered that this, or any woman, should not see me—the President of the United States?" springing to his feet, in a rage.

"I did, and do. I was determined that the doings and reputation of this woman should be brought to your notice, in such a way that you must pay attention to them," in a quiet, low voice.

The iron-gray face of the President turned an ashen gray as he stood silent for a moment. Then, ringing a bell, he called for a secretary. "Order the Secretary of War here!" The secretary stood bewildered. "Mr. Stanton; order him here quick." And turning to the unmoved Baker—"I'll deal with your master. As for you, I'll turn you over to the courts, for the present." When, without any reply, the detective left the room.

A few minutes later a messenger from the War-Office reported the Secretary's response to his orders: "That the Secretary of War does not obey orders!"

CHAPTER XXXIII.

THE PRESIDENT AND HIS MINISTERS.

At his own time the Secretary of War, with his round, solid head, and dark, sad eyes, came very quietly into the President's room, and, slightly bowing—

"Mr. President, your request reached me in the form of an order. I am glad to meet your wishes—I am not accustomed to orders." The voice was low and rather soft, but it covered the will and purpose of steel.

"The fault was mine, Mr. Secretary. The fact is, I've permitted myself to be betrayed into a little warmth by that minion of yours—Baker."

"You're unfortunate again, Mr. President. I have no minions. Baker is a regularly-commissioned officer of my department, promoted by you to a brigadier-generalship, and more independent of me than any other man in it." This was a little more deliberately said, indicative that the Secretary might be soon slightly on his nerve. The interview did not open well. "May I know what your complaint of Baker is, and what I can do?" The low, measured monotone somehow was like the placing of a poniard at the bosom of the President, and pushing it very slowly but firmly in. The President began, and in a few clear sentences placed the entire transaction before the Secretary, and with fairness.

"May I know the name of the lady involved?"

"Certainly. Mrs. Croly."

"Ah! I've heard of her—and seen her also. Perhaps I need not say, Mr. President, that, in this matter, Baker acted wholly without orders of mine, and without my knowledge."

"Indeed! It gives me pleasure to hear you say that." The remark was not fortunate in its betrayal of the President's suspicion, and met a look from the Secretary.

"May I know why this matter is brought to my notice, Mr. President?"

"Why? It is an outrage—a personal indignity to the President of the United States, by an officer of your department. I am astonished at the inquiry!"

"Indeed! I should suppose the President was equal to the care of his own honor in a personal matter; and it is possible that the honor of the people of the United States is involved. It is an ungracious task, Mr. President; but reflect a moment. Three months ago, one of the foremost men of the land was forbidden to appear in the Executive Departments of the Government for taking a small fee as counsel in securing your favorable consideration of a petition for pardon. Now, you are daily besieged by the corrupt traders in this 'unstrained' commodity. It is, as Baker pronounced it, a scandal. It is time that it was exposed; and, for exposing it to you and the nation, Baker is entitled to your thanks. I am glad of it!"

"I'll dismiss him!" was the hasty remark.

"Very well! I would put it on other grounds. This might be an unpleasant, even a dangerous issue."

"Dangerous!"

"Shall I proceed?"

"Certainly."

"For his conduct this morning, I know of no excuse, and it might be well to make an example of him, as well in the interest of morals as manners. A beautiful young woman, not celebrated for her severe virtue, favors the Executive with her presence, comes and goes when she will —is always admitted—"

"Go on, Mr. Secretary."

"Seems to have precedence of everybody, stops and dallies with your messengers, flirts with your clerks, coquettes with your private secretaries, and enjoys the favor of the Executive chief."

"Whose business is it, pray?" with energetic warmth.

"Not mine—certainly not, till you made it so"—in the same measured exasperating tone—"and she is the pardon go-between; and a man at your door impertinently thrusts himself between her and the President, and he commands the presence of the Secretary of War. Punish the man, if you may, and can."

"I've already ordered the civil officers to proceed against him."

"You have? Will you expose this thing, its inside? you, the President, and this woman connected with it?"

"She's been insulted, robbed, assaulted, and imprisoned, and on my account, for a mere business transaction, in which she is without fault. I'll prosecute him, and let those who excuse or shelter or sympathize with him beware! I swear, I say, let them beware!" with the emphasis of his fist on the table. "I've known for some time what I had to expect. I've felt the air grow chill and freezing about me. I've known that men, whom I could push from their stools with a breath, were not friends of mine. If they care to be enemies, that is their business, and it will be mine."

"Your breath, Mr. President, made none of these. Breathe as dissolvingly as you may, they will be likely to remain till their mission is performed."

"This to me! Do you threaten me here? Has the rupture come now? Very well, very well, I'm prepared."

"Hush! this is too idle. Send up a name to the Senate; do, and at once. I was not called to the place I occupy, at your bidding. I shall not consult your pleasure as to the time or reason for leaving it. Send up a name to the Senate, and see what action you will invoke."

"Am I not the President?"

"You don't let me forget that, however glad I might be to do so. But look about you and try your power. Congress in a single day can, by constitutional law, tie you hand and foot. They may, by law, require the assent of the Senate to a removal, as well as an appointment. Be advised, and don't try conclusions with such a body."

"Do you threaten me—mean to bully me?"

"I would admonish. I never threaten;" with a voice that had been growing softer, deeper, and its accents more measured. "Were I indeed an enemy, I would urge you to prosecute Baker—dismiss him, and by all means to champion this distressed woman. Good-morning, Mr. President," and he went.

The President ordered his carriage, and with a frown on his brow, that from this time seldom left it, he was driven to the Department of State.

The Secretary of State, with the fine conservatism of a philosophical mind, and optimist as he was, shrank somewhat from the practical logic of his doctrines. As an opposition senator, and more a man of thought than of action, with fewer revolutionary elements than Sumner and Wade and Stevens, he would have been glad to meet and deal with the new difficulties with the old methods, however inadequate. He did not sympathize with the first views of Chase, to permit the seceding States to establish their own empire, nor had he the decided convictions of Blair and Lincoln. But, ductile as well as versatile, he would do every thing, keep every thing, and change nothing. His fine-fibred nature shrank from war and blood, but in a moment he felt the reins of control break in his hand, and saw the President, cabinet, and Congress, lifted and dashed from the seats of authority and power, and were governed and controlled rather than governing and controlling; and, like the new, fresh Lincoln, whose great power consisted in his rare docility and ability to learn from the hour its demands, he reluctantly abandoned his theories, and resorted to expedients more or less sagacious. He properly appreciated the Secretary of War, and came nearer doing him justice than any man of that day, unless it was their lamented chief. He was little less than shocked by the coarse, rough-fibred nature of the present Executive, his short views and superficial expedients, his arrogance, his ambition, his vulgar belongings, rude associates, and his seeming incapability of adhering to any settled line of policy, however deliberately entered upon. For himself, he knew that his opportunity for the first place had passed, and he had ceased to regret it. He knew very well that, when the present struggle should really cease—when the revolutionary wave had spent its force—that he would be left on the shore where it died, and he looked forward with eagerness to that day. No man saw clearer the inevitable separation between the President and Congress, and no man deplored it more. To him there seemed no help for it, and for him, with his views of personal duty, to control and shape, as far as he might, public affairs, until he was finally stranded, he decided to remain at his post, though it might involve him in a seeming acquiescence in the President's policy, and the odium with which he would be visited. He shrank from the bolder course of Stanton, which he could not reconcile to his nice sense of the personal relations of a President and Secretaries, to remain in the cabinet and oppose the Administration.

He listened, with a bland serenity which completely hid his disgust, to the story of the President, and, so far as he could, disabused his mind of the suspicion that Stanton had set a trap for him; said that Baker must be neither dismissed nor prosecuted. He said that, what would be hardly an imprudence in private life, came to be almost a vice in the President of the United States, and that, especially in the present delicate relations of the President to Congress, "we cannot afford to have a scandal at the White House." His manner and language were the decided language and manner of a master, whose word was to be heeded. He spoke as decidedly of the pardon business, and said that a general amnesty had better be prepared, and that he would bring the matter to the notice of the President more formally, at an early cabinet meeting. The President had been thrust into an old cabinet, with its fixed habits and traditions, and, everywhere outside of the War-Office, the Secretary of State was quite dominant; the President fell at first completely under his sway, and, had he been capable of any steady course, this would have saved him and the country many calamities.

On the present occasion the President, from the nature of his mission, and partly as his own messenger, was completely in the position of an inferior, the full sense of which he realized, as he went away abject and humiliated in his own estimation. He went back, to find a deeply-injured woman, beautiful and in tears, who again told her tale, and appealed to his honor as well as justice. It was the old, old story. Baker was that night arrested for robbery, and the next morning's papers spread the story, with pleasant details of exaggeration, before the gossips of the capital. A day or two later, a sharp doggerel from Miles O'Reilly denounced Baker and the Secretary of War, and the President entered fully upon his unfortunate war against the head of the War-Office, which finally involved him with Congress, and conducted to innumerable woes, culminating long after the Croly had ceased to be spoken of.

CHAPTER XXXIV.

SAP AND BARK.

Lent with its penance and Easter with its new dresses were passed, and light spring overcoats, with their new, open styles, were already a burden. The sensuous, lazy days of March were lengthening and lapsing into the longer and lazier days of April. The flags of the two Houses often drooped in the still heat, the crowds thinned out, and the Northern winter sojourners departed. The Berwicks went with the first; and yet the debates and wrangles, projects and counter-projects, the lobby with its schemes, the rings and their plots, boiled or simmered, roared or murmured on toward midsummer.

Alice, in her new home with her new friends, could only anxiously wait the development of events, over which she had no control.

Teed and Ward rallied about the injured Croly, and eminent counsel were retained to aid Carrington, the distinguished district attorney; and yet for some reason the case went over to autumn.

Mrs. Thompson and Millie were still with Alice, who had recently been sought out by wealthy friends of her father in Connecticut, now sojourners at the capital, a lady of whom was an early and intimate friend of the unhappy Rachel Withers, who made the bequest to Alice, of which so much has been said; and who told of her early loves, faults, and sorrows, to the tender-hearted Alice, whose being and fortunes she had so much influenced. Mrs. Boardman —her husband's family being one of the old, well-known Connecticut families—took the liveliest interest in the orphaned girl's welfare; had invited Alice to spend the summer months with her at her sea-side residence on Indian

Neck, and, becoming acquainted with her two friends, Lucy and Kate Lozier, she included them in her invitation, in which, ere she left the capital, her husband warmly joined, and it was arranged that the young ladies should go North in July, and return in the cool of the coming autumn.

On the forenoon of one of the lazy days when more life in the open air is a soulful luxury, Millie, with an unusual sparkle in her eye and face, stepped with a message to the lolling, lazy Grayson, who was lounging about home on this Saturday from school. "Misto Grayson, Mrs. Thompson says, will you please step to Mrs. Warren's a moment; Miss Alice is out, and she wishes to speak with you on somethin' very particular," and the smile became a grin, and deepened into a decided laugh, which involved her whole person.

"Something particular? Thunder!"

"Somethin' *very* particular, an' you'll miss a heap if you don't go," with another convulsive laugh. Something of mischief was in it, and Grayson languidly complied with her wish, and was shown to the little parlor, one of Alice's suite of rooms. He found the expectant Thompson in an effervescing state of mind, giggle, blush, and effort at restraint. The door was closed by the laughing Millie, and the wondering young man sat down.

"Misto Grayson, you'll think it quare"—which he did, decidedly—"but I sent for you, for, after all, I thought I could trust you; an' Alice, you know, is a flighty, onstedy thing. Now you won't tell—you sartin won't?" The young man, as gravely as he could, assured her on his honor he would not.

"You know Misto Smith?"

"Who—that lop-eared, Down-East Yankee, that Yank of Yankees?"

"Of course—good Yankees is good, you know. You hain't got no prejudice, have you?"

"None at all," with gravity.

"Wal, you see, Misto Grayson, me an' him is kind of two lone persons, you know—"

"When you're not together—yes, I see," with an elderly air that, though above, still could tolerate such young follies. "Proceed; you are alone, when apart."

"Yis, an' he's bin sort o'—sort o'—of course you know what," tucking the end of a handkerchief into her mouth and looking down.

"Courting you?" with an immense effort of containing himself, and putting it very directly and magisterially.

"Yis, sort o' courtin' an sort o' not, and he's writ me some varses, just the sweetest in the world. Wal, he's guine away now, and I want to show them to you. An'—an'—I want some writ in answer," she finally said, looking up when it was over, though not in time to see the convulsed face suddenly relapse into its frowning severity.

"Oh! that's it, is it? Let's see 'em. Lord, the dry old mullen! I'd as soon expect poetry from an old boot, or tears from a dried herrin'."

Mrs. Thompson looked a little alarmed, but the frank, handsome baby-face was grave, though a little of its severity had gone in spite of him. "Wal, you see, he's quare; he's writ a good deal, some on Scripter subjecs, an' one quite a long poem, on the Ole Testiment, that he calls his 'compound extrack!' An' he said when the spring come, and the sap run—"

"He'd run poetry, I suppose. It happens to many, I'm told," from the magisterial heights. "Let me see it."

With an averted face, she held out a rose-tinted sheet of note-paper, on which, in an exquisite hand, were transcribed the following stanzas:

"TO SALLY T——.

"The speckled frog sits alone on his log,
   By the side of the yaller Potomac;
And the little tree-toad sings alone by the road,
   While my heart is a goin' caslommac.

"O dear Sally T—— I'm a-goin' for to be
   Far away over hill and over vally;
And dearest Sallee you must ever think o' me—
   Sally Thompsin, Sallee, Sall, Sally.
              "JEDUTHAN PORRINGER."

The impulse of the young imp was to leap up and butt his head against the ceiling of the room, and utter an Indian yell, and why he did not he could never tell. But he maintained his seat and gravity, and ran his eye two or three times over the lines. At length—

"Why, Mrs. Thompson, your beau is a real poetic old cuss, and no mistake; every line of it is genuine sap, no doubt about it."

"Wal, you see," said the pleased lady, overlooking the rudeness of the remark, for its hearty appreciation, "Misto Smith will call round to-night, an' can't you write me two or three lines just by way of answer for 'im? He'll expect somethin', you know."

"You won't expect me to equal these gems! I don't believe there's another poet in America that would have written these."

"Wal, no, somethin' like what you'd like to git from a girl, you know."

"Like what I'd like to get from a girl, eh?"

"Yis, only make it more like what a widow would say, you know; they know wat's wat, mor'n girls—is not so kind o' timid like."

"Oh! I understand. Make it warm, eh? a little on the female Barkis order, I suppose?"

"Wal, somethin' that'll—that'll—you know, Grayson, don't you?"

"Exactly, something that'll—" and, feeling as if he must get away or die—"good-morning, Mrs. Thompson; I'll bring you round something before sundown, if sap'll run."

And he went, compressing his lips, with something like this running through his wicked pate: "The old hedgehog fell off the log and rolled into the water; and the mud-turtle he climbed up a tree, and kissed the hedgehog's daughter. Eh, m—m—m."

With an air of immense gravity, weighted with the importance of the undertaking, Master Grayson marched away from Mrs. Warren's; and, instead of going home, he took his way directly to General Lozier's. The enterprise was too much for one, and he thought it would be as much as he and Sam could both do to keep the secret. An observer would have seen him occasionally throw out his arms, and several mental whoops were uttered on the way. As he approached, Sam saw symptoms of fun, and called out:

"Hallo, Gray! what hen is on now, old fellow?"

"All the flock, old cock and all. Anybody at home?"

"All out."

"Let's go to your room. As the girls say, 'I shall die.'"

When they arrived there, he put down the windows and closed the door, and burst into a boy's hearty, animated laugh, of utter *abandon;* the overflow of wild, sensuous life gushing out in fits of mad mirthfulness. The more he laughed the more tickled he was. So genuine and infectious was it, that Sam, from a broad grin, broke into a hearty laugh, which he deepened into uproarious mirth, and, thus accompanied, the two imps of mischief exhausted themselves till Gray began to catch his breath, "Oh—oh—

dear—dear!" and off he went again with his accompaniment, until they subsided from pure exhaustion.

"Well, old fellow, and finally, what is it; and to conclude with, what's up; and, sixthly, what the devil is it all about. It's too funny for any thing in this world, I'll own," running off down another sore ripple.

Gray sat breathing short, puffy breaths, and wiping his red face and tearful eyes. Finally:

"You know Mrs. Thompson—Alice's and Millie's aunt? for she's about as much related to t'other as she is to one."

"Yes."

"Well, thunder and lightning, she's got a lover!" which ran off up an ascending scale of laugh, and ended in a guffaw. A thing so laughably absurd, Sam never would have conceived, and he fairly screamed at the idea. When he recovered—

"Who is he," which ended in another.

"Oh—oh—don't ask—don't ask!" and finally, "did you ever see Smith—Smith? and there ain't but one on earth, and this is he. All the rest are shams. You never did? oh, dear! we must go and hunt him up, then. I can never mark him out to you, and you'll never see the full force of it—oh dear! Well, he is the Down-Eastest Yankee that was ever born! Oh, if you could see him as I did a few evenings ago, with a huge bundle of purple lilacs—'laylocks' as the Yanks call 'em—with that old blue coat, the collar on a level with his little old head, like the pictures of Robert Emmet, traveling along on his old thin spindle-shanks, pulling away at the bell like an old woodpecker—oh, dear!" and off they went again. "And the idea that she, the farthest off of Southern women, and he one of the old specimen-seed Yanks, and to be in love! But then she says, 'They is good Yanks, only they's quare' that's all.' But the creamiest of it all is, and where the laugh would come in if there was any left—he's a poet, and has written his lady-love some verses, and I've got 'em, and worst and more than worst still, I'm her confidant, and am to answer 'em for 'er."

This took Sam's remaining breath away, when Gray produced them, and read them through, intoning them with great effect; when the wretches threw themselves on the carpet and shouted like mad things, and kicked out their heels, and rolled and roared, like two young bulls of Bashan.

"And the worst of it all is, Porringer, Jeduthan Porringer, is the lovelorn name appended to them. Porringer! dear, darling, delicious Porringer; what a name to pipe from the lips shriveled like the picture of famine! Porringer a poet!" and then they rose and went on with the lines separately, and dwelt on their several sweets, and then sang them to a melancholy old air; and then, in his boy-way, with much exaggeration and exquisite mimicry, Gray told Sam the story of Sallie's interview and of his momentous undertaking. This they both agreed was a solemn and important matter, to which they doubted whether they should be equal, but they resolved to go about it at once. Sam remembered that all the ancient poets always commenced a great poetic enterprise like this with a solemn invocation to the gods, and he suggested that, after the classic rule, they take a stroll down by the Potomac, and gather up such inspiration and suggestions as Nature might put in their way. Accordingly, taking their hats, they started off in the summer day, down past the old Van Ness House, down to the river, and so across a river slip on some old scows, and made the turn around the bank and took discouraging views of the Washington Monument, which always had a depressing effect, but all in vain. It seemed no more inaccessible than the flighty steeps of the Parnassus which they must mount. They started a hundred lines, made half a hundred rhymes, without catching the spirit and jingle of verse-making, which, when it opens, runs as easily and incontinently as a brook, which it often resembles in nothing but running water.

Finally Sam proposed to adjourn to Sardou's for a lunch, which was unanimously assented to, and with a quickened step they made their way to that appetizing resort. Sardou recognized the young bloods, and in person conducted them to one of his choice rooms, and awaited their order.

"Well, Mr. Sardou, bring us some sardonic sardines straight from Sardis, hot on ice, if you please; we have a desperate brain-labor to achieve this afternoon in the poetic way."

"Certainly, certainly," said the smiling and admiring Sardou.

"Which, being translated," continued Sam, "means stewed oysters for two, in your vulgate. And, stay—what have you got, that a fellow can swallow without chewing, and not die of immediately?"

A wine-bill was handed him, and, with a wonderfully practical air, he pointed to a brand. The truth is, they were not often at Sardou's, and seldom drank wine; but they were very young, and just now needed inspiration. The oysters and condiments were dispatched, as only hungry poets of their age could do it, and the wine cracked, when they called for paper, pencils, etc.

"And, Sardou, it must be the finest rose-tinted, gilt-edged, lavender-scented note; surmounted with a blind Cupid, rampant—mind!"

Then they closed their door and went seriously to work. It is possible that guests in the adjoining rooms and the loitering servants may, from time to time, have been exhilarated by the boyish peals of merry laughter which their poetic throes produced; when, after about two hours, a bell summoned a servant, who brought a check, and the mad-caps gathered up their somewhat numerous scraps of paper, and went out humorously discussing the merits of their performance, as compared with that to which it responded.

Just before sundown, Grayson, with grave face and deportment, called upon Mrs. Thompson, who was nervously awaiting his approach, to whom he produced a small and neatly-addressed note, directed to "Jeduthan Porringer, Esq.," and, taking out the joint production, remarked, that he was but an inexperienced poet, and hoped his little effusion would meet the occasion, and proceeded to read it

"To JEDUTHAN PORRINGER, Esq.

"The pecker-wood he is sitting by his she,
Little white-winged darling red-head;
And the shy katy-did with the hopper-grass is hid,
But where—oh, where is my Jed?

"O Jeduthan, my Jed, pray open your head,
Don't dilly, shilly-shally in rhyme;
I am very sorry, my dear, darling Porri-
Nger, you don't come to any better time!
"SALLY."

These lines he read slowly in lugubrious sing-song, and was pleased to notice that the head of the gentle Sally moved and swayed with the run of the moving lines. When he finished, she gently said, "Read 'em agin;" when he proceeded to render them still more effectively, and would have transferred his entire interest in this world, if his brother-poet could have witnessed the effect upon the lady whose sentiments he thus daringly translated into numbers. When he finished, he ventured to remark, that the second stanza put it pretty strong—he trusted not too much so, as she was a widow.

"Rather strong," she remarked; "but, on the whole, an' considerin', an' takin' every thing into view, an' come to reflect on't, it was very satisfyin'. She believed it just suited her feelin's, and she didn't think she could a-done better herself, and she was very much obleeged to him; and, of course, he wouldn't say nothin' about it."

To which he gave ready assurance—took his leave, and met Sam by appointment, whom he regaled with a graphic account of the reception of their work by the tender Sally.

"Well, she may be satisfied," said the serious Sam, "for it's pretty good poetry."

"So 'tis," assented Grayson.

CHAPTER XXXV.

THE STORY OF HAYM SALMON.

The Republican caucus of the two Houses sat several nights through April, and had many long and earnest discussions, and not a little fierce and angry wrangling. It is in these party private family meetings, to harmonize views and action upon great measures, as well as take order of mere household matters, that the real feelings and motives of men, their loves and hates, hopes and fears, jealousies and suspicions, reveal themselves, and also the character of the individuals, great and small; bringing to light, too, the imaginary difference which often exists between the great and small. How difficult to bend in hero-worship, when one has mixed and mingled familiarly with the heroes—been slapped on the back by them, listened to their coarse jests, and seen laid bare the springs and motives of their greatest actions!—learning that the deciding votes for a great measure, which bears the nation forward on its real progress, were given from hatred of a man, and to thwart his measures; that a change in the system of revenue was to gratify a spleen against two or three unimportant officers, or to spite a Secretary of the Treasury, whom the President would maintain; and that a needed reorganization of the judiciary was carried, after all, to get rid of an obnoxious judge, whose purity could not be impeached.

Not only amendments of the Constitution, reconstruction of the States, great revenue measures, but the policy in reference to the immediate claims of Southern patriots for spoliation of the war, were to be settled. Plundered and outraged by the rebels, plundered and unredressed by the Union armies, the greatest sufferers by the war, robbed by the South for loyalty, robbed by the North because they lived at the South, their claims remain at this writing unrecognized and their wrongs unredressed. It soon appeared that the Thirty-ninth Congress would adopt no policy of justice, however narrow, toward these starving sufferers, and by a solid vote of near three-fourths it was decided that this whole subject should be laid on the table.

For two evenings Mason had striven for the floor to secure attention to the claim of Alice Brand, and two or three others, as of such exceptional merit that they ought to be admitted and paid. But Mr. Brasson, who had constituted himself his enemy, was in the chair, and refused to recognize him. Pursuant to the caucus order, the bill for her relief, as well as all others from the South, was sent to the table, with the understanding that, if they were called up, they should be indefinitely postponed. Watching his opportunity, Mason called her bill up, on private-claim day, and, with a notice for such action, that the Speaker ruled him entitled to debate it, he having introduced the bill, when he proceeded to address the House in a thoroughly-prepared speech. He had one full hour of sixty minutes, and, for that hour, he lorded it right royally.

In a few happy sentences he stated the case with such forcible clearness, that argument upon its merits was impossible. In the same way he stated the whole case of the South, and brought it to the direct and unavoidable issue of a flagrant denial of justice, coupled with a bold and graphic sketch of the condition of the claimants, and of their whole country. He then turned upon the Republican majority, and arraigned, condemned, and denounced it, directly and in set terms, severe only for their truth. This brought a number of gentlemen to their feet, with angry questioning, whom he sharply answered back. I quote from the *Globe*, in part, for what follows:

"Mr. Brasson wanted to inquire if the gentleman did not know that he was expelled from the Republican party.

"Mr. Mason: 'I did not know it, and, next to the gentleman himself, there is nothing that the sun shines on, nothing that darkness hides, that I care so little about.'

"Mr. Brasson: 'I wish to ask the gentleman if his Republican constituents did not recently hang him in effigy?' with a triumphant look over the House.

"Mr. Mason: 'I am so informed, and it is not an unpleasant way of undergoing that elevation. I would admonish the member — named from his face — that, when his constituents mete out justice to him, they will demand the real thing—though the difference between it and any other bundle of soiled rags may not be worth considering.'

"Mr. Cox: 'I call the gentleman to order. He has referred to a member by name.'" Which brought the House, through a laugh, to good-nature again.

However the majority smarted under the assault of the young orator, they greatly relished the discomfiture of poor Brasson, who had an unhappy way of poking his metallic nose into every affair that occurred.

Mason was not interrupted again, and he spoke of the duty of nations to individuals, and of their proverbial injustice. He did not mean ingratitude, and, unfolding a bundle of time-stained papers, he read a promissory note, signed by Robert Morris, the Revolutionary minister of finance, to Haym Salmon, a Polish Jew, for one hundred thousand dollars, the last sum which enabled him to put Washington and Rochambeau in the field, for the campaign against Cornwallis, with other proof from the president of Congress, and Revolutionary generals, to the same effect. He then read a letter from James Madison to Haym Salmon, thanking him for various advances which enabled him (Madison) to remain in Congress and the public service. After the reading he paused a moment, holding the Morris note shivering in his raised hand, unable for an instant to command his voice. When he could, he went on: "Haym Salmon impoverished himself that this nation might not perish. For seventy-five years this promissory note of Robert Morris, with these vouchers, has lain in the pigeonholes of the American Congress, and is still unpaid and unacknowledged. A gentleman of this House, now present, says that, during the third year of the rebellion, Haym Salmon, Jr., a solitary, aged, and infirm man, the sole descendant of him named here"—holding up the note—"died in want in this capital.[1] Is it a wonder that the sons of such a nation turn their hands against her bosom? Is it a wonder that the very walls that hid this thing in their darkened crevices should have been scorched and crackled in the fierce flames kindled about it, that from dome to foundation it should have trembled and been shaken in the mighty struggle that convulsed the continent? Should we not beware how we add to these accumulating instances

---

[1] The papers mentioned above are still in existence, though some of them have been robbed of the signatures, which gave them such importance, and the last of the Salmons was well known to the author.

of national wrong to individuals, and may I not be excused for at least reminding the House that nations, no more than individuals, are exempted from the primal bond of justice?" and sat down. The House had few men bold enough to venture on such a flight, and fewer still who could have sustained themselves in the attempt. But the House was taken by surprise, and an old-fashioned feat of bold, passionate eloquence had been achieved in spite of it.

It was an idle effort, however. On a call of the yeas and nays, the pledged majority indefinitely postponed the claim of Alice Brand, the seat of whose patriot ancestors had become the site of a Union fort in the great struggle between freedom and slavery. A secret fiat went forth that the intrepid young representative should, if possible, be defeated at the approaching election—not the fiat of the Republican party, by any means, nor of any of its considerable leaders, who were, in the main, men of just and generous natures, who saw much to admire and respect in the young tribune.

No interest of my little story, if such it may claim to have, requires further attention to the two Houses, which, notwithstanding the anxiety of the representatives to return to their constituencies, to canvass for the pending election, worked and wore, toiled and moiled on, till the last burning days of July.

The Conservative Convention had assembled at Philadelphia, said its say, and did its do—that mighty flash in a mighty pan, and its mighty smoke, with its mighty noise, had subsided to the mighty nothing from which it so mightily sprung, leaving but a faint odor, and that not of sanctity, on the trackless air.

Mason remained faithfully at his post till the last closed-out details of his unfinished business at the departments, and then, with a heart burdened with its own sorrow, turned his way homeward, where the cause of it had her home, and where nothing but fierce personal and doubtful war could await him.

CHAPTER XXXVI.

A MINE PREMATURELY SPRUNG.

The quiet of the capital was broken by a small ripple in mid-June, an incident having an important bearing upon some of the characters and course of my narrative.

Leibenthal, the active agent in the colored soldiers' bounty speculation, which the reader may remember as a venture that had ripened to promised fruition, was arrested in New Orleans and returned to Washington, and held to bail in the sum of one hundred thousand dollars, to answer for alleged enormous frauds. He appeared on the street one day with his counsel, gave a lunch on the Avenue at the corner of Eleventh Street, and the next day died of the cholera, as was said, and was buried, followed by a procession of seventy carriages. A day or two after, Smith called at Ward's rooms, where he found business quite suspended, and was told that Ward was suddenly called to the Indian country, to which he replied, with apparent surprise, "Du tell!"

The scrubby-faced Teed had a pallid look for some days, as if he too had suffered from an attack of the disease fatal to Leibenthal, whom many people in Washington, to this day, believe to be living, although an administrator duly closed up his affairs.

No other arrests were made. Baker darkly hinted that the seizure of Leibenthal was premature. Whether that was so, or the conspiracy was so well arranged, and Leibenthal so isolated, that the real connection could not be made, or whether that connection was cut with gold, was never certainly known. Curiously enough, George Kramer within a few days left the department and the capital, to the detriment of the civil service. If any one is disposed to complain of a want of justice in his case, I can only say that such is the rule of the service, which this narrative cannot violate, and preserve the semblance of probability; no member of that service, above the grade of clerk, ever having yet been called upon to do more than resign, and usually with the thanks of the head of his department—thus proving that the popular estimate of the service is a mere prejudice, for which newspaper correspondents are in the main to blame, of which the people ought to be ashamed, and to correct which this little story is mainly written.

During all this time where is Frank? If any one cares, it is only the interest which one takes in a scapegrace, and not at all commendable. He must take care of himself. As I am now soon to journey northward from the summer-leaguered and festering capital, I may hope that the intervening months will mature the incidents of this slowly-moving story, so that, when I return in late autumn, I may find them ready to develop.

CHAPTER XXXVII.

ELLEN.

Two or three days after the receipt of Mason's note, Ellen met him in one of the Capitol-corridors. She saw him approach, and would have recognized him, but, chagrined at her own conduct, and shy with the new consciousness of her love, and hurt by his rude repulse of her overture, she stepped, with a cold, grand air of pride, past him, and yet feeling that she received a quick and pained glance from his eye. This was to each the final adjustment of their relations—past, present, and future. They were not even to be acquaintances, and each accepted and acted upon this as conclusive.

Never before had the young girl thought, really, upon any thing. Every thing had come and gone with the golden haze of present pleasure and enjoyment. She was, in the main, good, from the abundance of a rich nature of glad impulses, and an absence of all temptation to evil—kind and charitable from her abundance of wealth and kindly sympathy; religious from the education of her mother and aunt, and the instinctive reverence of her nature. She had never thought of what her relations to a possible lover should be. She had somehow adopted the notion that a lover was to be true, devoted, and generous; and the more rudely treated, the more neglected or abused, the more docile, patient, and forbearing, he was to become. That he could resent any thing in the conduct of his liege lady, never entered her head, and in her maiden meditation, when fancy free, several wild caprices had occurred to her, as the things to be done in a given case; of course, she knew that the time would come when all this would end; when the claims of true love would be truly met, and in every fibre of her loyal woman's nature she felt that, when this came, no breath or shadow of fickleness, doubt, or disloyalty, could exist. She knew that Mason was the one man who met her fancy, realized her dream, and was always near her heart, and who was to be fully admitted into it some time; and when she walked with him, the evening before the Chief-Justice's reception, she was a little annoyed to find his strength and hold upon her, and in her mind had determined not to admit it—at least, not for the present. She did not forget her engagement to ride with him, but it occurred to her that going off with the chevalier was one of the predetermined things to do, and with what a wild, half-wicked impulse she did it! Oh, dear! It was all over now. Had he come to her as she knew he would, she would at once have owned her fault and asked his pardon, and she didn't know what she might say or do besides. She knew that she should always love him, and nobody else; but she did not mean to die, or pine away much. She should live, and the world would some time grow tolerable again. Then the idleness and uselessness of her life came to her. What a frivolous life it was! But then she was very young, or was two or three days ago. How old and experienced she was now; and how hard and real all at once life had become!—and with deep and earnest prayer she turned to it. She cried, of course, and once or twice her eyes showed it, to the tender, watchful aunt, but she was self-contained, and quite equal to any emergency of life—a little toned down, a little more thoughtful and considerate, more lovely and attractive, subdued and quiet; and those who met her at the capital, and had been struck by her beauty, and the little sort of womanly dash which she seemed to have, on meeting her again, were charmed by the sweet, womanly dignity of her manner, and the gentle, quiet reserve which, after all, was the basis of her real character.

In her quiet reflections, Ellen recalled the image of a sick, humble, girlish friend, Minnie Winter, the sister of General Mason's orderly, who was killed by his side in the war, and who lived with her mother, just out of Berwick Falls, in a little cottage, poor and straitened. Mason had told her of them, and she went with him to see them, and found them very poor, and the young girl suffering from consumption. All their means came from a small pension to her mother, and the provision made further by Mason. Ellen had at once taken them off his hands, and provided for them. How tenderly all this came to her now! And this was still something that she could do, and in some way for him. He might hear of it, and would at least know that she was not utterly heartless. She wrote to Minnie, inclosing her a hundred-dollar bill for fear that she might want, after all, and on her return home she went at once to see her.

Ellen was greatly pained to mark the progress of the disease, and awed and elevated by the exalted religious fervor which sustained the suffering girl, and raised her to the beautiful and touching realm of ideal beatitude and saintliness. Minnie was so glad to see her dear Ellen, and wept and murmured prayers of thankfulness at her return. A bad cold had made her temporarily worse, and she said, when the roses bloomed, she would be better, and that she would live through the beautiful summer, and die when the leaves fell, with the last notes of the birds in her ears. How sweet and holy, how deep and certain was her faith! Going to meet her brother, she said, and sad only to leave her mother and friend, and Mr. Mason; but then they would have each other.

Almost every day through the deepening season Ellen was there. Her answers about Mason were evasive, until the sick girl's attention was aroused to her manner, when Ellen, in a gentle, self-deprecating way, told her that her dreams and hopes for her friends were idle, and that it was all her own fault.

"Why, Miss Ellen!" with her preternaturally large eyes turned with surprise upon her friend. "He loves you, and love forgives all. I know how it will be when he comes home. I shall have you two here—I shall not go till then—"

"O Minnie! you are never to say a word to him of me. It was my fault—a grievous fault—and it must be left. Think—think—had you a lover, whom you had by your folly offended, could you bear that any friend should go and ask him to return to you? Oh!" dropping her face into her hands, "it would kill me—never, never one word—let me suffer! I deserve it. It will do me good."

"And he, too, Miss Ellen; must he suffer?"

"He may not suffer much, Minnie;" for which speech her heart smote her as a treason against love. "Some time, Minnie, I will tell you all about it, and you won't blame him a bit; and you'll see that he don't—or can't—or ought not—to love me."

When the season advanced, and the young girl began temporarily to gain strength, Ellen proposed that she should try a change of air, and wished to provide ample means, as she had in the autumn before. She was now, as then, deterred, by the advice of able physicians of its uselessness, and that it would only expose her to fatigue and discomfort, which would probably hasten the catastrophe.

"And, besides," said the faithful Minnie, "I must be here when the general returns."

Isolated, Minnie was spared the pain of knowing much of the fierce war waged all about her against him, and only dreamed of her joy at beholding him, and the certainty which she felt, in the power of reconciling the two—next her mother—dearest to her on earth. Yet so wholly and peremptorily did Ellen reject this idea, that she rarely referred to it in her presence again.

The intensity and bitterness of the popular feeling against Mason, which Ellen could not help hearing of, and with whom she could not help sympathizing, and all the more for her own act of folly toward him, were exceedingly painful to her, and the more especially, as her father was, in a measure, a central and prominent figure in it, and, so far as came to her knowledge, Mason seemed to be without friends or supporters. She knew that he had resigned, and she saw his card, in which he promised to meet his accusers face to face, and she fancied him making the onset single-handed, as she had before fancied him charging the rebel lines alone. For the first time, she read the local newspapers enough to pick up the charges brought against him, and was one day stung to a womanly rage, and chagrined to mortification, by the following editorial paragraph in the Berwick Falls *Republican:*

"THE REAL REASON WHY.

"We are informed, on good authority, that the real reason for the extraordinary course of our late representative on the tariff bill was the failure of his suit with the beautiful daughter of our most prominent citizen, too well known to be further designated. In revenge for which, he attempted the ruin of that gentleman's immense interests. There are some souls in the world capable of such conduct."

A few moments after, very cool and collected, the young lady, with the paper in her hand, walked very directly to the editorial office of the *Republican*, and was shown into the editor's presence, who personally knew her.

" Are you the editor of this print ? "

" I am."

" Am I the lady referred to in this paragraph ? " pointing it out.

" Well—yes ; I suppose so."

" As I am much interested in it, may I know on what authority the statement in it is made ? " all very cool and quiet, but in a voice of decided firmness.

" Well, Miss Berwick, you see, now, really—one cannot always reveal the name of an informant. That is confidential, you know."

" You then assume it as your own, probably. It is of

little consequence. I came to say to you, Mr. Editor, that the statement is utterly untrue—that no such thing ever happened; and you must contradict it."

"Really, Miss Berwick, consider a moment. How can I do that? Think of the position it places me in."

"Think of the position it places a much better man in—to say nothing of a 'woman,'" with some flash in her eyes.

"And—and if I can't see my way clear to this, Miss Berwick?"

"I think you will. If you cannot, I will deny over my own signature the truth of your paragraph, and say that you refused to do it. Good-morning, Mr. Editor. I shall await your next issue." And she left, leaving the exponent of public opinion with a confused idea of Mary Queen of Scots and Joan of Arc.

In the evening of that day Mr. Berwick sought his daughter's room under a little excitement.

"Is it possible, Ellen, that you have been down to the editor of the *Republican* and ordered him to correct that statement about General Mason?"

"I did not order him, I requested it."

"Is it possible? And you threatened to publish a card correcting it if he did not?"

"Certainly, why not?" now arising with a calm, serious face, and approaching her father.

"Why not? Have you thought how that would compromise you?"

"I haven't thought much of that; I think only of the lying injustice to him. But could I be more compromised than I am now by it?"

"How are you compromised now, pray?"

"Why, father, can you ask? Suppose this was true that I had rejected Mr. Mason, how could that ever be known unless I had published it?" dropping her voice and face. "Can you bear to think that your daughter—your wife's daughter—should be so unworthy, that a man could not intrust his secret—his honor to her? O father!"

"I had not thought of that," affectionately. "And what would Mason think of it—if he knew that this came from you?"

"He need not know it if Barlow makes the correction. If he does know it, he will at least feel that I mean he shall have some justice from me. I cannot afford that he should think more meanly of me than he does now," with her voice falling and face sinking again.

Her father sat down. "Come to me, my dear child," and she knelt by him, putting her hands on his knees, and raising her great tender eyes to his own, full of tears.

"You are your true mother's true daughter—beautiful and wise, strong and tender like her, and it shall be as you wish. This correction shall be made."

She laid her head down and sobbed in grateful relief, and then raised it wreathed in teary smiles. "And, father, you won't have this war carried on in this way against him, will you? Let him be fairly and openly met as a brave man should be met."

"And so your sympathies are with him?"

"Father, if you had wantonly injured a noble man past forgiveness, would you not feel that at least you should be magnanimous toward him?" He looked down upon her with a proud admiration. "I don't know about the real merit of this controversy, but I will never believe that he has acted from any but high motives. And I believe he is destined to a brilliant career, whatever is the result of this contest," she added. "There, father," rising and throwing her arms about his neck and placing her cheek against his whiskers, "I've defined my position, as the politicians say, and I want to thank my own dear father for his considerate kindness. And so the editorial Barlow referred the matter to papa, did he?" she asked.

"Yes, and the poor fellow was really perplexed."

Two days later, in its next issue, the *Republican* had this:

"CORRECTION.

"We are glad to say, and this time on undoubted authority, that the statements in a paragraph of our last issue, headed 'The Real Reason why,' are entirely without foundation; and the gentleman referred to is entitled to this correction."

CHAPTER XXXVIII.

HANNIBAL IN ROME.

MASON returned to what had been his home, early in August, and was very much surprised at the bitterness and strength of the feeling against him. He knew and felt the coldness of his correspondents. He supposed that it was probable, however, that he might have some friends. The paragraph in the *Republican*, of which he received several copies, significantly marked, he felt the most pungently. Nor had he seen the correction. He could not contradict it, for of course Miss Berwick had chosen to give this interpretation of her conduct toward him; and he despised himself, that he could still love the woman who could thus publish herself and him. That it was an invention, he never suspected; that it could come from no one else, he knew. So bitter was the popular feeling adverse to him that threats of personal violence had been made against him; and, when his return seemed to be delayed, it was reported that he dared not return, and he was advised to leave the train at the upper station, as he might not be safe at the depot.

He disregarded this prudential warning, and reached the depot a little before noon, sent his baggage to the Bond

House, and walked his way up the principal street. He was not long in discovering the change in the climate. He who had been the one local idol, to meet whom, less than a twelvemonth before, the whole population had gone out, with banners, bands, and acclamations, who had been escorted to the depot by a procession with a band, when he left for his duties at the Capitol, not only found no man to welcome him, but the few acquaintances whom he met greeted him with uncivil coldness. No man heeded him on the street, and the clerk of the Bond House hesitated to receive him. He felt, long before he reached the hotel, that he was in the camp of the enemy, and he resolved himself to make the onset. It was war, one against one hundred and thirty thousand, and he resolved that it should be relentless and exterminating.

What a glow and stir he felt as the strong, fierce elements of his nature were so suddenly aroused! The town was divided quite equally by the river, traversed mainly by one bridge, over which a large proportion of the active population passed almost every day. Within an hour of his arrival, each end of this bridge was placarded with this announcement:

"Charles Mason will speak at the City Hall at half-past seven this evening."

An hour later he was waited on by the mayor, who told him that in the then state of the public mind he could not permit the use of the City Hall, as undoubtedly his attempt to speak would occasion a tumult, and might lead to a riot; and he advised him not to attempt it anywhere.

"Mr. Mayor, I would recommend you, out of regard to the continuance of the city government, not to be present if such are your fears; of course I need not apprehend the presence of your police. I shall speak from the steps of the City Hall to-night. Good-morning, Mr. Mayor," who had no choice but to withdraw.

During the afternoon he went out to the Winter cottage and was shocked at the change for the worse which he found in the sick girl. Though dressed, she was unable to move about much, and spoke of her departure as not remote. When he sat down by her, she put her wasted arms about his neck and wept tears of joy at seeing him. She was quick to discover by his manner that he was much disturbed, and had caught faintly the echo of the clamor against him. With a few gentle words he passed that matter over; when she spoke of Ellen, informing him of what he was very glad to hear, that, with her father and aunt, she left for the seacoast about the middle of July, and would not return till in September; and then in a very direct way said how grieved she was that any thing had arisen between him and Ellen, and was going to say—what he did not permit her to say.

"My precious, precious child! If there is one in the world who cares for me, it is you; and I have to ask but one only thing of you, and, as it is the only one, I hope you will grant it."

"Gladly—oh, so gladly, General Mason!"

"That you will never again, under any circumstances, name Miss Berwick to me."

She turned and looked him fully in the face, and was shocked at its hard and relentless expression. She put her almost transparent hands over her eyes—"Oh, don't! don't! I know now how you look in battle. Oh, my God, how wretched!" and she lay back moaning on her pillow; and a moment later, "How glad I am that I am not a man, with his hard, cruel notions!"

"My poor girl, I would not pain you for the world. I would shelter you with my heart, as I sheltered your poor brother with my body," with exquisite tenderness.

"I know you would—I know you would! But I had so set my heart on this; and as it was not for me, only in little part, I thought God would grant it to me, as the one thing, ere I left." The sorely-distressed young man soothed her as much as was in his power, and carried an added burden away from the cottage.

All the afternoon groups of persons were gathered about the placards on the bridge, and wondered at the boldness of the young man, and his very audacity interested the common men very much; they wondered what he would have to say, and they wondered whether the men from the iron-mills and furnaces would be on hand and disturb the meeting, and thought the thing would be worth attending, and in some way their hearts turned to Mason again.

Long before sundown the people began to gather about, in the large area in front of the City Hall—a good-natured, curious, and anxious crowd, which amounted to many hundreds, ere the time arrived. It was actually known to but few that Mason had returned, and many doubted it. A rumor was put afloat that he had not returned, and that this was only some wag's practical joke, and some noisy fellows began to call for Mason, and ironically called for three cheers for him, which were responded to by all manner of cries; and, just as the clamor grew loud and boisterous, Mason himself stepped upon a small box on the upper broad step leading into the hall, and, uncovering his head, sent his quick eyes, in inquiring flashes, over and through the crowd.

"Who calls for Mason?" he demanded, in a loud, peremptory voice, that went startlingly over the suddenly-hushed throng. It was still broad day, and all eyes fell wonderingly on the proud and haughty form that so suddenly and defiantly confronted them. "Was it you, or you, or you?"—fixing his eyes in turn upon the faces of three or four different men in diverse parts of the crowd, and catching sight of a well-known man who escaped to Canada during the war, to avoid a draft, and who, since his recent return, had been among the noisiest of his detractors—" or was it my patriotic friend Morgan, there," —pointing to the man—" who invaded Canada? I'm glad to see him, and if he has any business with me, pass him up." The hit was a good one, and raised a laugh. "We wanted him badly at Stone River and Chickamauga, and everywhere else. But he's on hand now, when lies are to be told, and a man hunted. Where are the men who said I dared not come back where my only home was?"—with a shaking voice. "Where are the men who threatened me, if I did come? I am here, alone, unarmed; and, of all the hands which I trained and led, not one is here to defend me." This sentence was pronounced with a defiant, yet pathetic energy, and smote upon the cowed and awed throng, with accusation and rebuke, that made men hang their heads. "Where are the men who would commence a riot if I, Charles Mason, should dare to say a word to my once friends, old neighbors, and fellow-soldiers—should dare to utter a word in vindication of myself—of truth and our common rights? What has come over you? What change have you met, that your mayor dare not open your own hall to you, dare not let you into your own house for fear you would tear it down, or burn it?" He then singled out by name some of the more conspicuous of his defamers, and denounced them personally, and from them to the men in a mass. There is nothing that men so like to hear as personal assault and invective upon others. Mason showed himself a perfect master of the weapons of personal warfare, and surprised his auditors quite as much by his ability, as a bold and dashing speaker, as by his courage and daring. From this and these he turned to his action in Congress, and in a few, clear sentences placed it broadly before the audience, now increased to thousands of silent and eagerly-listening men. From this he passed to the course of his constituents, and, in sarcastic, pungent ridicule, sketched the actors in the scene of his execution and cremation. He said he had come back, and, in the face of the world, demanded that his constituents should thoughtfully pass upon his conduct. Had vacated his seat so that it must be passed upon, and, with a strong and felicitous peroration, he closed.

It was so utterly unlike what was expected, that his audience were taken completely by surprise, and surprises followed each other until they were surprised into cheers—faint at first, and finally hearty, and, when he ceased, three unanimous cheers, loud and full-voiced, broke spontaneously from them. After which, without any acknowledgment for the applause, Mason announced that, on the following evening, if the condition of the mayor should permit, he would make a speech at Forge Hill; and he wanted this brought to the personal attention of the proposed rioters, and all such as had expressed kindly intentions toward his person.

He went away, but many of the crowd remained to talk the matter over. Not a voice had been raised against him. Not a hiss given, or murmur. Men were powerfully impressed—at first held captive, as a crowd usually is, by a strong, masterful will, and, when fully cowed and subdued, set to thinking by the new thoughts so forcibly and easily dropped into their minds. Here was a man—every inch and fibre a man—brave, true, and just—abused as no man known to them ever was. He was a force, a power, a man to lead, to be followed; and should they be parties to an attempt to crush him out? What had they to gain? And then there was a large sprinkling of his soldiers, and many who had fought under other officers; and one of their number called them to order, and, forming a procession, they called out the Berwick Cornet Band, and took up their line of march for the Bond House, where they played several pieces and called Mason out for a speech. He went upon a little balcony, and, as he stood in the strong light just over their heads, those nearest him could see that he was profoundly touched—the solitary young man—by this mark of consideration and return of popular favor. After one or two ineffective attempts, his soft, sweet, and powerful voice, tremulous with emotion, went out over the hundreds who came to honor him, not angry, fierce, and defiant, as an hour ago, but gentle, moving, and tender. What he said nobody could recall, but almost in a moment the sympathizing mass were softened and melted to tenderness, and many shed tears profusely. The words conveyed the emotions of a noble and tender soul, touched and grieved by a gross injustice, of which it was too proud to complain, and yet could not wholly repress its sense of the wrong. When he closed, a great number of gentlemen came in, and he held an informal but a warm and spontaneous reception, and, in the excitement of the hour, many unhesitatingly pledged themselves to stand by him.

The next was a day of excitement, such as the Falls had seldom seen. The leading and bitter enemies of the young representative were justly alarmed. So industriously and successfully had they manufactured opinion and prejudice against him, that no man was hardy enough to say a word for him, and in one hour it seemed to dissipate. The folly of violence was never contemplated by the leaders, and to-day they were as anxious to avoid it as any lover of peace in the city. The mayor had become an object of derision, consecrated to ridicule, by the sharp words of the night before. The first passers over the main bridge found at each end a conspicuous poster, announcing that Mason would speak that night at Forge Hill, now the heart of the iron-region, where, once, at an earlier day, one Pease had set up a forge, in the rear of which was a bluff, which had long since disappeared. A stand was erected against the extended wall of a building, and at nightfall about one hundred stalwart young men, many of them late soldiers, and most of them with serviceable bludgeons, gathered about the stand with "wide-awake lamps," and their numbers rapidly increased to two or three hundred, while a large share of the male adults gathered in the open ground about. No organization of the meeting was had. It was wisely left to itself in the hands of the spirit which had conjured it. While it was yet light, Mason made his way through the immense throng, alone, and with easy, smiling confidence mounted the stand. When he turned his fine face to the crowd, in its flush of still quite young manhood, he was greeted with exclamations. "Hush! hush! gentlemen—I beseech you! you will disturb the nerves of his honor; and possibly wake up the drowsy police—it is said that they watched the City Hall all night, and had a real tussle to save it." When the laugh subsided—" Where are the rioters—where are my friends the mob? Don't they know I'm here, in their very midst? The Romans vainly supposed that the Alps would save them from Hannibal. I crossed the Alps last night; I tarried in their sunny Italy of pig-iron, all one livelong summer day; and this night I am to riot in its very capital;" and then, dropping his saucy air of audacious banter, he entered at once upon the real question on which he differed from many of his constituents. He showed how it was a pure question of profits to the master and capitalist, which did not really touch the operatives and people; and explained how hitherto capital had dealt with labor as a commodity—one of its means—implements of production, and for itself, as it used steam or any other motor, and not at all in the interest of the workers; that in all the ages of the world the workers had invariably held the lowest plane, that of bare subsistence, and always must and will until the relations of capital and labor were readjusted, and they were placed on terms of equality; that capital now so held the control, that it chained the laborer to the hard necessity of toiling for a bare subsistence, for rude shelter, coarse clothing, and scant fare, just enough to supply the waste of bone and tissue; that in the United States this condition was modified only by the generally improved condition of the whole people, and not at all because capital held any but the old relation to labor; and turning to a swart group of iron-workers—" Your masters own you, do they not? You come and go, work or are idle, fare well or ill, as their interests dictate. Did you have any more wages under the late tariff? Do you receive any the less now? You had only what would sustain you then? You can have no less now. All the mills run. My vote reduced not your wages, not your food, but their enormous profits! They told you to hiss me, and you did, like gabbling geese. They told you to hang up a bundle of straw, and you did it. They told you to burn a bundle of rags, and you did that. They told you to throw another into the river, and you did that also. You, who call yourselves men, did these idiotic mummeries, at the command of your masters, and I am here to tell them and you this, in your teeth! Wasn't it said that this would ruin the iron interest? and yet the flames of your furnaces burn out the nights, and the roar and clangor of your machinery is the awful undertone of my speech. You hear it when I pause." And then he passed to kindred themes, parts of the same great argument, and showed the identity of interest of all workers, and the need of work for all; and, pausing for a moment with his mobile features working with emotion, he dashed off in a strain of lofty eloquence—an appeal to the best in man's nature—and sat down. The crowd had swayed and bowed, lifted and depressed their heads, with a common impulse, and when the enchaining voice suddenly ceased, and the spell dissolved, they stood in mute silence for a moment, and then broke into spontaneous and irrepressible applause—shout upon shout, such as Forge

Hill had never heard. And so the opening battles were fought.

Mason returned home to find that a Republican candidate had already been nominated by a party convention, that passed resolutions of condemnation against himself; a man of wealth but with some infirmity in his war record, as an unsuccessful officer, and who early retired from the service, was the nominee. In the hope of a division of the Republicans, the Democrats had also put a candidate in the field. The three Republican papers of the district were of course committed to the regular nominee, while the one Democratic paper adhered to the fortunes of its party, and the representative was thus remitted to the task of winning his votes from both parties.

On the morning after the Forge-Hill speech, he received a note from one of the officers of a bank, requesting him to call at the banking-house; and, upon his doing so, he was greatly surprised as well as touched upon being told, that from an unknown hand the bank had received twenty-five hundred dollars, with directions to place it to the credit of Hon. Charles Mason, which had been done; that with it came an open note, addressed to Mason, which was handed him, and which contained the words, "From a friend." A wild thought flashed across his brain, and he started at the idea that the thought should come to him. Nothing could be more opportune. His sole means had been his pay in the army, and the small compensation as a representative in Congress, nor had any man with money yet come forward to his aid, but now he would start a press. What a busy week that was, of speeches, interviews, visits, and calls! At the end of it, a saucy little tri-weekly sheet, neat, sharp, and spicy, made its appearance—the *Campaign Times;* under the management of two young lawyer friends of Mason's, with incisive, trenchant articles from Mason's pen. The *Times* was sent all over the district. Men with money and character soon came forward, the great reserve of the unpolitical, so hard to reach, and who ordinarily take no part; and men from both parties, generous, impulsive men, men of cool, shrewd judgment, and all the dissatisfied and disappointed of all parties and factions; and the Mason headquarters became a lively and thronged resort. During August, Mason, now attended by one or more, spoke at every important point in his district.

The first week in September saw the Democratic candidate withdrawn, under the influence of the generous manliness that is usually found somewhere in the basis of the personal character of the bulk of men of that party. A convention, representing every part of the district, unanimously renominated General Mason, who delivered a noble and manly speech on the occasion, enunciating the principles for which he had fought in the war, and which he had maintained on the floor of the House. A thorough organization was made of his forces, and, under the inspiring magnetism of his character, eloquence, and presence, his supporters entered upon the brief campaign with activity and confidence. His enemies, though alarmed, had the prestige of old success, and the still remaining party organization rallied with determination to the contest, which was now wellnigh equalized. The election would occur on the second Tuesday of October.

CHAPTER XXXIX.

AN IDYL OF THE SUMMER SEA.

EARLY August found the Boardmans, with their Southern guests, in their cottage on Indian Neck. The young ladies went North in mid-July. The coast-cottage needed some repairs, and Mrs. Boardman took them to Newport for two weeks; and, if matronly heart had ever cause to swell with womanly glow at the homage of man to her sex, Mrs. Boardman enjoyed that luxury. Wherever she moved or paused, with her *protégées*, admiration moved and paused with her. In their first freshness and brightness, each in her style was no bad representative, while Alice might well dispute the first place with any. Curiously enough, almost the first gentleman they met was the Chevalier St. Arnaud, seemingly on pleasant terms with everybody, as usual, and ever ready enough to do the agreeable by Mrs. Boardman and her fair convoy. Mrs. Boardman had met the chevalier in Washington (as who, of any pretension, had not?) and accepted from him the little pleasant attentions to herself and party rather necessary as lady-luxuries, or even to existence. And, curiously enough, within three days, there was on the air an unvoiced whisper that he was the accepted suitor of the beautiful Mississippian belle.

When the Boardmans drove to their Indian-Neck cottage, who should be pacing up and down the veranda of the Montowese but this everlasting chevalier, and here, as everywhere, at home and at his ease; and here, too, the puissant lion, and on terms with all the knowable and noticeable people! Here, also, he became the golden marginal cloud of the Boardman party, on the beach, under the linden-trees, and on little boating-excursions; though, for some reason, he never quite established himself as other than a ceremonious caller at the cottage. Yet here, also, in some mysterious way, there soon came to be a misty impression that he was the favored suitor of Alice.

Indian Neck is a narrow strip of the continent, of a mile or two in extent, formed by the Branford River, which flows into the sound almost in a line with the coast, leaving a peninsula between it and the sea. It is some nine miles from New Haven, and, seventy years ago, the mouth of the river, a beautiful land-locked harbor, was the entrepôt of an immense West India and other foreign trade; while now it carries out only food to the extensive oyster-beds, so carefully preserved and cultivated all along the shoals of the sound. The Montowese was one of half a dozen sea-side houses at the base of the Neck, with a beautiful elm and maple shaded lawn, reaching from its front to the abrupt bluff, which, protected by a sea-wall, abuts on a beautiful sandy beach, which bends pleasantly into the land for a quarter of a mile in extent. All along the bluff were large clumps of fine basswood-trees, surrounded with platforms and seats, and stairways leading down to the beach, where were bathing-houses, boat-houses, and the usual appliances of sea-side life. The Boardman cottage was a dozen rods beyond, or up the coast from the Montowese. A mile and a half back, and across the river, is the beautifully straggling and stragglingly beautiful old town—half town and all country—of Branford, with its railroad-station, post-office, churches, stores, and dwellings, among its wonderful old elms and maples, surrounded by hills, among which, and superior to all, rises Cherry Hill. As might be expected, the Montowese and the houses about it were a favorite resort; not so much of demonstrative fashion and showy wealth, as of the quiet, refined, and cultivated element, which seeks rest and health by the sea, on some of its tamer and more secluded shores. To Alice and her friends the whole was a lazy, sensuous little paradise, of sun and shadow, green earth and green sea, of flowers and fish, fruit and clams, boating, bathing, and oysters, where one long, bright, idle day lapsed to another as long, bright, and lazy. Days of strolls on the beach, of climbing among the rocks, of excursions among the islands, rambles among the hills, of cool nights and lapping waves, unannoyed by beaux, and free from the little pests of flirtation. It is true that this blessed nook was not wholly free of young men and mosquitoes, but both were in a comparatively mild form—the former not numerous and audacious, and the latter not very penetrating.

The Montowese mustered a large number of guests from New Haven, New York, Brooklyn, Philadelphia, and even from the West, with a fine show of well-dressed ladies and many very beautiful young girls. Among them were the three Morans from New Haven, two sisters and a cousin: the latter, Maud, was a decided belle, and much inclined to practise the prerogatives of bellehood; another young lady was with them, and Maud had two brothers and her cousins one. In mid-August the young men were coming over from New Haven accompanied by a classmate of Maud's brother, and a real hero of the war, handsome and brave; and a band was to come, and the hoppingest kind of a hop was to be had and held at the drowsy and staid Montowese. What a flutter it made! All the ladies, old and young, at the Neck, were excited, and all the men, too. It even extended to the Boardman cottage, whose inmates were on the pleasantest terms at the Montowese. Even the grand chevalier condescended to be interested in it.

The day came, the band came in its carriage, and then a wagon with luggage—and finally, in the cool of the day, a landau, with the four young gentlemen, bright and sparkling with spirit and gay and happy with youth, and the *abandon* of unthinking, unknowing, uncaring, impulsive young manhood, than which and whom there is nothing in the world that young womanhood so intensely sympathizes with, and is so powerfully drawn to. What a flutter they made when they drove up! Their rooms were waiting, and very soon they were ready to introduce the war-hero to their cousins and lady friends. Soon after, a little procession, headed by Maud and the young officer, went down the walk toward the lindens, where, facing them, sat the young Southern ladies, not wholly indifferent to the now approaching company, which had at least four unknown young gentlemen, of whom they had heard a good deal within a few days past. Not all unknown were they. Alice was the first to make the discovery, and rose, with a little pallor about the lips, a little distention of the eyes, and moved back. And there, within a dozen steps of them, with little Belle Maud clinging to his arm, with his pleased face bent down to catch her idle words, was Frank Warbel—looking any thing but a war-battered veteran. A little thinner, and, though browned, he had a fresh look, swinging his hat in his hand, with his splendid head set off with its hair, now in long waves. His eye flashed over the group he was approaching, and his smiling lips compressed, as if a rebel battery had suddenly uncovered before him; and, had Miss Moran been observing, she would have felt just one spasm of a tremor in the arm which she held in both her hands, and that was all. The party reached the walk and carriage-way along the beach, and turned into it, and passed.

"Frank Warbel!" gasped Lucy, which alarmed the observant Mrs. Boardman, who was with them, and who had admired Frank's splendid approach without knowing him, and who now instinctively arose, as if to cover her tender charges from the menaced danger.

"And this, then," she thought, "is Frank Warbel," and how utterly unlike her idea of him! "A proud, tall, dark, mysterious-looking man of thirty, something like the chevalier. And here was this slender, frank, laughing, open-browed youth, whose deep, honest eyes any woman would trust—and yet, he had for the favor of a —— betrayed his honor, his trust, the girl he couldn't help but love, and then fled the capital in disgrace." And her eyes followed him along as he walked gracefully away by the innocent young girl, who was hanging on his every look. She, at the least, must be alarmed, and set upon her guard. For once, Mrs. Boardman realized the perils of her sex, exposed all unknowingly to these handsome depravities.

As she turned, she saw Lucy and Kate, still staring after the passing forms, seeing no one but Frank; and, when they withdrew their eyes, it was to turn them toward Alice, who, perfectly composed, had turned, and was coming to the front of the platform. After the promenaders had passed beyond the walk leading to the Boardman cottage, Mrs. Boardman and the young ladies returned to it.

The hop was a success, though pained hearts were, as usual, present. Alice and Lucy did not dance. Mrs. Boardman and the chevalier stood guard over Alice, while Lucy was much of the time on picket-duty or acting as a scout. In some way Frank managed to have it known to his immediate set that he was not to be presented to Mrs. Boardman and her *protégées,* and without any explanation. And Lucy, with the consistency and logic of a woman, was piqued and incensed that "during all the evening Frank never turned his eyes toward the spot where Alice sat or stood. As if it was not enough that he should be such a traitor, and go and break her heart, as he knew he had, and compel her now to remain in the background, but he didn't even look at her—had no thought of any thing but this little, romping, pink-faced Maud, but he'd get his pay for it all," which was one comfort. Frank was one to bear himself well under the cloud that darkened and the eyes that scanned him. Proud and gallant, with the lightness and grace of youth, and the quick spirits of a nature still fresh and elastic, the partner of the conceded belle, admiration followed him, and light and joy waited on his footsteps. Little gushes of laughter sprang up where his bright and sparkling words fell, and, to the eye of a stranger, he was one of the gifted and favored of Fortune. Compared with him, the studied and elaborately-natural chevalier was battered, worn, and *blasé*. These gentlemen had met in Washington, and the chevalier was disposed to claim Frank's acquaintance, but somehow that personage seemed unaware of his existence. He finally asked a gentleman, who had been presented to Frank, to introduce him, an honor which the latter declined. Late in the evening, while some of the ladies and gentlemen were in the billiard-room, with the assurance which, with him, amounted to the sublime, he approached Frank in his superior way, and, in the presence of ladies as well as gentlemen—

"Colonel Warbel—I believe?" directly facing him, and bowing.

"The Chevalier of Castle Como, I believe," in precisely the same tone and voice, with a cool, steady look of his eyes and no motion of his person. The chevalier had not calculated his man, and had perhaps over-estimated himself; and there was nothing for it but to turn and walk away. Frank may have expected something further from it, but the chevalier had that night, in some mysterious way, received a message, which took him away to meet the early train to New York in the morning, and the Montowese saw no more of him. The incident made quite a little ripple, and, while it enhanced the admiration for Frank, it in some way cast a little haze upon Mrs. Boardman's party, who were in some sort thought to be under the chevalier's patronage.

The next morning the young men took a plunge from the "flat rock," up the sound near a solitary tree, and were laughing and shouting back to a seven-o'clock breakfast, and then in Captain Pond's boat were off to the islands. Then, after a latish dinner, back to New Haven, Frank carrying half of the hearts of half of the young ladies of Indian Neck with him. It is the last and best half of a young girl's heart, that is so hard to win, and that so richly repays the deserving for his labor in its acquisition.

Just before Frank went, he saw Millie, for whom he had much kind feeling, flitting around under the lindens by the beach. He approached her, and, as he did so, thought that she wished to speak with him. He took her hand and kindly asked after her welfare, and made no further inquiry. She seemed to expect that he would ask something more, but he did not, and was about to turn away. "I did not know," she finally said, "but that you would like to inquire about Miss Alice."

"I'm not at liberty to do that, my girl; she has forbidden my very name to be mentioned. Had I known she was here, I should have remained away."

"But this chevalier — you might have heard what is thought or said about him and Miss Alice—"

"No matter about that, Millie; that don't concern me the least in the world."

She looked up, surprised and pained. The tears came to her eyes as she said hastily: "Colonel Warbel, you won't mention my speaking to you. She would be displeased if she knew."

"Certainly not. Good-by," and, shaking hands with her, he turned away. Millie continued to stand where he left her, with her great, swimming, tropical eyes looking wistfully after his retiring form. Bright child of Nature and poor woman that she was, her instincts, after all, may have penetrated the hazy mists that involved these young hearts, so impenetrable to others.

CHAPTER XL.

MINNIE'S MESSAGE FOR THE ANGELS.

THE war in Mason's district raged with great fierceness and increasing doubt as to the result. The Republicans had many able speakers, and the advantages of organization, but they had no one who dared to meet this young representative, whose friends had greatly in excess zeal, courage, and activity. From the first, Mason put his opponents on the defensive, from which he never permitted them to escape, and fought them at all points, and in all modes, short of detraction and misrepresentation.

Toward the end of the canvass, his opponents made a false movement. They secured for a few days the Republican member of Congress from an adjoining district, of unusual ability as a speaker, and regarded as dangerous in the personal warfare of sarcasm, invective, and ridicule, to which Mason subjected all his leading opponents. They made four appointments for him, and it was intimated to Mason that he was a man entirely willing to meet him in debate, which the best of the speakers on their side had declined to do. This man was challenged at once. The first encounter was to be at the Falls. Each party was entitled to one hour and a half, and might, if he chose, divide his time. In the first encounter, Mason, as the challenger, was to open. The speaking was on the Fair-grounds in the open air, in the presence of many thousands.

Mason opened with a sarcastic reference to his opponents, who in their feebleness had been obliged to call in a foreigner to their aid, a confession shameful to themselves personally, and most damaging to their cause. He then paid his respects personally to the gentleman who had thus volunteered to come into the district of a colleague, to aid the malcontents who made war upon him, not for any crime against his party, not for any violation of trust or betrayal of confidence, but because he differed from half a dozen iron-mongers about the eighth of a mill in the price of a pound of pig-iron! He said, as modesty would prevent the honorable gentleman from saying much of himself, he would inform them who and what he was. He opened the *Congressional Globe* and reviewed the gentleman's whole congressional record, from the journal of the House, making many grave and striking points, and with a fiery blast of sarcasm and ridicule he pitilessly pelted him for three-quarters of an hour, and sat down.

This was not the feast to which the gentleman and his backers were invited, and the spectacle which followed was most pitiable. Surprised, enraged, and wholly unprepared for the attack upon his career of seven years, many incidents of which had gone wholly out of his memory, he found himself bound to the hard, and for him fatal necessity of a defence of his whole public life, never before seriously assailed. He did what he could. At fault in his memory, worse at fault in his temper, and most unfortunate of all in his defense of some points wherein he had really blundered, he sat down, at the end of his full hour and a half, under the mortifying sense of discomfiture and failure.

In his reply, Mason read extracts from a speech of the gentleman, who represented an agricultural district, wherein he had taken ground quite as obnoxious to the iron interest as any thing he had himself advanced; and then, turning to the *Globe*, showed that the gentleman dodged the vote on the final passage of the bill, when, had he voted, as the record showed, and for the interest of his retainers, the bill would have failed. This finished the unfortunate gentleman; when, apologizing for this waste of time, upon a subject of no earthly importance, Mason held the vast crowd, for his remaining thirty minutes, in a brilliant discussion of the real question, and, with a happy closing, took his seat. This was the last of the aid from abroad, who went home, to meet as he best could the damaging effect of Mason's assault upon him; as his speech was printed and largely circulated among his constituents. Mason's enemies never fully recovered from their overthrow on this occasion, and maintained as they best could an apparently losing battle.

On the afternoon of one of those wondrous early autumn days, after the noon of summer, at that delicious pause of the season, with an equilibrium of temperature, when balanced sunlight and shadow bear rule, and Nature marks one of her rarest changes, by the ripening tints of fruit and foliage, ere she detaches them from spray and bough, just when the sky takes a deeper, serener shade, and the sigh of the breeze swells to the moan of the wind, when from out the azure depths drop the farewell notes of the blue-bird, like pearls of melody from ascending angels—in that restful pause of the seasons so sweet and serene to the poetic and contemplative nature, and which is never lost upon the most matter-of-fact, and now doubly sweet to the long overworked Mason, who found the whole of one calm, sweet autumn afternoon, to be followed by a night of absolute surcease of labor, and he devoted it to the failing Minnie. He had only seen her for a few moments at a time, and at rare intervals, since his return, though he sent her flowers and little pleasant reminders of his kindness often when in the neighborhood. Now he meant to devote all the latter part of this beautiful day to her. He found her in bed, unable to remain long from it; sweet, beautiful, tranquil, happy, and hopeful. She was very glad to see him, so glad that she could only clasp his hand and murmur a ripple of broken girl-words over it, while tears came to her eyes. And then she told him how she had been, and all the little world of her monotonous life, and recalled in their order all the small presents he had sent her, and the kindnesses he had done, and of the pleasant happenings about her, of all the calls made to see her. The warm, quick sympathy of the rich-natured young man was a blessed manna to the languid, worn spirit of the poor girl. In the world's pharmacy, there is nothing so grateful to a sick woman as the strong, fresh, sustaining tonic of an appreciative man's sympathy, and that finds its only equivalent in its counterpart, the tenderness of woman for man.

When she had murmured out all her little histories, and had all her questions patiently and pleasantly answered, she paused—and turned—was restless, with something that she must say.

"What is it, Minnie?"

"May I tell—and all that is in my mind?"

"All, every thing—every thing that is in it."

"It is about Ellen Berwick—I must tell it," noticing the sort of spasm that involuntarily contracted his hand which hers still held. "She and her father will be home in a few days; and we shall be so glad, and you must be glad too. I know what she did in Washington. I teased it all out of her. It was as foolish a thing as girl could do, and yet a brave, generous man could, I should think, forgive her."

Mason had determined, for her sake, to indulge her, and he answered: "It was not a thing of forgiveness, little Minnie. A woman rejects you: what has pardon to do with it? The matter is ended. You would not have a man go back, would you, especially when so rejected? I fear you won't understand it."

"If he loved her, and she loved him—"

"Oh, indeed! Then, love will forgive love to the end."

"And would you do that?" very brightly and anxiously.

"Of course I would; every lover would do that," with fervor.

"Oh, I'm so glad! She loves you."

"And that is just what she does not do. She never would have done what she did. No mortal would have done so—faugh, little Minnie! Let us talk of something else."

"No. I will talk about this; a woman understands this matter instinctively. Had she not loved you, she would not have acted so. It was one of the outrageous things that a girl in love could only do."

"Love does not forget the loved one for a stranger. And how could it have been known that she had rejected me, had it not in some way been derived from her? O Minnie!"

"She didn't reject you, and so she could not tell of it. Do you, in your thoughts, think so meanly of her? O General Mason! I thought a man was not only just, but generous, and so they are toward men; when you deal with us—it is so hard and cruel! Let me ask you of a thing: how came that miserable statement in the *Republican* to be contradicted, do you suppose?"

"I never heard that it was."

"You never heard of that?" in surprise. "It was; and because she went personally to the editor, and required it."

"How—what! What do you say? Minnie," starting up earnestly.

"She came here on her way back and told me. She went and told the editor to contradict it, and threatened to do it herself if he would not, and he did." Her visitor regarded her in mute surprise.

"And, General Mason, may I ask another thing? Did

you receive something through a bank, and a note with it?"

"I did," with increasing surprise, "and have the note with me now," producing it and handing it to her.

"You didn't know the hand, did you? You would have known hers, and I wrote it for her; of course she don't care any thing for you!" covering her face with her hands while tears stole through her wasted fingers. Just then came a light, clipping step, with a little bound into the room, and a ringing, cheery—"O Minnie, Minnie, Minnie!—" and a sudden pause, and hush, when the general and the absorbed girl turned, and there stood Ellen Berwick, herself flushed, warm, and beautiful, with her eyes staring wide at the sight of Mason, who, bowing in profound silence, stepped back from the sick girl.

"Oh, I'm so glad you've come!" holding out her hand which Ellen took, and bending over her, kissed her repeatedly ere she raised her face, which had tears upon it when she did.

"Charles Mason," said the sick girl, "come here;" and as he stepped to the side of the trembling, unknowing Ellen, she took his hand and placed the hand of Ellen in it. "You love one another, and, with failing breath, almost my last, I declare you shall not be so cruel to each other."

"Minnie, you mistake," said Mason, deeply moved, "you utterly mistake; you pain and embarrass Miss Berwick beyond measure."

"And, now," said the girl, unheeding him, "put your lips together—as lovers kiss each other. I want to carry the story to the angels, that I saw a pair of true and beautiful earthly lovers join their lips in love, as pure and eternal as the love of heaven; and that the world is full of love."

Tremblingly, the beautiful girl lifted her face, without raising her eyes, turned her lips toward her lover, and received upon them the thrill of his; when, throwing herself on her knees, she clasped the shrunken form of the sick girl in her arms: "Oh, you darling, blessed angel!" and covered her face with tears and kisses. The young man with the electric touch as of heaven flashing from heart to brain, threw out his arms wildly with an audible groan, cried—"Oh, my God, my God!" and dropped on his knees by the kneeling girl, and laid his face in the bed-coverings. For a moment there was absolute silence, save the murmurs of Ellen, and, when she raised her face, a little cry recalled her lover, and both thought that in her gladness the spirit of the sick girl had gone with its message; and, just as this thought took possession of them, she breathed again, and, opening her eyes, said faintly: "No, I could not go yet. I would not so mar your happiness, and I wanted to see how beautiful you are; and now stand up, and let me look at you two together. O God, how I thank thee that I have been permitted to do this great thing!" Clasping their hands with fervor, and pulling them each down to her, she kissed each of them, and, touching a bell for her mother, she said, "There, go now out to your own, dear, precious selves, and leave me with my joy!"

CHAPTER XLI.

THE LOVERS.

THEY went out, the maiden and her lover, into the mysterious twilight, that hung like a dark golden fringe upon the robes of passing day, and bordered with half-translucent glory the gloom-mantle of oncoming night—the low, ominous hush of Nature, while her dusky fingers were weaving the deeper mysteries of silence and darkness.

It was a lovers' night, with full moon and new, large stars, and the soft airs of lingering summer lisping off to sighing sleep in the dewy foliage. One willing, clinging hand lay in his, with his other arm, all unreproved, about the consenting waist. Hardly dared he trust his voice when he now felt, in the free, dusky twilight, how entirely she was his, and how fully she accepted him. Naturally enough they took the way that would lead to her home by a very long line indeed. "What an incomprehensible thing is this heaven of your love, which so fills the world to me! I used to lie in my tent, and wonder if this—this love, a true, noble woman's love, would ever be mine, that I should be glorified in it; and now, you whom I love more than I once thought was in the depths of my passionate nature, bring and give me its full and blessed return. Surely these wondrous capacities to love and be blessed, could come only from God."

"They do—oh, they do, Charley!" fervently murmured the loved and awed maiden. "Let us accept and be grateful for it, as from our Father;" and they walked forward in reverent silence.

"Do you really, and from the bottom of your very heart and soul, forgive me, Charley?" came the little quivering voice that had only learned to call him by that dear name within the hour.

"Forgive you? it was not a matter of forgiveness, but of love. Love would forgive love forever and forever, for it would know the blessed compensation which it would receive."

"I don't quite like to leave it there. I give you my whole heart now, and I must feel that I fill every part of yours. I must search out every sore place in it. Charles, a girl is strange in her nature, and with your warm, poetic imagination you might understand her was it worth your while. Cannot you imagine a wayward, proud, and willful girl, who is willing to be loved, and feels that she shall more than return it, and yet who tries in her capricious soul to withhold her heart, who is angry at herself when she finds she is going to surrender, and half angry with her lover for compelling her, and who delights in dashing away from him, and putting him in a sweet wretchedness, while she is more unhappy still, and who joys in her secret soul to think of the reward she will in her own way and time give him if he is faithful? But you would not come to me, and this is all stuff to you."

"You did not ask me to come, and it is precious stuff."

"Of course my foolish note meant nothing else in the world. How your face haunted me when it was turned up with such pain?"

"And your horse dashed the spilth over me."

"I saw it, and would have given the world to have undone that foolish thing. The truth is, Charley, I was a little alarmed the day before, to find how much you were in my heart, and I could not bear that you should press me then. It half floated in my mind that this summer, when we were at home here, if you were very, very good and very, very ardent, you know—what an absurd idea I had of a lover! and what a horrid day that was to me, and all the days, and you would not look at me, and then I sent you that note and knew you would come; and I feared to have you, for I feared myself. Then came your answer, and I knew it was all over; you had only loved me a little, for I could not for a moment believe that you would think that I could purposely do such a thing. I fancied that a wise, superior man would know me and learn why I misbehaved as I did. See how I trust you now with all my wild-girl folly."

"O Ellen, how sweet and precious this all is! How should I know you? A man never fully understands a woman, and that is one of the charms of love, to perpetually read without ever fully understanding. We judge woman as we do man, I suppose, and that which we do not comprehend, which is pretty much the whole of you, in our man's way we call caprice or perversity. I thought you had grown weary of me, found that you did not love me, and was ready to shake me off, and not unwilling perhaps to humiliate me."

"Charles Mason, do I deserve this? I thought I was sufficiently punished," with a real anguish.

"And then, after your return home, came the *Republican* paragraph," he went on.

"Surely you did not attribute that to me? You could not."

"No, I did not, and yet—I am trying your young love sorely, Ellen—and yet, I could not help fearing that this was your translation of your own conduct—an intended rejection."

"Is there more to say to me, Charles? You certainly saw the contradiction of that miserable paragraph, and might suspect that it would be as likely to come from me as the other," in a low, hurt voice.

"I never saw that. I never heard of it till this afternoon, from that blessed Minnie," with fervor.

"She is a blessed Minnie, and our blessed angel, Charley. Would we have ever met and understood each other had it not been for her?"

"If we were to, we should."

"If we were to, she was the appointed angel to do it," said the maiden, "and what a sweet surprise to us both, wasn't it?"

"And most to me, for I did not dream that you loved me."

"Really and truly? That hurts me a little, that you should have thought me incapable of loving."

"Not incapable of loving, but I was incapable of inspiring you with love."

"I am glad you are not over-vain, but I don't want you to think too meanly of yourself, Charley."

"When she spoke as she did, I felt an agony at the painful position in which she placed you, and, had the Goddess of Liberty turned her lips to me, I would not have been so amazed."

"I couldn't help that," in a low, little voice, "nor you either, if I remember right," piquantly.

"No; and I didn't try, and—" there was a little pause in deep shadow, and when they passed on, the happy girl had her lover's tears on her face. At length—"Minnie told me another thing, all about a little note accompanying certain greenbacks. Oh, it was the most precious deposit ever made! And Nellie, I thought of you—just one wild, absurd thought of you—when I touched the note. I didn't hesitate to use the funds, and received it as a good omen; and it came to me ere I had broken the tide that would overwhelm me. I wonder how you got so much?"

"I asked my father for fifteen hundred, and wore my old dresses and saved a thousand. He little suspected that I would use it to arm a knight against him, undutiful child that I am."

"And your father, Nellie?"

"You will go to him like a man, and he is a man, and at heart loves you, and scolded me sharply for my foolish act; and Charley, dear, is that really atoned for?" and another little pause in the lonely way brought her the answer. They finally found themselves in the populous part of the town, and had to proceed along the principal street ere the Berwick mansion could be reached. They were recognized by many, and, do what they might, the air of vast content and joy, which surrounded them like the atmosphere of newly-wedded love, in a sort betrayed them; men and women turned with a glad and pleasant surprise to these two, and a little aromatic, indefinite whisper, like a faint perfume of violets, that evening and the next morning, pervaded the town. As for the lovers, they now went very directly to Ellen's home, and learning that her father was in the library, she conducted the general directly thither, where she deserted him and fled. Mason advanced at once to Mr. Berwick, and held out his hand, which that gentleman as frankly took. "Mr. Berwick, my presence undoubtedly surprises you."

"I am surprised, general, but not unpleasantly—I do assure you."

"Thank you. But what I have to say I greatly fear will: Mr. Berwick, from the moment I met your daughter on my return from the war, I have loved her deeply and profoundly, as a man loves when his first wish is to devote himself to the happiness of a woman's life. I was led to suppose that my suit was not favored by her. We met this afternoon, and an explanation ensued, and I am most happy in her assurance of love. I make this known to you at the first moment, and venture to hope that at some time, when the bitterness of this contest passes, you will kindly regard our wishes."

"General Mason," said Mr. Berwick, deeply touched by the direct manliness of the young lover, "I have always respected and admired you—I liked you—I do now. I was aware of your attachment to Ellen, and I fear that she conducted herself in a way which must have repelled you, and I was sorry; and now, from my heart and soul, I am glad that it is made up, and I've no idea of permitting a moment's quarrel to stand in the way of the happiness of a lifetime. Where is the runaway?" ringing a bell, and ordering her to be called.

Ellen soon made her appearance, with the splendid color flushing cheek and brow like a summer sunrise.

When she left Mason's side, it was to take refuge with her dear, good aunt, by whom she knelt, clasping her arms about her, and, hiding her blushing face, she cried in a smothered voice:

"O aunt! I'm the happiest girl in the world!" and had not done murmuring her love-talk when the father's summons reached her.

"And so, traitress," said the smiling father to her, "you not only give material aid to the enemy, but you propose to go and adhere to him, giving him comfort also?"

"Yes, papa, please," looking down.

"Do you love the scapegrace—much?"

"Yes, papa, very much."

"How much?"

"As mamma loved you when she promised to be your bride."

"Oh, dear! It is a gone case, sir," and, taking her hand and placing it in that of her lover—"General Mason, she's to be yours in her own time; and, believe me, no man need hope for a nobler or a truer-hearted woman." At the last words the father's voice faltered and broke.

"My blessed, blessed father!" and the young girl threw her arms about his neck, while Mason pressed one of her hands to his lips, leaving his tears upon it. Then the true-hearted aunt came to mingle her joy and happy tears with them, and to congratulate the fortunate and happy lovers.

That these events had some influence upon the contest now drawing to a close is quite certain, and probably in favor of the young representative. It is true that Mr. Berwick, who had been absent from the actual struggle, but who had contributed liberally to the expenses of the party, and yet had somehow fallen under the charge of being lukewarm, now announced himself quite decidedly, and really imparted a new vigor to his side. But it is also true that it came to be known that what was supposed to be the old relation of Mason to Miss Berwick was restored, and after some romantic vicissitudes. As might be expected, she was an immense favorite, and universally conceded the fittest bride for Mason, who was rapidly recovering his old popularity, and a very general interest had been felt in their supposed mutual attachment, and no little anxiety at the known estrangement; concerning the cause of which, as nothing was known, many absurd rumors, more or less romantic, were afloat. Now it could be seen that, so far from there being differences between them, the young lady, so maidenly coy and reserved toward her lover, made no pretense of concealing her partiality for him, and of course none in expressing a wish for his success, among her immediate acquaintance. Her relations to him naturally enough imparted a new interest to him, and from being first favorite with such ladies as paid the slightest attention to the struggle, many who had not, from their sympathy with the lovers, came to feel a lively concern in his success, and this romantic element finally gave much zest to the last days of the canvass, and enlisted the active sympathy of whatever existed in the gallantry of man nature where the men were not themselves committed against the political fortunes of Mason. The fact that Ellen's father opposed her lover was not without its influence in his favor. Upon the personal bearing of Mason himself, this dawn of happiness had a marked effect. It was willingly remembered that he had never spoken unkindly of Mr. Berwick in his bitterest moods, and now there was a charm, almost a sweetness, in his manner of dealing even with the most offensive of his opponents, and which certainly lost him nothing.

Finally, to-morrow was the day; the last speeches were made, the latest slander contradicted, the last handbills sent off, and the hosts encamped over against each other only awaited the coming day, with challengers and poll-lists, committees and carriages.

The day itself was much like all American election-days under a great local excitement. A general election never can be a matter of indifference. The little, frail, almost imponderable slips of paper are often more potent than shot and shell. At the least, they appoint the *personnel* of all the officers of a great State. When questions of expediency are involved, they change or maintain a public policy. When a great principle pulsates in the ballot-box, they produce or defeat a revolution, and are always the safety-valve of the dangerous impulses of an excited people, the accumulated stores of which might otherwise be destructive to society.

On the whole, the election was generally very fairly conducted. The Democrats, to a man, voted for Mason, and so large a number of Republicans that the battle seemed a very equal one. The latter, however, or some of them, were guilty of an outrage, not only a palpable violation of law, but it arose to the turpitude of a blunder, and, as was afterward thought, was the cause of their defeat. Means were taken on both sides to ascertain, and, as far as was possible, to note the seeming success of the respective parties at the polls as the election progressed. In the most populous ward of the Falls—the third—and latish, a ticket, in imitation of the Mason ballot, with the Republican candidate's name on it in room of his, was set afloat, and found, of course, in the hands of his opponents, many of whom, understanding its character, voted it, while his partisans early detected it and avoided it; a good many Republicans, unaware that such a *ruse* was being played off, were alarmed at the apparent Mason vote, and, in their anxiety, started the rumor that this important ward, so confidently counted on for a large majority for the party candidate, had certainly given a decided majority against him. How many were implicated in what followed, or who first proposed and directed it, was never known. But just as the poll was closed, in the dusk of the early evening, some twenty roughs made an onset upon the officers of the election, seized the ballot-box and poll-books, destroyed the latter at once, and carried off the former. The excitement was intense in this orderly community, and, while there was no doubt in whose supposed interest the outrage was committed, it was certain that the great mass on both sides equally condemned it, and were alike zealous in bringing the offenders to justice. But for the present, at the least, that ward passed practically out of the contest. Nor was there any ready means by which effect could be given to the votes cast in it.

What American has not stood up all night at headquarters, hailing or cursing, shouting for or hissing, the returns? The Falls, and the county of which it was the shire town, had apparently given a small majority for Mason. So much was quite certain. At dawn returns from the nearest of the contiguous counties showed a small majority against him—enough, however, to elect his opponent. Toward noon returns from the others made it exceedingly doubtful, and the matter remained in the clouds until the official count settled the matter, that Mason was elected by a majority of seven. Innumerable pencils went up with the twenty-seven or twenty-eight thousand votes, and many times, with this unvarying result. And now it came to be pretty well understood that very many of the seeming Mason votes, the spurious, cast in the Third Ward of Berwick Falls, were really for Mason's opponent, and the stupidity of the blunder, intended to insure his election, was perfectly apparent. On the returns, as made to the Secretary of State, the Executive issued to Charles Mason a certificate of election to fill the vacancy occasioned by his resignation, and also for the Fortieth Congress. As for the victors, who does not know that they held a grand celebration with tar-barrels and torchlight processions, while the mourners went about the streets!

The autumn deepened, the frosts came, the leaves fell, the birds departed, and then the first snow, followed by the Northern Indian summer—and I may linger from the capital, only for a moment, for the departure of Minnie, bearing on the wings of her released spirit her precious message to the angels. Ellen and Charles were with her at the final moment, and, with her mother, were chief mourners at her simple and touching obsequies. Her serene and hopeful spirit, with its boundless love and trust, softened and elevated even their high natures, pervading them with that sweet religious sacredness that was the perpetual charm of the love that bound them to each other.

They finally left the bereaved mother, with one or two friends, in her lonely cottage. After the funeral, and amid the starry darkness of another night, went these two, with the sad sweetness of their chastened love, over the same ways on which they journeyed that memorable night of their revelation and reconciliation.

CHAPTER XLII.

SUMMER AT THE CAPITAL.

WHEN Dick, Harry, and Bob, go off for a summer lark, they say everybody is out of town. When Mrs. Shoddy, Mrs. Snobby, and Mrs. Noddy, with the rest of the Shods, and Snobs, and Nods, pack and start their baggage-train for Saratoga and the sea-shore, they do actually leave nobody in the city; and summer roasts and bakes and festers and stews in silence and solitude. When Congress adjourns and goes, with all the visitors, rings, and lobbies; when the foreign fancy of both sexes hurry off to high carnal and carnival at the Northern meets and hunting-grounds; when the great Secretaries and—as the President now does—all hurry off, and the heads of bureaus and clerks, with their thirty days' leave, go off pell-mell—Washington is dull. Then, with the heat steady at 85° to 98°, and not falling below 80° at the coolest; when the Avenue is a broad desert under the glare of a perpendicular sun, and the Goddess of Liberty contracts her eyes on the Capitol-dome, and the iron dome itself sways as it expands and contracts, and the shapeless Washington Monument glimmers and burns like the chimney of a blast-furnace at white-heat; when the sidewalks are silent, and the hotels are solitudes, and cards with "Rooms to let" and "Table-board" disappear from all houses, the capital falls back upon itself. Its wealthy go, as the wealthy go from other cities—the high-toned Southron to the White Sulphur or Rawley Springs, where the sulky rebels still talk over, and walk and wonder over, the incidents of the war, the males chewing tobacco and finding solace and inspiration in Southern whiskey; and the feminine, in faded finery, and in fancy still lift the scornful skirt in the imaginary presence of a Northern officer. Many go to beautiful Berkley, Piny Point, or find delicious retreats in the sweet homes, under the beautiful old trees, of the Friends of Montgomery, or in the many pleasant resorts and cool, quiet nooks of the Virginia side of the Potomac. The Vanes and Loziers were at Berkley—save the two at the North—and Cousin Margie, as the graceless Grayson said, went to Rawley to nurse and hoard up venom for the next winter, with the rattlesnakes and copperheads of that salubrious region. Mrs. Thompson remained at her boarding-house, wondering what had become of Mr. Smith. Drybow, with his hungry, dissatisfied eyes, was a fixture in the capital. Colonel Gordon, in ample coats and pants, with a profusion of fresh linen, mopped and juliped himself in the city. The Bardlaws took a month at Bedford Springs. The Chief-Justice of the district was at his Cleveland Home, and yet the great mass of the people, as of all cities, remained at home—had to. The President lingered at the White House, with drives out to the old Soldiers' Home, and a trip to Fort Monroe, and the routine and tape of the departments went and wore on, tired or untired, as usual. In the warm evenings innumerable carriages made processions all through the beautiful drives about the city, nightly excursions down the river to Glymont, Marshall Hall, and lonely Mount Vernon; while the mass—the working, sweating, festering mass—without cessation toiled and wore and worried on unrelieved, and with no surcease. The huge marble Capitol was as silent and almost as desolate as Tadmor, but all along the declivity of Fourteenth Street, between F and the Avenue, a faint life beat languidly on, among the young and pensive band of journalists sentenced to remain and watch the President, and drone and droop about the departments, and listen to the feeble pulsations of the political heart that almost ceased to beat. Day burned into day still hotter, and languid night was succeeded by night more enervating still, with a dim cloud of dust drooping over the sun-doomed city, where the turbid Tiber, too feeble to grapple with the garbage that gorged its hot, reeking bed, filtered its festering filth into the rotting canal that, like an open, gangrened wound, gaped wide and ghastly through the southern half of the wretched city—in whose putrid depths were hatched the obscene brood of malarious diseases that smite alike the infant and bosom where it feeds. Those were the pre-Board-of-Health times, ere the world cursed Governor Shepherd for rendering the capital of the republic a habitable city.

Fiery July poured its hissing length into more fiery August, and the summer emptied its accumulated evils into hot and malarious September, the worst of all. October, with its cooler nights, autumn skies and foliage, with its chills and fevers, still brought grateful relief. Sojourners away for the summer came back to their dust and mould lacquered homes. Along the Avenue, and leading streets, carpenters and painters were repairing and ornamenting shop-fronts and interiors, and half the houses in the city were ornamented with their advertising cards of rooms and river herring.

The Vanes and Loziers were back, and the young ladies returned from the Northern campaign. Teed and Tazewell were in full tide. Ward's rooms were unopened. The Bardlaws, with their office thronged, were busy in the autumn courts.

Frank was at the capital in October, and had a neat but cheaper back-room on F between Eleventh and Twelfth Streets, and walked listlessly about in the beautiful autumn evenings seeing Beau Hickman by the Metropolitan, and the mysterious Duval, that silent and eccentric athlete, posed movelessly against a pillar or door-post, by the old Frank Taylor book-store, standing at early night, with his splendid and carelessly-draped figure, with one shoulder lightly against a wall, and his rapt gaze on vacancy. Deep midnight often found his moveless form and changeless gaze, like a rare sculptured statue, in the same place.

In mid-November the senators and representatives, who had residences in the city, began to return, and later, others who were merely to reoccupy old or look up new quarters. The busy tide refiled along the Avenue, and surged into and about the hotels. On the first Monday of December the two flags were rolled out over the two Houses, two chaplains made proclamations to Heaven, two gavels descended on two desks, and the two Houses entered upon the old life and strife; and life and strife at the capital fretted on at old tide.

Mason reached Washington only the night before the House opened—remaining near Ellen as long as he could, who with her father was to follow him early in January. On the opening of the House he was resworn and resumed his old seat, in spite of the vehement opposition of Brasson, whose constituents had not elected him to the Fortieth Congress. They excused him, and Mason said that he ought to be all the more grateful for it, as he did not ask to be excused. Stanfield, Mason's competitor, had finally given him notice of contest, and much of the intervening time had been spent in taking the evidence of the actual vote polled in the now famous Third Ward, by calling some hundreds of the voters themselves. In this labor the Republicans had the disadvantage, not only of having destroyed the poll-books and ballots, but were under the added difficulty of stemming the now popular current; and, in more than one instance, men who were supposed to have voted for Stanfield declared on oath that they voted for Mason, and they were driven to that unallowable legicide of impeaching some of their own witnesses. The evidence, when complete, was unsatisfactory and contradictory, and nothing but party devotion, never a cardinal doctrine with the Republicans, could be relied upon to unseat the re-elected member. The memorial of Stanfield, with the evidence, was presented to the House, and referred to the committee, where the zeal of Brasson, a member of it, as may be remembered, and the urgency of Mason, promised an early disposition of the case, which, by arrangement between the parties, was to decide it both for the Thirty-ninth and Fortieth Congresses.

CHAPTER XLIII.

SOME BEGINNINGS OF THE END.

The proud and sensitive Warbel, though he received the curt order, under Alice's own hand, to withdraw from her affairs—
> "Take your beak from out my heart;
> And take your form from off my door"—

declined to do so; and the Bardlaws, for some inscrutable reason, continued to trust and permit him to act with them. Perhaps he was endeavoring to make amends for his past misconduct, and in some way redeem himself, and they were willing to give him a chance, and especially as he was really now powerless to do further harm. Whatever the reason was, he had used such diligence that the evidence in the great case in the Court of Claims was taken and printed ere midsummer, and it was placed on the trial calendar for December. It was among the first trials at that term. The evidence was voluminous, and, as the senior Bardlaw tried it with care, there was no doubt of its merit, and the court rendered judgment for Miss Brand for three hundred and seventy-six thousand nine hundred dollars. The Assistant Attorney-General, perhaps for reasons that may shortly appear, appealed the case, on behalf of the United States, to the Supreme Court, which would delay it about three years.

Alice and her friends were much elated at this success, and bright visions of rebuilding Magnolia and gathering her scattered people about her again took full possession of her mind; and she was greatly depressed at the threatened delay incident to the unjust action of the attorney of the United States. Another source of anxiety, in the skillful hands of others, arose, to occasion her much distress. It seemed that Colonel Warbel was still connected with the case; and, although Mr. Bardlaw assured her that the whole matter was beyond his (Frank's) control, and that he had only acted for them at their instance, and much cheaper than they could do it, still Colonel Gordon, under the influences which inspired him, was wholly dissatisfied, and was brought to believe that Frank, under his specific and irrevocable power of attorney, could and intended to sell and transfer the judgment, or in some way realize upon it. It was under his influence that the poor girl was induced to execute a new power of attorney in blank, so far as the person appointed was concerned, with other important provisions, also in blank, which were to be filled up and used as exigencies might require, and which were lodged in Colonel Gordon's hands for safety, while all parties, for prudential reasons, were to keep it a secret.

As may be suspected, some of the persons and influences, already under the reader's eye, brought about this new complication. The breaking up of the pardon business, which was the result of the arrest of the Croly, and the collapse of the colored soldier bounty conspiracy, were blows which the "Heart of Midlothian" never recovered from. Ward, in alarm after the latter event, left the capital and never returned, and the main conduit of innumerable profits, great and small, the fountain of information and means, George Kramer, had resigned, and the united influence of the Pangborns and Josephs and Pymptons and Brassons failed to secure a competent and proper successor. The expenses of the association were immense, and the squandering profligacy of the admitted and unknown partners fabulous; and when the broken fragments reassembled at the capital, in the fall of 1866, their personal prospects and fortunes were desperate. On a full consultation it was determined to get direct control of the Brand judgment, which the reader will remember was always a prominent object with Ward, Teed & Co., nor in the present aspect of things did that appear so very difficult to the survivors of the summer collapse. In any event the attempt must be made, and, if not the whole, as much of the proceeds of the judgment as could be clutched, was to be secured, which would at least furnish the means of escape out of the country. Rymer had been already bled to depletion, and but a few thousands more could be wrung from him, even if his case terminated most successfully. Gordon was the medium of this final approach, and having induced the Assistant Attorney-General to appeal her case to the Supreme Court, she was now asked to name a sum which she would be willing to give if a dismissal of the appeal could be procured and the money paid, and she finally consented to pledge the sum of twenty thousand dollars; and, to give effect and power to accomplish the undertaking, she executed the power of attorney, mentioned above, with another paper, to be used if found necessary. Mrs. Vane, Margie, and Colonel Gordon, were of the council that came to this determination; and Mr. Smith, who put in a sudden appearance at about this time, and who had become known to Gordon and Miss Brand as a man of much real shrewdness, and who was consulted on the occasion, "wouldn't wonder, on the hull, if that wasn't best. 'Twas purty strong commission, but nobody could tell how much greasin' the darned thing would want ter make "er go," was his judicious comment.

Unexpected difficulty arose in the final arrangement with the Assistant Attorney-General, who, as may be suspected, was of a speculative turn, although his chief was of undoubted integrity, and not very well advised of some of the rules that governed the practice of his nominal subordinate, who had charge of the Court of Claims.

When the distinguished head of the T.'s signified to

that incorruptible officer that he was now ready to go forward, and required the formal dismissal of the appeal, the representative of the United States affected to understand that the only thing he was to do was to take an appeal; and many days, with fruitless interviews, elapsed before he could be made to remember the terms of the agreement, which, like many of those virtuous compacts, was one of winks and nods, and by the use of two or three terms of art which the necessities of this branch of the public service had invented, and were known only to the most advanced, and which a free translation would hardly render intelligible. At the close of a perfectly good-natured but seemingly ineffective interview between the high contracting parties, Teed went out of the office, which was in the Capitol, leaving a small package of white official envelopes, well known to the departments and the prosecutors of claims—apparently part of a full package, which he had laid on the table of the Assistant Attorney-General, and forgot to take when he left. Soon after they fell under the eye of the law-officer of the Government, who seemed to have some curiosity about them. They were apparently empty and never used. Curiously enough he removed one from the package, and, casting his eye furtively about his empty office, peeped into it and found, to his surprise, doubtless, that it actually contained a one-hundred-dollar Treasury note, and, singularly enough, each of the other white, virginal-looking things was quick with a similar burden, and there were five in all. The official, so far from running after the forgetful Teed and returning the package, withdrew the bills from each, placed them in his vest-pocket, and threw the envelopes among a quantity which they resembled, on his table. On the next morning, Teed called quite early, of course, to inquire for the lost package. It was very strange, when his quick, eager glance failed to see it on the table where he left it, that he should say nothing about it, nor did the Government attorney mention it. So far from it, he was now able to remember that the terms of the original stipulation were as Teed had claimed, and executed the required paper which was filed in the clerk's office of the Court of Claims, who made him the required transcript of the judgment, which, under the statute, still might not be paid until after ninety days from the day of its rendition. Upon this transcript, the Assistant Attorney-General also made a statement to the effect that the United States waived the ninety-days, which rendered it payable immediately, a practice which, in this case, induced the Controller to make a rule that in no instance thereafter should a judgment *vs.* the United States be paid till after the ninety days had expired.

I may observe that, soon after this incident, an Assistant Attorney-General resigned, and another officer was placed in charge of the Court of Claims.

Judgments of the Court of Claims are paid at the Treasury Department. They fix the liability of the Government and ascertain the amount, but they still have to pass the accounting officers of that department, and especially the First Controller, who was apt to look with suspicion upon every man who demanded money from the Treasury, and he construed statutes making appropriations as highly penal. Ordinarily, it took a judgment seven or eight days to work its way through to the result of a draft on the Treasurer; and Teed had no influence to shorten up the time in the Controller's bureau. He filed his transcript, and was obliged to wait. These seven or eight days will be ample to develop the now rapidly-ripening incidents of this little narrative.

CHAPTER XLIV.

MRS. CROLY'S LAST APPEARANCE.

IN the Criminal Court—Judge Fisher presiding—the district attorney came in and had the case *vs.* Baker set peremptorily for trial, which, with a flourish, the papers announced, and it made a little shiver through the capital, where it was in some way understood that the real contest was between the President and the Secretary of War. The President, with much frank directness of nature, was inveterate in his enmities, and at the bottom had lain and rankled the suspicion that the Secretary had inspired Baker's conduct in the wretched pardon-broker business. During the summer a marked estrangement had grown up between the parties, and the Secretary seldom met the President except when some matter concerning his immediate department was involved, or when, at the solicitation of the Secretary of State, he attended a cabinet meeting; while, on the President's part, he no longer sought the counsel of the great Secretary of War. When Congress reassembled, the gulf that divided the President from the governing majority of the House, and which necessarily governed the nation, as that majority usually does and must, was wide and palpable. And, of the whole cabinet, the Secretary of War was the sole minister who stood directly with that majority. This necessarily pointed and intensified the feeling of the President toward the favorite of the House. Personally the Secretary was not popular with the resident population of Washington, and mortal man never gave less heed to the words, the likes, and dislikes of others, though few had in their natures so deep and pure a well of tenderness, and few really more prized the genuine love and real confidence of men. On the contrary, the President was very popular, and, on the day set, his friends mustered at the court-room in force, to witness the legal contest of their favorite *vs.* the Secretary of War.

General Carrington, though present, left the management of the case in the hands of the distinguished gentlemen associated with him, while Baker, who was put on trial for a malicious arrest, was defended by F. P. Stanton, who made so fine a record in the Kansas imbroglio, and was aided by others of the local bar. The case for the United States was opened by Judge Hughes, a prominent politician and lawyer from Indiana, in a sharp, telling speech, one passage of which was greeted by the vast crowd in attendance with the outrage of loud applause. The court, in an impressive manner, stopped the advocate, and directed the marshal to distribute his bailiffs through the room, and arrest the first man who gave any sign of approval or disapprobation of any part of the proceedings; with orders, if any such manifestation showed itself again, to clear the room at once, saying that the prisoner would be tried by the court and jury, and not by the outside mob; and then, in the most courteous manner, directed the counsel to proceed in his own way. No further popular manifestation was made, although the patience and forbearance of the President's friends were sorely tried by the counsel for the defense.

Mrs. Croly, with her great beauty and rumored relations with the President, the victim of the machinations of the infamous Baker, backed by the austere Secretary of War, was really with men quite a heroine, and the rumor of hæmorrhages of the lungs suffered by her, attributed to the harshness of the monster Baker, made her an object of great interest. When placed upon the stand she removed her veil, and, with the utmost composure and absolute *aplomb*, gave to the sympathizing admiration of the crowd a face whose rare beauty had gained by the languid softness of real ill-health. Estimating at their full value her personal advantages, she had not—what woman ever had?—the least objection of adding them to the other conditions, so decidedly bearing against the dark, swarthy, taciturn defendant. An offshoot of one of the oldest and most aristocratic families of colonial New York, with misfortune rather than willful sinning, and dazzled with the hope of winning a fortune, and the position through that which she had lost, but powerfully attracted, as we have seen, by the handsome young man whom she was to betray, lifted by the high manliness that, to her, seemed to surround him as with an atmosphere; vain, luxurious, with eyes that had looked unwinkingly on other paths than the one, and with feet that may have touched some of them, under the awful pressure of the social and moral—shall we call them Christian?—forces which surround only to entrap, and that sustain only to crush and kill such as they have already betrayed, she found in this youth, whom the pure had cast out, a protest against her life and folly, and a powerful magnet attracting her to a purer if a colder atmosphere. How almost bright and roseate the rugged way of purity, to a solitary woman, betrayed by early unkindness and actual want, in the thoughtlessness of girlhood, through her beauty, under his guidance and on his arm, now seemed to her, and how strong and invigorating his presence was! And the very grudgingness with which he doled out little pittances of sympathy, only made the high, craving hunger the greater. How she loathed the tasks she had undertaken, and how she came to abhor the persons and presence of those she was to influence! Even the kind President became an object of absolute dislike. She reconciled to her awakening conscience her pursuit of Frank, through her resolve that when he was her own—when his love beyond question was hers—she would escape with him to a better world and a better life. Though she was not free from the healthful tradition of her sex, that a man thus won was hopelessly lost, still she felt that here was a nobly exceptional nature, with which formal and outward compacts gave no sanctity to the sacraments of the soul and heart. He went off, and, to her, as others, his absence was unaccounted for, and though he went with scarcely an implied promise to her, had she not rendered him all he sought? And he would come at some time. He did come —but hardly to her. He was cold and changed, and accused her of coqueting with the President, and made that a cause for absenting himself from her, when she determined that the case should be tried for the purpose of clearing herself from all imputation; and she came forward now, gladly, to vindicate herself in the eyes of the only man whom she loved. Was there ever a woman who, under circumstances which admitted of her being influenced by surroundings personal to herself, was indifferent to the admiration of men, and who was not made somewhat her best self, at the least mentally, by it—if that self was worth the being? And as she now cast her eyes carelessly over the throng, a thousand eyes shot admiration, made tender by sympathy, back into hers, and, with one quivering, long-drawn sigh of relief, she turned her head toward the questioning counsel.

I deal with this somewhat celebrated trial only as it concerns my narrative. Mrs. Croly testified to the facts already known, exhibiting much spirit toward the defendant, and was turned over to the torture of Governor Stanton's cross-examination. Poor Croly! She had never been informed of the scope and power for torture of a cross-examination. She was asked about her name, about her marriage and relations with her nominal husband; and then about her former life and history, over which many fierce battles were waged by counsel, and the court steadily held with the rules in the books, and the inquisitor, like a stanch murderer, firm in a fell purpose, went on. Through all this the earnest, kindly faces of the crowd triumphantly bore the witness, and her eye flashed with its old power along the electric chords of kindling male sympathy. Then came her relations with the President, and fiercer struggles of counsel, and the steady ruling of the court, and the head of the unhappy woman went a little down, as one thing after another was stated, in themselves nothing, and yet so many and capable of such sinister construction, that men, from steadily regarding her, turned and looked at each other. As these were gleaned up and grouped in long and embarrassing questions, their weight and force were felt by the poor, tortured thing, while the reckless exercise of the pardoning power by the President, under her approaches, was most damaging to him. She gave a clear account of the transactions of the night of her visit to Baker, and swore that she was arrested. She was then asked about the ring—about the place known in these pages as the "Heart of Midlothian," and of various men and things connected with it. Her examination by Baker had admirably prepared her for this, and her old force and courage came back to her with her old triumph.

"Did she know Le Grand?"

"Who is Le Grand?" she asked, by way of answer.

"That is what I want to find out," was the response.

"I sympathize with you, Mr. Stanton, most sincerely."

"Have you ever seen him, Mrs. Croly?"

"I never saw a man and heard him called Le Grand; the name to me is a myth—a mere sound, like so many questions put to me here."

"Did she know Colonel Warbel?"

"Very well, indeed."

"Had she had a—a some sort of a business transaction with him?"

"Yes, a—a some sort of a business transaction!" mimicking the dry voice and tone of the counsel with fine effect.

"A business transaction—what sort of business?" with a meaning.

"If the court please," in a pleading voice, "is the name of Colonel Warbel to be brought in here? I wish to say of him," with a softened voice, and a quiver on her lips, "that, were women always treated by men as Colonel Warbel has treated me, there would be fewer broken hearts and wretched lives in this miserable world." There was a real pathos in the voice, that touched many of all parties; and she was permitted to go.

Other witnesses were called, and when the Government rested, the defendant called Johns, who directly contradicted Croly as to the matter of arrest and imprisonment, and then the contest of the advocates came off, the counsel for the Government assaulting the Secretary of War, and those for the defendant, under the guise of eulogy, dealing the President many stinging thrusts and ringing blows. The jury, as was expected, returned a verdict of guilty, and the court, with dignified gravity, sentenced the convicted detective to pay a fine of one dollar; and Baker took his revenge on the President by publishing a report of the trial in his history of the secret service, written by Headley, and so the farce ended.[1] The trial was unfortunate for the President, as it exhibited him in the undignified *rôle* of the champion of a woman with a history and reputation, with whom he at the least seemed to be compromised, and who had evidently made a commerce of his weaknesses. The unhappy Croly, wearied and exhausted, was permitted to depart from the court-room, unattended, for her now mean rooms, crushed with the conviction that she had destroyed the last hope

[1] "History of the Secret Service," L. C. Baker, Philadelphia, 1867.

of the return of her lover. He had not been near the trial, and in her dreams of that night she saw him borne away on a radiant cloud, with his reproachful face turned with a saddened tenderness toward her. While she yet looked, a solemn bar of black night fell between them, growing thicker and darker about her, and forever hiding the tender face and the cloud from her eyes.

CHAPTER XLV.

OLD NANCY'S NOTION OF AN ANGEL.

THE outward manifestations of the excellent Mr. Rymer's devotion were somewhat intermittent, and his celestial communings, and heart renderings, and rendings, were never so abundant as when in a period of great or threatened pecuniary disaster; a panic melted his heart, and bankruptcy would change his head to a fountain of tears as certainly as a hay-fever. Since the betrayal of Frank Warbel by Mrs. Croly, and the removal of Alice's principal witness through the crowning mercy of Providence, the good Rymer had become not a little unmindful of the attributed source of these blessings, or restricted his out-gushings to the sanctity of his closet, to the loss of that edification to others which he had so unctuously shed about him in the preceding hours of distress. And the pious Teed had sad misgivings as to the Lord's exchequer, dependent upon any celestial assessment that may have been made upon Rymer in the mean time. Like other forgetful ingrates, he received a rude admonition finally. This came in the form of a notice that the case "John Doe, *ex dem.* Brand *vs.* Richard Roe with notice to Rymer," was absolutely set for trial on the following day. It must be admitted that the T.'s were also thrown a little aback by the note they received. The case had been pending for a year, and at no time had the Bardlaws seriously spoken of attempting to try it. It is true that, at the call of the October term calendar, it had been set for trial, by Teed himself, in a careless way, and when reached it was nominally passed to the heel, as the lawyers call the end of the calendar, and of course would not be reached; but it was, and at evening young Bardlaw sent them a note that the case must be finally disposed of the next morning, as the term would close on the Saturday following. When called upon, he said that they expected to have a jury pass upon what of merits they might be able to show. What did it mean? True, a notice had been served on them to produce the original will. And yet it was as certain that, although this difficulty might in some way be met, and the signatures to the will proved, it was not possible that the plaintiff's devisor could be shown to be the party named in the will. Perhaps Bardlaw had found the family records, and perhaps he was only to try the case nominally—suffer a verdict to go against him, and so end the matter. But this was not like him. There was mischief in it. Tazewell was in consternation, and Teed even was in trepidation. There was no excuse for a continuance, nor could even Teed invent one which, in the cant of the bar, would " hold water." Rymer came with almost a paralytic stroke of piety, wringing his hands and rolling up his eyes in a frenzy of silent adoration, and so the night shut down upon them.

The junior Bardlaw called in person on Alice, whom he found at Mrs. Vane's, with a request that she would be at their office at half-past nine the next morning. His arrival interrupted an animated discussion of the Baker trial, which closed the day before, the details of which filled the papers of that day, and were the one topic in all circles at the capital. That which excited the liveliest interest at the Vanes was the pointed declarations of the Croly in reference to Frank, and reëxcited all the painful interest that had ever gathered about his hapless name.

Margie was as unrelenting as ever in her denunciation, although violently sympathizing with Croly against the monster—her one name for the detective—and whom she believed when she swore strongest to implicate him, and whom she disbelieved when her testimony bore upon the President, or exonerated Frank. The considerate Mrs. Vane went so far as to hope that it might be true, and also that something would occur to clear up the mystery, if it was. Grayson accepted it as conclusive. "What did I tell you? I always knew how it would be. I always told you Frank was all right."

"You are always a fool," was the rejoinder of Margie. "And you are a Sark—a cut—" the door-bell fortunately interrupted this interdicted formula, and ere the conversation was renewed Mr. Bardlaw was announced, and smilingly remarked: "You are discussing the trial. I came to notify you of one much more important—Brand vs. Rymer;" and when he got them to comprehend that the case was actually to come up the next morning he explained the necessity for Miss Brand's personal attendance, and hoped that as many of her friends as could make it convenient would accompany her; that so much had been said about the case, that both his father and himself wished that they would be present. "Call at our office on your way, at half-past nine," and he went away leaving them still much surprised. All was anxiety, doubt, and uncertainty, with everybody except Margie, who knew just how it would come out— "You'll lose the case, Alice"—and Grayson, who knew that she would win it—" and Colonel Warbel will do it "— with an absolute confidence beautiful to behold.

The anxiety of Alice and her friends, Mrs. Vane and Lucy, attended by Grayson, brought them to the office of the Bartlaws on time, where they found Drybow and Colonel Gordon in a very earnest argument, which was suddenly dropped. The elder lawyer received the party with his usual cordiality, and they were immediately shown to a large parlor over the office. The first object that met the eyes of Alice on entering the room was the form of Frank Warbel, posed against a window-casing, with his face to the street. He turned, and their eyes met for an instant, and Alice received from him a pained impression of stony resignation; and as she paused, surprised, a loud "Lord bress the chile; O bress the Lord! Bress the bressed good Lord!" and the arms that had carried, pressed her close to the faithful bosom that nursed her; and tears and sobs and murmured blessings of the Lord poured over her.

"O mammy, mammy!" exclaimed the astonished girl, delighted beyond the power of more than exclamation as she returned the embrace of her recovered nurse, "my own blessed, blessed mammy!" and for a moment the pain-burdened heart, that had not for years poured itself fully out to mortal, went with a great throb to this faithful breast and stood for an instant still. After a moment's hush she turned to see who with sobs was pressing his lips to one of her hands which he held. "O Peter! and you too?" she cried to an elderly, white-haired black man, who it was, "and so we all meet—meet again," throwing her arm about his neck, and kissing his withered cheek.

"Yis. Amen, bress de Lord!" was the fervid answer.

"O mammy," said the still wondering girl, "how is this, how came all this? How did you get here?"

"Tro' de howlin' fire an' de burnin' wilderness," was the figurative answer, "he brought us."

"He—who?" eagerly, with a glance toward Frank.

"Dis yer bressed Gen'ral Warbel."

"He's a cunnel, Miss Alice," said the more correct Peter, "Cunnel Frank Warbel, he bring us yer, tro' de divine bressin' ob de Probidence ob de Lord Almighty; yer see, Miss Alice, we's—"

"Get along, Peter! let me tell.—Yer see, 'oney, that a man come an' said yer sen' fer us, so he tote us up de riber, an' then he tote us back, an' say you'll be in Memphis. Thar we staid an' staid, till I 'clar, I tho't yer an' the Lord must 'a forgot us, an' then we's tuck up to—to—"

"St. Looy," put in Peter.

"Be still, Peter, can't yer?—to St. Looy. Thar we's tuck to a little out o' one side alley an' put in a shanty wid low, mislable cullud pussens, an' low down white trash, an' thar we staid an' we begun (I 'n Peter) to 'spicion somethin's wrong. Well, an' thar I's tuck with the small-pox as de debble would have—".

"The Lord," put in the pious Peter, in a solemn and convicting voice.

"I said de debble! De Lord ain't gwine roun' an' do sich tings. Well, eberybody squandered 'cept me 'n anuder sick woman. Lord, how they did squander off, an' Peter hardly stayin', I neber seed no more ob de man! I's powerful sick an' full ob misry, 'n grew wus an' wus night'n day, till I don't know nothin', an' don't remember no mor'n —hush, Peter! don't put me out. An' wen I come to, t'odder woman lay dead, an' thar was that precious angel of the Lord—"

"A angel o' massy," put in the correcting Peter; "the bressed Lord's angels don't have mustaches."

"I says tha does!—don't they, chile?" to Alice.

"Yes," said Alice, warmly, not daring to look at the specimen referred to, and perhaps not well up in the natural history of the species.

" Well, Gen'al Frank—he is a gen'al—Gen'al Frank bro't a docto an' men who toted off the dead woman, an' bro't tings an' staid wid me an' nussed me mor'n a week afo' a mortal dust 'a come back, when ole Pete yer come roun' again—"

"I's dar all de time," put in Peter.

"I know you were, Peter," said the kindly Alice, quietly.

"Wal, mebbe," said the nurse, "I 'low dat fer the week wen I know'd nothin', I didn't see yer any way. Wen I got well 'nuff to be toted, Misto Warbel tuck us to a nice place out ob de city, an' thar I got well, an' he never left us a day till 'e bro't us yere. I know'd 'e come from yer, for 'e know'd all about yer, and wanted us to talk all about yer. Lord, I know'd 'ow it was," with a knowing look, "tho', Lord bress 'im, he's bery much cast down an' sad like; thinks I, ' My young missus knows wat's wat, an' it'll be all right.' "

This last she would say in spite of interruptions and warnings. Alice learned that Nancy and Peter had arrived in Washington early in August, and had been kept at Mr. Bardlaw's country-seat in Maryland. During this narrative the group were seated, and remote from the window where Frank stood. How the overjoyed and sorely-burdened heart of the young maiden went out in a mute throb of anguish to that cold, stony form by the window! this youth charged with having betrayed her, and with this woman; and when he fled in infamy it was to go down into darkness and pestilence to unclasp the arms of festering death from the form of this her old mammy, and bring her back to her; and she arose under the impulse of true woman nature to go to him, but he had left the room. Lucy, who had kept her eyes on him as well as her excitement would permit, afterward told her that, when Nancy sprang to her, he seemed much agitated, and that soon after he hurried from the room with his face wet with tears. The truth was, he stood at the window watching for the Vane carriage, which approached from the other way unobserved, and he was thus surprised in the room, intending of course to avoid meeting Alice. Just as she arose from her seat under her impulse, Mr. Bardlaw, Sen., came to the door and announced that the court was waiting, and immediately conducted the ladies to the Circuit Court room. What did Alice now care for a square of the city of Washington?

CHAPTER XLVI.

THE TRIAL.

THE Chief-Justice of the District Supreme Court was on the bench—with a tall, full, and personable figure, in the English sense; a large, finely-formed head, with its masses of raven-black hair; full, liquid black eyes; a pock-marked, striking face, which with his remarkable power as a public speaker, on a great field-day in a Western political campaign, where with his wonderful voice he had put forth his full strength, had won for him the title of the Mirabeau of the West.

When the Republicans reorganized the judiciary of the District of Columbia, to get rid of the incumbents on the bench, he was appointed Chief-Justice of the new Supreme Court, where his strong native vigor and real ability, his love of fair dealing and justice, united with his force of character rather than much law learning, soon gave him not only a commanding position in his court, but marked prominence among the leading men at the capital, where he was well remembered as a distinguished member of the House. One noticeable thing there was in the Chief-Justice's delivery of speech, which sometimes gave a racy piquancy to the original forms and modes in which he often gave expression even to his judicial opinions—a sudden hesitancy, hitch, or pause, in his utterance—and which, when it appeared, always came in the middle of a word, which, under the force of any extended delivery, generally disappeared wholly.

It was known that the "Alice Brand" case would come up this morning, and an unusual number were in attendance, of a somewhat different class from the visitors of the courts. There was much curiosity not only to hear the case, but to see the plaintiff; and, as her senior counsel conducted her to a seat with her friends within the bar, a marked sensation ran through the room. She put aside her veil and met the very kindly but expressive eyes of the Chief-Justice, and just inclined her head as if in recognition of the presence of the law of the land, in his person. The action was noticed, and for some reason gave great pleasure to the observers. The Chief-Justice politely acknowledged it, and in a less marked manner recognized the presence of the other ladies. On the left of the bench sat the jury, twelve intelligent-looking men, and Alice's glance ran along them until they fell on the form of Frank standing back of them in the recess of a window, with a cold, abstracted air, as if unconscious of what was occurring about him.

The case was called, when Teed, who appeared with less than his usual confidence, asked that it be continued. He was taken by surprise, as he said; the case had been so conducted by the plaintiff as to lead him to expect that it would never be tried, and now at the last moment it was suddenly sprung upon him for trial. Bardlaw arose to answer, but the court intimated that it was unnecessary; and in a very felicitous way disposed of the motion, and said that "counsel should have the full benefit of his sur-cr-prise on a motion for a new trial if it became necessary." The jury were sworn, and the elder Bardlaw stated the plaintiff's case, in substance, that square No. 367 was conveyed by the original commissioners to John Withers, who, by will, bequeathed it to Rachel Withers; that the title thus far was, by written stipulation of counsel, admitted. It was claimed by the plaintiff that by will, duly executed, Rachel Withers devised this land to the eldest daughter of Edward Brand, and his wife Helen Craik Brand. The plaintiff would undertake, by competent evidence, to prove the execution of this will, and would satisfy the court and jury that the young lady then present, the plaintiff, Alice Brand, was the daughter of Edward and Helen Craik Brand.

Teed told the court that he would reserve his opening until the plaintiff rested. Mr. Bardlaw then asked Teed if he had brought into court the original will, saying to the court that, as the defendant, who was one of the executors named in the will, had advertised in the streets that he had the will, he had served notice to produce it, etc. Teed, who had appeared as if quite undecided, hesitated a moment, and then produced the paper, saying that if he had ever seen the original will, it was the paper he now produced, and, when asked if he produced it under the notice, he said he did; it was all he could do. Bardlaw took it, opened and examined it with care, amid breathless expectation on the part of the audience, nearly all of whom had heard the story of the will, and the scandal which connected Frank Warbel's name with it, and hundreds of eyes were directed to the seemingly unconscious young man, and his name ran about through the crowd and reached the ears of Alice. Mr. Bardlaw, when he finished his examination, remarked that the paper produced was not the will. "It is, however, a very clever forgery of it, and would be quite complete if it had three subscribing witnesses."

Mr. Teed demanded to know "if the counsel pronounced that paper a forgery?"

"I certainly do," was the response, "and Mr. Teed will admit it in a moment. The will, your honor, purports to have been executed in 1846, and the last page is written on paper manufactured in 1863, as appears by the water-mark date in the body of the paper itself, as any man can see." Teed took the paper, and held the last page to the light, and turned ghastly, under his stubbly beard; for there, in characters half an inch long, was the maker's name and the fatal 1863, in the body of the paper. The Chief-Justice examined it and said there was no doubt of it, and that "that sheet was undoubtedly sp-u-rious." An immense sensation, which a moment later was increased, as Bardlaw went on to say that "the will was probated in Connecticut, with two attesting witnesses, and recorded in the register of wills office of the district with but two, and doubtless for the purpose, through that seeming defect, of defrauding the first devisee, if she ever claimed, and the legatees, if she did not, of the proceeds of the land on a sale; that Rymer declined the trust as executor, and pretended to buy the property in dispute; that for some reason the executor, Williams, subsequently delivered the original will to Captain Brand, at his house at Magnolia, near Vicksburg, and went down to New Orleans, and died as was supposed immediately afterward. During Captain Brand's lifetime, he and the plaintiff were, as is known, very wealthy, and made no claim under the will, but the war swept their very subsistence away, and the original will came to my hands from the plaintiff. Miss Brand's business agent was pursued by the emissaries of the defendant, and by some means induced to deliver to them, perhaps, this paper; I knew nothing about it then, and very little of it now. They got a paper from him, which I presume they thought was the original will; what they expected to do with it I don't know, and he may have obtained important facts in return. I would not make this statement, had not this paper been produced under my notice; and I would not have given the notice unless to test the truth, and fathom, if possible, the real intentions of my learned opponent."

At this moment Frank came forward and examined the paper with some care, and whispered something to Bardlaw, and returned to his former position, when the latter said to the court: "I am just assured, by one who knows, that this last sheet of the paper now produced has been placed in the document since the defendants received it; that on this same sheet, when delivered to their agent, there were three subscribing witnesses. As I said, I know nothing of any part of this matter."

The effect of these last statements was very great. The Chief-Justice remarked: "Mr. Teed, are you not now surper-er-ised again? The co-ourt is, very much."

But Alice! "Why, Frank had never given up the will!" "How could she ever think he had? and how cold and distant he stands! and she did not wonder at it."

Mr. Bardlaw said that having, as he thought, exposed some part of the tactics of the other side, he would proceed; and calling Senator Foster, of Connecticut, who was sworn, he placed a paper in his hands, and asked him in whose handwriting it was, who answered that it was in the hand of a former clerk of his, and written in his office; and, to further questions, that it was the will of Rachel Withers; that the third subscribing witness was himself, and he swore to the signatures of the others; that he transacted the business in due course of his profession, and that his attention had never been called to the matter since, until about a year ago; that the Witherses were old friends of his, and came quite a distance to have him do this, which was perhaps the reason he never heard of any trouble about the property; and as his name did not appear on any recorded copy of the will, very few would suspect that he knew any thing of it. Bardlaw then gave the will in evidence, and produced a certificate, properly attested, from the American legation at St. Petersburg, of the marriage of Edward Brand and Helen Craik, in May, 1844; and called Nancy and Peter Craik, who, to Teed's absolute horror, came forward and were sworn. Nancy swore that she was raised in the Craik family, and was the maid of Miss Helen, and that she and her husband Peter went abroad with them in 1843; was present at Miss Helen's wedding, etc.; that the plaintiff, Miss Alice—"the good Lord bress 'er!"—was born the 3d day of June, 1845, at Florence, and that her mother died within a day or two; that her own child was then but a few weeks old, and that she nursed Alice, etc.; had always lived with her; and then went on, although it was objected to by Teed, to state the facts of her being taken to meet her mistress, already brought to the reader's notice; and she dwelt with much fervor upon the conduct and kindness of "General Frank," that "bressed angel ob de Lord, if dere eber was one!" Peter, on being called, sustained Nancy fully, except Frank's personal relations to the Lord, which he set right—when Mr. Bardlaw, explaining that the Brand family records had been lost, as before stated, rested his case.

As may be supposed, Teed had no possible way of meeting the case—had not the hardihood of attempting it. The discovery that he had been utterly sold by the pretended will; the revelation of his own fraudulent alteration of the paper he received; and, finally, seeing old Nancy walk into court—were a succession of calamities that even he could not stand under, and he submitted the case. Mr. Bardlaw left it, without further remarks, to the jury. The Chief-Justice observed to them that the plaintiff had fully proved her case, as she had declared, and directed them to return a verdict accordingly, which was done. He then told Teed that, if he had any motion to submit in the case, the court would hear it the next morning, and the court adjourned over.

The spurious will was compared with the original, by several, and proved to be an exact fac-simile. But, curiously enough, when inquired for, it had disappeared, nor was it ever afterward recovered. It was popularly believed that Mr. Teed ate it up in open court!

When the court adjourned, the judge came down and was introduced to his fair suitor and her lady friends, while the released and gratified crowd stood compact until her party moved, when it broke out to see her enter her carriage and drive away. Many came forward to congratulate her—all who knew her—but one. How eagerly her heart and eyes ran over the throng of persons for one form, which was not there! By her side, clingingly, was the tender Lucy, whose thoughts, with pungent self-reproach, were wholly with the solitary youth; more wronged, as it seemed to her, than one could be, and she came to feel that even Alice was hardly a sufficient reward for his fidelity and suffering. She more than forgave him for his *hauteur* at the sea-side, a few months before, and, had it not been treason against love, she would not blame him at that moment if he refused to Alice a further place in his heart, blameless as she was. There were still many things to be explained, but she knew that he could not be in fault in any of them.

His name reached the ears of the ladies as they went out. Some one said that he had been appointed in one of the cavalry regiments, and was going to the Plains.

Rymer, contrary to Teed's orders, was in court, and, at first, in a state of chronic mental ejaculation, which sometimes escaped in groans. He collapsed with the exposure of the spurious will, and became nearly insensible when the original was produced. The direct blow from heaven, in the form of old Nancy, rendered him unconscious, and he barely crawled shakingly away, for the time a practical atheist. What faith could endure the shattering effect of such blows? Surely, submissive meekness would fail to discover any good to be extracted from such providences, and might well doubt the providence itself.

As might be expected, the non-political circles of the capital were much excited by the disclosures of the trial; and, next to Alice, the central personage was Frank Warbel, if indeed he did not take the first place.

CHAPTER XLVII.

GRAYSON'S VIEWS.

On the evening after the trial, two or three interviews were had among the personages whose histories are recorded in these pages. General Mason and Frank met two or three times since their return to the capital, on pleasanter terms than when they parted in the spring. Frank congratulated Mason very cordially on his double success, of which he had learned, and with much of his old friendly warmth, which induced Mason to change the subject to Frank personally. This was unfortunate, for Frank at once grew cold and distant, and soon put an end to the interview, and afterward seemed not much inclined to encourage any return to the old confidence so dear to Mason. During this day he heard that Frank had received an appointment in a cavalry regiment, and determined to attempt to dissuade him from accepting it; and at dinner he heard much of him mixed up with the trial that had closed, and went off to his room, where he met Colonel Gordon, who had just called to see Frank, who was out, and, as a servant said, for the evening. Gordon seemed much excited over the revelations of the trial, which had utterly dispelled the clouds and delusions enveloping the conduct and character of Frank, and he had called to make what amends might be in his power for his own treatment of him. He seemed also to be on a sort of mission from Miss Brand, or rather Mrs. Vane, and was to urge Frank to call upon that lady, and as soon as possible, should he find him in a placable mood. At Gordon's request, Mason accompanied him to Mrs. Vane's, where he met Alice, and was struck by the almost ecstatic light in her eyes and countenance, dashed as it was with anxiety and cruel doubt. Yet nothing could wholly repress it. The brightness of her hero's form was fully restored; it seemed to say that was safe, whatever else might happen; and, in addition to the profound relief which Mason felt at the real state of the facts, he was charmed by the young maiden's frank and ingenuous appreciation of Frank's noble conduct—dashed, as much of it was, with what seemed a needless mystery. She did not hesitate to say that she had done him the gravest injustice, which was a great offense in her, because in her heart she did not really believe him guilty, or could never realize that he was, and she said that there was no reparation in her power to make him that she did not owe to him; and this was said in that exquisitely conscious, maidenly little voice, that seemed to warrant that the words were meant to convey all that their most liberal construction would imply. And Mason felt that really all that was needed was to bring these two together, and that their hearts would do the rest. Alice went on to say that, though she had acted under the advice of others, she was not inclined to ask any excuse on that account, and she hoped that Colonel Warbel would at least permit her to acknowledge her wrong and ask his pardon. And she would be greatly obliged if General Mason would convey her wishes to him, which, of course, he was very glad to undertake, and he had little doubt that Frank would call on her at once, though he did not know how many or just what personal causes of offense she had given, nor did Alice herself. Before he left he had a few words with Mrs. Vane, to whom he said some things about the proud and sensitive nature of Frank, that would take deep wounds without complaint, without asking explanations, and yet which would be likely to rankle long. He would see Frank before he went to the House the next morning, and hoped he would call at Mrs. Vane's the next day. Before he left, he was asked about the rumor of Frank's appointment in the army, and said he thought it was true; that Frank was without a profession or business, and was poor money-wise, and that the frame of mind under which he must have suffered would naturally incline him to the service; that he was living very cheaply in Washington, and would perhaps feel compelled to turn to the army for a livelihood. Had he known how these words went like so many stabs to one bosom, they would not have been uttered. The impetuous Grayson did not hesitate to give them a needless emphasis. Beyond merely saying, "What did I tell you?" when the result of the case was spoken of, he had maintained silence. So clear was the whole matter that, in his profusion of language, he would not waste words on it. To the general's remark he added: "Of course he'll go into the army. I'd go to the loneliest—to Alaska; I'd leave Washington, and never think of it, or any thing it holds. I hate it for him"—and his voice trembled with indignant grief for his friend. "If he's like me, he'll never see one of you." And Mason, with alarm, thought that Frank would be found to be a good deal like this generous and impetuous boy. Nothing more was said, and the visitors departed.

Margie sat in dark and almost spiteful silence all the evening. She had been at home all day, and the idolized St. Arnaud had been with her for two hours that afternoon. All her old wishes and aspirations, her piques and hates, were revived and aroused anew; with secret joy she hugged to herself the visitations and the fates which she always felt and even knew would soon fall on those stupid things, whom she almost pitied. Well, she could wait—it wouldn't be long.

The words of Grayson produced a real depression, from which no one who shared it, so natural, bitter, and strong were they, recovered, and Alice and Lucy stole silently away to their room, and on their knees turned to the prayers both of thanksgiving and for grace in times of distress, and then in their night-robes, long Lucy's tender voice murmured to Alice, what she had noted during the day of Frank's deportment—how, in tears, he went from Bardlaw's parlor, and his distant, cold, and haughty bearing in the court. Then they talked up his course. Why couldn't he let Alice know what he was doing? She couldn't be trusted with her own secrets. Then Alice told her of the little things which had occurred between them, and which he might have construed into rebuffs; and explained that, in some way, Mr. Ward, who had once or twice visited her aunt, must have got from her some information, and as to where Nancy was, and probably it was thought that the only way was to let her know nothing, and then she would not tell any thing. And both felt what an humiliating judgment of women that was, and they did not know but that it was just; and Lucy knew, if it was, that it was the fault of their education and not of their natures. Then they spoke of the Croly, and didn't believe any—certainly not the worst—of the story; and Lucy said, if it was true, she thought Frank should be forgiven; and Alice murmured back that she thought so too; and then they lapsed into silence, and then into silent prayer; and, finally, with their checks on their moistened pillows, just ere dawn, to maiden's slumbers.

———•••———

CHAPTER XLVIII.

LE GRAND.

"Since the world went wrong, which was always," he went on to say, " there never was such a sell. I'm a d— good mind to take to virtuous pursuits in disgust. You see, Le Grand, this Croly, as bewitching as Cleopatra, instead of hunting, was hunted, and, instead of being the seducer, was the seducee—and there was in this case all the difference that virtue can draw between them. She got a spurious will; but then that would have deceived the very elect—and he got the hiding-place of old Nance and Pete. Why, the scamp is a man of fine genius, and I warn you that, if you go foolin' about him, you'll get bit—I'll bet a thousand dollars!"

And so this other chap is Le Grand, whose name has been mentioned, and whose shadow has once or twice fallen so ominously on our page? The light is dim in the room, but he may turn his face this way.

" And this forgery—they'll move on you." Somehow the voice sounds familiar.

" Devil a step! In the first place, it's a forgery of a forgery; and in the second—I've got it. Gus was a gentleman spectator who examined it with others, and, when their attention was abstracted, he abstracted, and both went off together. Then in comes old Nance, who didn't die. You see, the small-pox broke out in Bone-alley, and old Nance was taken, and a woman died, and my d—

fool was glad to make the mistake that it was Nance. As for Pete, we always s'posed that he was Nance's second husband, and didn't know any thing any way. Oh, dear! Now about this case in the department. You see, old Spinner will not deliver the check until he knows that this d— Warbel is paid; and he'll block the universe—and if the cuss won't sign a receipt, why, Smith must sign one for him, that's all. That'll be a plumper, and if that's done, Saturday's steamer must take two of the d—dest, deadest beats of this capital of dead beats that ever left it for the mutual benefit of all parties; and I tell you, we'll have to use it, and the thing must be got through to-morrow. Old Gordon, that invaluable goose!—oh, how the world depends on its geese, and how lucky that there's always a supply—the world wouldn't go a day without them! So drop your eggs, all oviparous mortals, no matter where, the big-bottomed Gordons will be sure to find and hatch them. He and his precious pigeons don't expect this thing will be through till Tuesday of next week at the best. Now, will we take the whole?"

"Yes, in one shape or another. I've a plan."

"D—n your plans, Le Grand!" Then came a pause, in which some figures were run up—a huge column of immense sums, received and squandered, showing but a very small balance, and the eyes of the two significantly met.

"Can nothing further be squeezed out of Rymer?" asked Le Grand. How that voice haunts one!

"There's nothing left in him; of course he'll have to go on a foreign mission. The A. B. F. M. will have an addition to its corps at once. Poor old sanctimony! And then there's that she-darkey and four or five children of his—for, like the rest of us, North and South, we are all fond of tropical luxuries. I'm very sorry for them—no, 1 ain't either. They'll be better off without 'im, he's so d—d stingy. You'd better see Warbel in the morning, if you're bent on that tom-fool errand, and let me know. I'll go into court with my motion for a new trial, and we'll see who's surprised then."

"What is to be gained by it, anyway?"

"Nothing is lost by a good, bold face. I can make a good showing that I had no reason to expect a trial, and that is true—I did not."

"And that is a good deal for you," from his companion.

"That's true, too—which is a good deal for you to say, little as it is. Then I'll show letters from two parties, who will write that they interviewed old Nance and Pete, who told them the reverse of what they swore to; and the fact is, I did have this prepared, and the men are here; but they hadn't the nerve to go on to the stand, and I believe I lost my own head a little, too."

"Did you miss it?"

"Good! Ha! ha! You may well ask that. But I'll have it in the morning, and keep up some excitement at the City Hall; at any rate, it may distract attention."

Le Grand now arose and walked out at an opposite door, with much of the air of a man whom we have all seen about the capital. After his departure from Teed's room, the latter sat with his head down for a moment, and, raising it, let his thoughts drizzle out in words:

"Was there ever such a magnificent fool? Were brains ever so wasted? With a splendid person and address that nothing has ever resisted, a perfect Napoleon in strategy and execution, till some d—d woman—some pink-faced, wall-eyed girl—crosses his fancy. When he should have been in New Orleans he was here, smelling about this—faugh! and his message was betrayed, and Leibenthal arrested. And then all last summer he was on his wild-goose chase at the holes and hells North, and the biggest devil in them. Oh, dear! it's up—up—up, and I'm down—down—down, lower than the sun 'on Linden.' Where the devil is Smith, I wonder?"

And so do I.

CHAPTER XLIX.

VALERIE'S LEAVE OF HER LOVER.

As Frank was leaving the court-room, the following note was placed in his hand:

"*Thursday Morning.*

"DEAR FRANK: It will do no harm to call you so, and it does me much good. Will you come to me this once? I hope to escape from Washington soon, and from the world ere long. I want to forgive you for some suffering, and I want you should forgive me for the injury I intended, for much which I have caused. Be as kind to me as you can, that its memory may be my one treasure.

"VALERIE."

Why shouldn't he go? He went, and without asking himself the question. In a poorish back room, on Fifth Street, he found her, pale and thin, but in no way less beautiful, reclining in an easy-chair, with Mrs. Harbeck—no longer in her useless masquerade—with her. He took a low seat by Mrs. Croly, and she took his hand in both hers and kissed it. "Frank, you are to be my lover just this once, for one little brief hour; and you need not say that you love me, and must not say that you do not. I know all where your heart is, and I don't blame you. In my soul I am sorry—sorry sick that in my wickedness I involved you in the darkness that has come between you and her. I didn't know or dream of it, till Harbeck told me yesterday; and now I see it all, and when I can't help it; and you so good and true and noble."

"Mrs. Croly, don't, I pray you, say this. I'm not pure nor good nor noble. I am a mere man, passionate, weak, and foolish—as ready to go headlong to the devil as the most unfortunate youth of us all; and if heart and soul and—"

"Hush! I know it, and I don't want to hear you say it. It was so fortunate for us both that it was so! Nothing else saved us then. Let me thank God; I can't thank this fortunate and beautiful angel. Some time you'll tell her of me, in the—in the—oh, I can't!"

"There will never be such a time, Mrs. Croly. She does not love me, and I've long ceased to wish for her love," in a voice of utter desolation, as if sounding down from an inaccessible ice-cliff. "Pray," he went on, passionately, "don't—don't speak of her, nor any thing connected with her. Say that you will not, or I will leave you now."

The two women heard him with surprise, and one at least with great pain.

"Colonel Warbel," said Mrs. Harbeck, "that is a man's unwise speech from the depths of a hard, bitter nature, which will doom itself to starvation and death, if it can also blast the heart of a woman whose only fault is loving him. It makes one tremble, for I—"

"Mrs. Harbeck, am I to go, or remain a few moments longer?" almost fiercely.

"I beg your pardon, Colonel Warbel," with a cold humility which her flashing eyes belied. Frank had been strung up for a long time, and, though he knew that he was behaving like a brute, he took a savage pleasure in it. In a moment, however, he changed and said, "Both of you forget that I am Mrs. Croly's lover to-night."

"Call me Valerie, then, please," in a plaintive tone; "I

won't ask you to say dear Valerie, but just poor, little, plain Valerie."

"Valerie, Valerie, Valerie," in a soft, musical voice of varied inflection, was his response.

"Thank you, love, thank you." Then he inquired all about her health and plans. She was going to her old home near Albany, where was one poor, dear friend, who would give her shelter till death should hide her in the ground, though she hardly knew how she should get to Albany, even if her health permitted. Then she asked Frank's plans. He should take an appointment in the cavalry, and go upon the Plains, and hoped to get away by the middle of the coming week. Croly wanted he should remain while she staid, though she would not ask to see him; still she could not live in Washington if she knew he had gone.

Then he arose to go. "It don't make any difference, Frank, a few minutes, and you have been so dear and kind to me that I am willing you should go now, ere any thing occurs to rob me of its memory." She arose—"Just one moment," she said, and put her arms up about his neck, and laid her head on his shoulder. "I want to do this just once—lay my head on the shoulder of the only man whom I have ever loved, and feel his arm about me." He placed his arm gently about her little waist, and great convulsive sobs shook the bosom pressed against him. Then she sank back into her chair, and, without a word of adieu, he went.

Mrs. Harbeck accompanied him with a lamp down the otherwise dark stairway. When at the door, he placed a hundred-dollar note in her hands for Mrs. Croly, saying that it was his last of that denomination, and he went out into the warmish wintry night.

He went down Fifth to Louisiana Avenue, and thence down Sixth to the Avenue, too heart-sick and lonely to go home. He only thought to lose himself for a time in watching the various faces and catching the broken words of the thoughtless throngs he knew he should meet with. At the National the asking eyes of Drybow rested on him, who placed his arm within his, and finding out his mood, turned the tide of his talk into and finally beguiled him of it.

CHAPTER L.

SURPRISED.

THE Circuit Court was in session on the next morning, disposing of motions, settling exceptions, and closing out its term; and perhaps the hope of hearing something more of the Brand-Rymer case had filled the bar with many of its active members, among whom privileged outsiders were mingled. Teed placed his motion on file for a new trial, on the ground of surprise, and, the pending cases being disposed of, he arose with a calm assurance, so touching in the manner of the insidious advocate, to support it. He assured the court that the whole story of pursuing the callow agent of the plaintiff with the allurements of beauty was a figment of pure fancy; that the defendant, a religious monomaniac, had been approached with an offer of the original will, and closed with it, which, as proved, was a mere trap for him; that when it came to the notice of his counsel, they advertised the world generally that they had it, so that the plaintiff would know where to look for it, and on notice produced it. If the thing was spurious, somebody, not in the interest of the defendant, forged it— did it to mislead the defendant, who was taken by surprise, alike by pushing the case to a trial now, and by the ready detection of the counterfeit will by the counsel whose side did it. Of course he knew, or was told, where to look for the marks of detection. He then produced two letters, with the names of the writers, and envelopes, with the postmarks from Memphis, detailing what Nancy and Peter said about the parentage of Alice—that she was the child of the second Mrs. Brand, and not of Helen Craik; and had arranged to produce the witnesses on the trial, and should have done so, had he not been misled by the course of the plaintiff's counsel. He also told of having heard of the death of Nancy, who he supposed was the principal witness, and was surprised by her appearance in court, and denied all attempts to conceal her. Not a bad showing.

With a wave of the hand to Mr. Bardlaw, the Chief-Justice, who had never withdrawn his eyes from the truculent face of the plausible advocate, proceeded to dispose of the motion on its merits, amid the profoundest silence.

"This is a motion predicated of a surper-r-ise, and a surprising motion. It rises almost to the di-ignity of amazement. It lacks one of the elem-ments of a good motion, for it does not state that there is the shadow of a defense to the plaintiff's case. To set aside a verdict on such a motion would, of all surprising judicial action, surprise a lawyer the mo-ost. As a surper-er-ise, how does this thing fare? It is conceded that the title to this square was in this Ra-a-chel Withers. It may excite some surprise that she should have devised it to this plaintiff, and appointed this Williams and the defendant her executors; but she did, and died—naturally, the court will presume. And here the surprises commence. This will was probated in Connecticut, with only two attesting witnesses—all that the law of that State requires, as we are told; and here, with two, where the law requires three, to pass the title of land. The counsel does not claim that the-e thir-r-d w-itness was suppressed by the plaintiff, although he makes the plaintiff, through her agents, guilty of the folly of delivering to the defendant a will, with only two w-itnesses, and a forgery at that. This surper-cr-ises the court. One of the executors—this religious monoma-a-niac—refuses to act as executor, and becomes vendee of this property to the other as ve-endor; and, for some reason not made known, Williams, the executor, years ago deposited the will with the father of the plaintiff, which was calculated to surprise the defendant's counsel, though he does not urge it at this hearing. That father did not prosecute the rights of his daughter, which ought also to excite at least his suspi-i-cions. The father died, the war came, and devoured the substance of the orphaned plaintiff, who in time made her way to Washington with the will, and this suit was commenced; and the defendant's counsel comes into court knowing all these facts, and the other facts which emphasize them, and he is surprised that this suit was brought with any idea of pushing it to a trial. This certainly pushes the doc-oc-trine of legal surprise into the region of legal impudence. When it is commenced, harlots are set to course the plaintiff's attorney in fact, and kidnap-ap-pers to hunt her witnesses. In the first of these enterprises the hunter becomes the hunted, and gives up the hiding-place of the witnesses, and gets a copy of the will, instead of the original, and this surprises the counsel, and it does the court. It's a little in the line of one of the you-unger sons of Ja-a-cob. In the other, the kidnappers drove the plaintiff's witnesses into the home of the small-pox, and the religious monoma-a-niac tha-anks Providence for relieving him of her, when she walks into court. God went back on the defendant, and his counsel is surprised, and well he may be, with the exposure of these outrages, running through years, breaking in rapid succession, like the developments of the last act of a tragedy, only more startling, upon the counsel yesterday. He was taken by surprise, as were the court and bar, and that portion of the public who witnessed them.

"The law, as we administer it among men, is essentially common and vulgar; its plane is low and practical. It cannot mete out poetic justice, its arms are short, and its means are imperfect. In its way, it is rude and strong and honest, and I may be excused for regretting that I can only overrule this astonishing motion, and order judgment to be entered upon this righteous verdict, which I now do.

"I deem it my duty to say, also, that the conduct of the counsel for the defendant, in the management of this case, will be the subject of judicial inquiry before the ensuing general term, so that he may not be again taken by surprise. Mr. Marshal, adjourn this court without day!" And so the case ended.

CHAPTER LI.

THE KING TAKES THE FIELD, AND IS CHECKED.

Lions at the capital are short-lived; few survive the first season. In official society, one wave follows another; and it is only now and then that one finds his day run beyond a winter, and many rule only for a night. St. Arnaud returned as fresh, as fastidious, as exclusive, as faultless, as perfect, as when he almost reigned, or seemed not to reign, from indifference to dominion, the winter before. He was the same—Washington never was, two successive seasons, the same. Perhaps he cared even less now than before; perhaps he had lost all interest in the capital. The very fact that he returned was against him. Men might acquiesce in a stranger, when they might question an old acquaintance. He certainly seemed quite at leisure; formally called on the Vanes; was quite assiduous to Margie; called on Miss Lozier; and failed to project his Newport and Branford cloud over Alice, though he evidently maintained a show of forces in front of her castle.

On this same Friday morning, Frank heard a knock on his door, and, without rising, directed the knocker to enter, and was very much amazed at the easy and assured entrance of the chevalier, whose graceful and suave bow he very haughtily acknowledged. "May I know to what I'm indebted for this—?" leaving the sentence to be finished mentally by his visitor

"A matter of much delicacy, and of personal importance to you and another, in whose welfare I am so far interested as to relieve my presence here from the appearance of intrusion. I trust you will believe this, Colonel Warbel." The air and manner were courteous, and as self-assured as those of one quite master of the position.

"Indeed!" with sarcastic gravity. "I am sorry to know that we can have any thing in common. I am quite prepared for it," with just a ping of contemptuous irony, which seemed lost on the chevalier.

"You may have heard, Colonel Warbel, the name of Miss Brand and my own mentioned together?"

"I have certainly heard the name of Miss Brand," said Frank, with the utmost composure, "and I may have heard it connected with yours. A matter of such utter indifference to me would be very likely to escape my recollection." The chevalier was not quite prepared for a, contempt so sublime, notwithstanding his experience at the Montowese.

"Possibly, colonel, but this paper may perhaps advise you, if you can bring yourself to notice it," with a voice and manner quite equal to Frank's own, "that these names may have been associated in a way which a gentleman of your nice appreciation will readily understand," extending a paper. Frank took it and read as follows:

"*Friday Morning, December* 23, —66.

"Eugène Edouard St. Arnaud is fully authorized to adjust with Colonel Francis Warbel all claims and demands which he has against me, on account of all business which he has transacted under my power of attorney to him, and all claims which may have accrued since my revocation of that instrument. Colonel Warbel's attention is earnestly requested to this matter at his earliest leisure.

"ALICE BRAND."

"In the presence of
HAMPTON GORDON."

It was a genuine paper, and made that morning. St. Arnaud had his heavy eyes fully on the young man's face, who looked the paper over, and coolly raised his glance and met them. A shock like a *rigor mortis* passed through Frank, but it was not betrayed. His look seemed merely to say, "Well?"

"I am here to execute this commission, and am prepared to recognize and pay your demands, whatever they may be."

"Indeed! Suppose I do not recognize your authority, and refuse to treat with such a high and mighty embassador?"

"You certainly do not question my authority and character?"

"Oh! Your character, if you have any, St. Arnaud, is a subject quite out of my consideration. Your authority, and your right to thrust this paper on me, I do question." As he spoke, he advanced with a downward sweep of his arm, and shook his finger close under St. Arnaud's mustache, while his voice and glance went through him like a flash of electricity. If this was the result of a design to throw his visitor off his balance, it was most successful, though it was doubtless the offspring of an impulse.

"This more fully vouches for my authority," said the

chevalier, producing and handing another paper to Frank, which he would have given the world to recall the moment it left his hand, and he could hardly hold himself from clutching it back by violence. Frank's eye took it in: a full power of attorney, from Alice to Eugène Edouard St. Arnaud, placing all her earthly interests at his disposal, dated that morning, and formally executed.

"Eugène Edouard St. Arnaud!" repeated Frank, in a mimicking voice. "My good sir," stepping close to St. Arnaud's side, and placing his lips near his ear and hissing into it—"why not say, *Jean Jacques Le Grand?*"

The chevalier, already betrayed into forgetfulness, recoiled, while his disturbed eyes started with an amazed stare, and a fully-drawn breath swelled his chest and raised his shoulders. "Take your papers," said Frank, throwing them contemptuously upon the floor at his visitor's feet, and turning disdainfully away. He arrested his steps, however, and turned suddenly back, under a new impulse. "Say, Jean Jacques, you understand English pretty well? You know what scoundrel is—what villain means—eh? Take them, as coming from me." Nothing could surpass the energetic scorn with which these epithets were delivered, and Frank witnessed with astonishment their seeming want of effect. "You don't understand—do you know what that means?" striking his face smartly with the back of his hand. The chevalier glared at him with a brute animal stare of rage and revenge.

"I care not for words," in a low tone, under perfect control. "The blow gives me a claim. Beware!"

"Ha! ha! ha!—A claim! Good! A sort of mechanic's lien, as the lawyers would call it, for work and materials furnished, and you've expended much of both on me, Jean Jacques. I shall acknowledge the claim, and honor it at sight, wherever you are."

With his recovered papers the chevalier strode out of

the room, and Frank sank almost helplessly into a chair. He had thought that Alice's power to hurt him was exhausted long ago, and now this came—the very next morning after she had heard his honor and his fidelity vindicated from the mouth of her nurse and others, and he sat utterly prostrated by the strength and depth of this new wound. One long, deep, awful groan of anguish escaped from him, and, with his head on his nerveless arms extended on his table, he lay, a quivering, aching mass of mere suffering. How long he was thus prostrated he never knew. Not long: the hitherto unsuspected depths and strength of his real nature were just beginning to make themselves felt, like a strange new auxiliary force; and under the reaction he arose, bathed his face and hands, and was pleasantly surprised to find by his mirror that his countenance, to his own eye, exhibited little trace of this new struggle. He thought of Alice with one great throb, and knew now that he had unconsciously cherished a clinging hope or expectation that, after all, when all was cleared up, she would find a lingering tenderness for him, and that some word or sign would call him back to her. That was over now—and an affianced lover had called to pay him off! And such a lover! He ought to be exposed, and she at least saved from him. And there came in a sort of reckless feeling, bringing a kind of ghastly mirthfulness, and he laughed and grew really excited at the sound of his laughter, and laughed on, a mere mechanical empty laugh, and then the sound pained him, almost frightened him, and he became silent.

CHAPTER LII.

MELODRAMA.

It was now near eleven, and he remembered that he was to go down and learn whether judgment had been entered upon the verdict of the day before, and taking his hat he reached the bottom of the stairs, when the idea of the judgment, and that he ever had felt any interest in it or in any thing else, struck him as so loathsomely absurd that he stopped at once, and was about to turn back, when General Mason and Colonel Gordon came up, and said that they called to see him specially, and hoped he was at leisure. "He had nothing under the heavens to do, think about, or care for," and invited them up to his room. When they were seated, Gordon remarked that they called the night before, wishing to see him. "In fact, Colonel Warbel, we come to congratulate you, to rejoice with you; and, for me, I come to apologize, to acknowledge and beg your pardon, for ever having suspected or doubted you, and I do it now, and here, as fully and heartily as a man can; I—" The colonel spoke very warmly, and with the manly sincerity of one determined to atone fully for any injustice; and Mason was a little disappointed at the indifference, positive apathy, with which Frank listened to and interrupted him.

"Oh, come, colonel," Frank said, as if bored, "that is altogether too much. I don't remember what I thought about it. It is all over, and it was hardly worth your while to be at the trouble to tell me this; I don't care a rag about it."

"Frank, my dear boy, I have hurt you deeper than I thought," said the pained colonel, sorrowfully; "I hoped that the old feeling might be restored, and then that it might ripen, till you should come to fill Hampton's place." " Hamp had a lucky escape, didn't he, Mason? though you can hardly see it. Well, colonel, I wouldn't wound you for the world, but as for the old feelings, you have read that a volcano sometimes in its eruptions kills and covers a whole village, mothers, men, and children, crisps vines, and buries all. After a long time, the surface of the scoria and slag becomes the site of new villages and vineyards, and new life and joy spring up over the graves of the dead. Let it be so with us. The past is dead and buried under ashes and slag. I don't want to dig down to the dead children and withered vines. I will be here a few days. I feel that this is all that is left us, and I cheerfully give you my hand on that. I never had any animosity, colonel; I never blamed you. The past, such as that to which you refer, is all dead.". Frank said no more to him, did not even refer to the papers of the morning, in the hands of St. Arnaud, which bore the colonel's name. The truth was, his presence and words merely annoyed him immensely. He had died out of his thought or care, and he was only anxious to be rid of him. The poor old man, suffering more than he could conceal, arose—" Colonel Warbel, I cannot complain; I know that you have a tender and noble nature. I regret that I have intruded upon you. I should have waited "—and moved toward the door.

" Oh, my good sir, don't be pained. I'm sorry I was away last night. The truth is, colonel, I spent the evening with Mrs. Croly, of whom you've no doubt heard. If you happen to see Miss Marston, mention it to her, with my compliments. Good-morning, colonel; look in when you feel like it."

Mason heard all this with surprise and pain, and something of it Frank saw in his eyes. " My dear Charley," said Frank, " I can't help it. I ought to be caned for this absolute cruelty—I suppose it must be—to poor old Gordon. I remember to have liked him very much away back, when I was a little boy, fifty years ago.

"What has really happened to you, my dear Frank?" said Mason, sitting near him. "Let us have an old-time talk. I begin to think I never understood you, and I don't well understand what you've been through with. Talk; let your feelings run out to me, and you will feel better."

"Well, Charley," and Mason thought it a good sign that he called him Charley, "I'm only just finding myself out, and I am a little surprised—ain't yet used to my real self. You know every heart has its inner recess, its blue chamber, where no other may enter, where it does not even ask for the presence of God. This used to be to me so sweet and so sacred, so full of light and beautiful things; and now it is a cave, an abyss, and opens to woful depths, full of shadow, where black passions and evil thoughts, like blind Samsons in the mills of the Philistines, are chained, toiling and groaning—turning out shapeless things of darkness. I am cruel and hard and harsh; feel as I did sometimes in battle, where a man like me is reduced to a brute, with a wish to slay. How I envy young Gordon! What a brave and beautiful boy he was! and how blessed to die so early, with the last light of day and the light of life going out together, and when the world looked beautiful and worth staying in! What a silly, melodramatic cuss I have become, Charley, like the ranters on the stage, only I seem to feel it all! I catch myself striding about, in that awful stagy way, mouthing the absurdest balderdash, or thinking it." And, rising and walking through the room: "Oh, what a luxury to find myself once more on my powerful, bony, homely old Mazeppa!" he cried, in a deeply-agitated voice, "and to charge a rebel battery alone, and feel its hot breath in my face; to have a leg torn away, so that I must bleed to death, though not all at once, but slowly; and, as life ebbs away, to feel the cruel hardness of my inmost nature melt out with it; to lie under the trees in the twilight, with a soft rain pattering down through the leaves into my face, and grow cool and serene; and then be buried naked, and feel the moist, cool earth press against me, and know that no word or throb could ever reach me! Funny, ain't it, Charles?" And when he turned his face toward his friend, Mason saw that he had been shedding tears, and he could hardly restrain his own.

"Frank, there is one thing I want you should do for me; will you do it?"

"Any thing for you, Charley."

"I want you should go with me up to Mrs. Vane's, and see Alice Brand—now."

"I won't do it! I won't see Alice Brand in this world again, if I can avoid her. Never! never!" and Mason was startled at the fierce depth of his declaration.

"Frank Warbel, you are laboring under an awful mistake. Alice loves you with the full love of a devoted woman. She sent me last night to ask you to come to her."

"Ha! ha! ha!—Ha! ha! ha! Well, Mason, that is good. She sent you last night with a message, asking me to come to her. Well, sir, she sent the Chevalier St. Arnaud to me this morning, with a note from her own hand, dated this morning, directing him to settle with and pay me off. O Mason, love indeed!"

"What—what do you say? This can't be!" in astonishment.

"It was. He not only had that, but also exhibited a power of attorney, from her to him, also dated this morning, placing all her affairs in his hands, and he in effect told me that they were engaged. O Charley! I think I'll go, wouldn't you? And on each of these papers was the name of this loving old Colonel Gordon, in his own hand, as a witness. I believe I didn't think of that when he was here. I'm not crazy, Charles," he said, as his friend examined him in surprise.

"Frank, he may have shown you such papers, but there is an awful mistake, or worse, about the whole matter. I'll stake my own hopes of happiness on her truth."

"So'll I, which is no great shakes. She rather wants to thank me, and express gratitude and regret and all that, and pay me by the hand of this——, as if I served for money."

"What did you say to the chevalier?"

"Slapped his face, literally, with the back of my hand, and he threatens to enforce some sort of claim upon me for it. It occurred not an hour ago, and in this room."

"That is grave," said Mason, thoughtfully. "He is a man never to overlook a blow."

"Mason, in my present mood nothing would suit me so well. Poor Alice! but it would be bitter for her."

"I tell you that the whole thing is a most miserable mistake; she is no more engaged to him than to the man in the moon, and I'll get to the bottom of it all."

"Charley, I'll not hold you as my friend if you move in this thing. Say to me that you will not. Don't send me off to the Plains without one friend to think of. Oh, I shall be so glad when I see that awful figure on the dome for the last time, and can bid a final adieu to the Washington Monument, and George's small-clothes, and his wooden face, that looks so stupidly down at me from everywhere in this abominable town! You see, I'm irreverent as well as mock heroic. By-the-way, do you want I should go with you to see La Belle Brand?"

"Not in this frame of mind, I do not. Answer me one question, on your soul: do you love Alice?"

"Do I love her? do I love her? That's a funny question for a happy lover to ask. Would you have me turn braggart? When Hamlet boasted of his love for Ophelia, that proved him mad. What have I done for the last year? Ask her nurse. Look at this mean room, and this worn suit, and think that there is but one other, not so good. What do you mean by this question? and who am I, to be catechised in this way?" After a pause: "Forgive me, my one friend. I don't know what my feelings are toward anybody but you. My love is hate, and my hate is maddest love. I'm full of unutterable sore, hurt feeling. Pray, don't press me; I'm weak and silly and foolish."

"I won't, my poor, dear Frank. God knows, I would give a hand if with it I could first pluck this wretchedness away from you!"

"I know you would."

"And, Frank," rising to go, "I'll wager a thousand dollars against a dime that you don't go to the Plains; and another against a half-dime that you'll—"

"Don't, don't; for God's sake! don't," with anguish; and they parted.

This conversation with Charles Mason had the usual effect. It relieved Frank, as this sort of unbosoming, as it is called, always does one overwrought as he was, and left him in a mood in which his mind worked in its usual healthy channels. And he remembered that, in running his eye over the power of attorney, shown him by St. Arnaud, he saw some allusion to a Treasury warrant, or something payable to Alice Brand, and his mind connected it with the Court of Claims judgment. He immediately took his hat and went to Bardlaw's office, and communicated his impressions to the senior, whom he found, and who was much excited over it, and who called a carriage and drove rapidly to the Treasury Department.

About noon, Mrs. Vane received the following note from Mason:

"*Friday Noon.*

"DEAR MRS. VANE: I had a long interview with Frank Warbel this morning, and found him in a most unhappy frame of mind, and sore and hurt in feeling, for which there is more cause than even we were aware of. A most inexplicable and unfortunate thing occurred just before I saw him. It seems that this St. Arnaud is mixed up in this thing, and may be at the bottom of it. Well, he called on Frank this morning, and exhibited to him a paper signed by Miss Brand, *and dated this morning*, authorizing him, St. Arnaud, to settle with Frank for his services and pay him off; also her power of attorney, placing all her affairs in St. Arnaud's hands, of the same date; and both were witnessed by Colonel Gordon. He also gave Frank to understand that Miss Brand and himself were engaged. You may well imagine the condition in which I found him. There cannot be the least doubt of the intensity of his love for Alice, and just as little of his high and generous nature. I'm hopeful. I would not have you send him any message at present. But let us get at the bottom of this new deviltry. I suspect that Miss Brand has at some time been induced to sign some papers which were left with blanks and now filled up and dated. I did not think of this till I left Frank's room this morning. I hope Colonel Gordon will remain quiet; he only makes matters worse.

"Don't let our precious friend be cast down—I'm sure all will end well. Will call this evening.

"Sincerely,   CHARLES MASON."

CHAPTER LIII.

THE KING CHECKMATED.

THE chevalier walked with his usual cool and dignified air from Frank's door to his carriage and drove away, conscious that he had the attention of passers on the streets, and conscious of two other things—one that he received and one that he did not. Yet, after all, his greatest mortification arose from the certainty of one awful blunder in managing the affair, and the assurance that he was known, and to a man apparently not predisposed in his favor. As he put it to himself, and as he coupled the scene of the Montowese with the recent interview, the brute-animal glare for a moment lit up his carriage. He knew, after all, that Frank was terribly moved, and envied his magnificent self-control, and exulted in the anguish he knew he had inflicted, and he doubted whether, after all, the young man took any particular idea from his hasty and scornful glance at the power of attorney which he had so foolishly shown him. He was uneasy. He had evidently underrated him, and his mind ran darkly on a line of fearful vengeance. That would, for the present, take care of itself. There was nothing now left but for his grand and final demonstration, for which he had been trying to prepare the way, and which lay in a field on which he could remember no rebuff. No time was to be lost, for, if worsted in this encounter, nothing but flight could remain. He was indifferent as to the fate which must now await Teed; for he had so arranged that any use of a receipt in the name of Frank Warbel, in the Treasury Department, would involve himself in no consequences, and, if fly he must, the way was open.

An hour later, in faultless calling-costume, careless in its finished art, he drove to the boarding-house of Miss Brand, when a servant showed him to Alice's own parlor. Fortune favored a private interview. Mrs. Thompson and Millie were absent, and when told, in her own room, that a gentleman was awaiting her in the parlor, a thought of Frank—a thrill of gladness and a sudden flush of hope—held her for a moment, when, subduing herself, but almost in a tremor, she stepped out—to be confronted by the chevalier. To him, and possibly to none, had she ever appeared so lovely, with hope and expectation in her eyes, and the beautiful flush on lip and cheek. It is more than possible that she had touched the fossil remains of what the chevalier called his heart; and vainly supposing, coxcomb that he was, that this radiance was inspired by him, he stepped forward with a profound bow, possessed himself of the confused girl's hand, and sank on one knee at her feet.

"Miss Brand, you must hear me—I implore it for one moment"—as the young lady, changed by surprise to a statue, stood fixed for an instant, with her hand in his. "An idler from the so-called aristocracy of England, under a name that obscured me, I saw you and loved you, deeply, passionately, and with a love that will speak out and not be denied; that will claim you as a bride, and bear you to the proudest courts of Europe; that—"

"Stop! stop! I forbid you," said the fully-restored maiden, drawing her hand from a gentle force that would detain it, and stepping back with the regal air of an injured queen. "How dare you! What have I said or done, that you thus approach me? To me, what can be your name, or position, or your—"

"Lady"—in a deep, troubled, but imperious voice, with hands clasped, and still on knee, with his handsome, sharply-cut olive face fully lifted to hers, and his great mysterious eyes, full of passion, flashing upon her—" they can be, and are, every thing; and who and what are you —more beautiful in your pride—that you should scorn me?"

"I am a woman!" with a lofty air as became that, the proudest title her sex can claim. "I am a woman!" with shoulders and bosom rising, and with head more lofty and proud than ever, " a woman who does not and never can love you; and who, if you have too little manly sense to leave, now leaves you." And, with a slight sweep of haughty grace, she turned to her inner room, and closed the door, ere the now discomfited chevalier recovered his feet.

The excited girl threw herself on her knees by her low bed, and buried her face in its coverings. Is it possible that mortal woman did ever hear the real voice of passionate love, pleading and appealing to her woman's heart and nature, wholly unmoved, and without at least feeling some stir of sympathy or compassion? And, however she might scorn and reject, does not the lover forever remain in her memory as one consecrated, and held, as savages regard the tree struck by lightning, as somewhat sacred? To Alice, the chevalier was merely the chevalier — elegant and handsome, gallant and courtly, admired by women, and admired and envied by men. If she had ever heard the whispers that had coupled their names, it was a meaningless breath. She had never thought of him as a possible lover; and now, like a fierce, bright flash of lightning, he came and blasted her vision for an instant, and only for an instant, when the quick, strong energies of her high nature sprang to her aid, and repulsed him, as he merited.

When the tumult of her feelings had subsided, a light step approached, which she heard and knew, and the next moment Lucy knelt by her, with an arm about her. "What is it, dear—what has so disturbed you?"

Lifting herself up from the bed, she cast her arms about Lucy's neck, and gave way to a flood of tears. Oh, blessed power of womanhood, to wash away sudden and often deep emotions and sorrows in a flood of tears, renewing the heart, like a summer-seared garden with a freshet! And she lifted her face, a few moments after, flooded with tears and dimpled with a bitter laugh. "Oh, nothing, noth—" but the convulsed bosom stopped her voice—"nothing but a sudden surrender to the—the doubts and miseries that, amid all my good fortune, lie in wait to leap upon me."

What natural-born dissemblers women are!

"I met the chevalier in his carriage, and thought that perhaps he had called upon you."

"Yes, just for a moment"—in the most indifferent way.

"Alice, that man is horrid, most horrid. He is in this, and at the bottom of it all. Read this letter, which mother just received, and which I came to bring you. Read it, and go home with me."

She placed Mason's note to Mrs. Vane in Alice's hands. As she read, her eyes distended, the color left her face; she arose without taking her eyes from the paper, and paused, with her features rigid as in a spasm, and, throwing up one hand, exclaimed:

"O my God! O my God! What can happen next? What else is there to happen? Those dreadful—dreadful papers, which we all thought I'd better sign! O Frank! O Frank! You will never, never know." And she sat down listlessly on the bed, with drooping head and nerveless hands.

"Read the rest, Alice dear. I'm sure it is not all bad. It has some good things—read."

And Alice resumed the letter. As she did so, her face suddenly lighted with a rich, warm color, and her drooping form rounded out to its full symmetry; and suddenly her lips went down upon the paper in grace for its blessed message. "He loves me! he loves me!" she murmured, as if to herself. "Oh, he loves me! And though I may never hear him say it, I am blessed and happy!" And she read over and over the words of assurance in Mason's letter.

I may not further trace the course of this day with Alice and her friends. A consultation was had that evening at Mrs. Vane's, at which, with Mason and Colonel Gordon, the younger Bardlaw was present, when all the aspects of the case were gone over, with one or two new features not yet placed under the eye of the reader. On the whole, Alice was almost happy, and lay on her couch, not only with Mason's letter under her pillow, but with the blessed assurance of his warm, tender words—a lover's interpretation of a lover's words to the ear of love.

CHAPTER LIV.

MARGIE'S VISION.

The dark Margie was not present, and, if missed, her absence gave pleasure. It had so happened that, in every thing connected with Alice and her absorbing affairs, Margie had come to be an object almost of suspicion; she was a counterplot and marplot, and grew to be one not to be talked to or trusted, and her presence was a clog, something more than a damper, and she found herself excluded; and one of a less inquiring turn of mind, and less persistent, would have often been at fault as to the status of things, but nothing eluded her. At first, she was the judicious friend of Alice, praising, suggesting, and encouraging, though always finding same ugly drawback, or some fatal obstacle. At length, the drawbacks and obstacles alone received her magnifying consideration, and ultimately these were supplemented with querulous and spiteful remarks, sinister suggestions and dark insinuations, until, under the sharp fire of Grayson, her covers were demolished, and she was forced into open warfare, or the sullen silence of an impotent enemy. To-night she was absent. No one had seen her since mid-afternoon. She was not at dinner, and, when summoned, sent out through her bolted door a sharp response. But then she had fastened herself in before, and nobody felt uneasy about it. Once Grayson fastened her door on the outside, with the remark that "the world had the greatest occasion for bolts on its side of her door." There she was, a little black coil of black robe, black hair, and black heart, silent and alone, in the dark. She was not weeping—had not been; was not one to be helped by a freshet. She had clinched her hands and glared and groaned with impotent rage—rage against herself. She had torn some of her clothes, which she could ill afford to do, and once or twice clutched at her hair, but then remembered that it was already thinning out, quite as rapidly as she could spare it, and then she sank down, in a little round limp bundle in black, down—down into an abyss of abject, helpless, hopeless humiliation. That afternoon she was out on the street, just beyond Alice's boarding-house, and saw the chevalier's carriage drive up to the door, and the coveted chevalier rang the bell and walked in. Suddenly she remembered that she wanted much to see Alice, or Mrs. Thompson, and, hurrying forward, she entered also. She was told that Alice was engaged. She said she would step up to Mrs. Thompson's room for a moment, and ran up the stairs. She had always been suspicious. She would now burst in upon them, and judge by what she saw—and what she saw was quite sufficient to justify the judgment which any beholder would have formed. She passed the open door of

Mrs. Thompson's empty room, and went straight to the door of Alice's parlor, which was a little ajar, and stealing to it, the inquiring eyes of the lady were applied to the opening, just as the flushed face of Alice came from her room. The opening kindly permitted the ambushing foe to witness all that occurred: the advance by the chevalier, his capture of the hand—of the good-for-nothing thing—and going upon his knee, the wretch; and though the earth shook, the air darkened, the heavens thundered, and she grew faint, heroically she saw and heard it all: the inexplicable drawing back of Alice, her proud bearing, and cold, haughty words, and grand turning away—"the artful hussy—it was all her doings!"—and the humiliated chevalier, his rising and turning—when she escaped into Mrs. Thompson's room until the chevalier passed out. She threw the door wide open and stood in it with the face and eyes of a fury, but her voice failed her, and she could only glare at him in mute rage as, unnoticing her, he passed. Then with a stealthy look out and around, serpent-like, she glided down and stole away into the street, and shrunk and slunk along the walls, and entered Mrs. Vane's by the back way, and vanished like a light-hunted shadow, into her own room, and all the way muttering to herself, "It's all her doings—it's all her doings," and, womanlike, ready to stab her innocent rival, and forgive her treacherous lover. For he was her lover—declared lover. She had heard in effect, though not so effectively delivered with knee on carpet, this same tale of the carpet-knight. To her he was the veiled prince chained by the invisible cords that she had artlessly snarled his heart up in, who was compelled to steal to her, almost under jealous, watching eyes, which had hunted him away North, and kept him there all summer. He it was who had filled her to the lips with the envenomed poison, with which she had so skillfully corrupted the atmosphere which Alice breathed—a labor of love in a double sense; and now it all came to her, that instead of being the favored one, the worshiped, who was to be borne from Washington within a few days to the courts of Europe, she was the mere mouth and hand to drive a dangerous rival of the chevalier from the artful, good-for-nothing Alice, whose doings it all was. It now only required that Grayson should hiss in her ear, "You are a Sark!" to put an end to her. And she would die, anyway; she wouldn't live in such a world—she would die, and let it get on as it might. And then she thought that that would be an incomplete satisfaction, and she would live. She would live just to spite the world, which she could much more effectively do if she was personally present in it, to take advantage of any openings. Then she remembered her threat to go into a nunnery, and had seen some of the Sisters in quite becoming dresses, though not fitted to her style, still with a little alteration it would do very well. The fare—she would think about it. She wondered that she did not shriek out to the chevalier his treason on the spot; and what held her from it she could not tell, nor can I. In fact, I thought she would, and I've several times wished that she had. But she would tell him that she saw it all. He wouldn't get off without that. After all, might it not be some sort of a horrible goblin scheme, in which it became necessary to make love to Alice. Not that. She ground her teeth when she recalled his intense ardor, and the tremor of his voice. "Well, it was all her doings." One thing came to her, just one opening to outside light and life. She would tell Frank Warbel how she had seen the chevalier kneel to Alice, and that she had thrown herself into his arms, and promised to elope with him. On this she dwelt, and found its flavor so reviving, that on its strength and hope she arose, lit her gas, washed her face, and made her way down-stairs.

After leaving the court, and getting the expected message from the chevalier of his failure with Colonel Warbel, Teed made his way to the Treasury Department, and found that an unaccountable hitch had stopped the case there ; and instead of going to the chief, who would deliver the all-important check on the Treasurer, he found a stoppage some bureaus back of that, and busied himself to find where it was. This baffled him. He could not strike its trail. A dozen men have to see the papers while on their winding way. Some put a few words or marks on them, and words and marks in a book, and then a messenger takes them to another room on another floor, and waits, and sometimes they are seen and marked again, and so on ; and though Teed knew all the ways and places, and all the clerks and messengers, he was at fault. Finally he went to the Controller, and Mr. Taylor sent him to his chief clerk, Colonel Jones, and he sent him to Mr. Claxton, and he sat him in a chair and went out—was gone till about the inevitable three ; and came back and told him that if he returned the next day at twelve, and would devote himself to it personally, he could get the case through. Teed then went to inquire of Mr. Taylor whether, if he presented a receipt in full, for all fees of the attorney in fact, who had been discharged, the new regularly-appointed attorney could receive the check. Mr. Taylor said that matter was wholly with General Spinner, the Treasurer; and General Spinner told him that the rule in force was only to protect the interests of the attorneys, and, when they were paid, the rule was satisfied ; that if Colonel Warbel had been discharged and paid, that was all the rule required as to him, and Teed went away quite reassured. He was not quite ready to go that night—would have all closed out by the next night. Every thing seemed safe, and he had already resolved upon the appropriation of the whole proceeds. If he could escape at all, he could as well take the whole as a part; and as he was to run the final risk, the chevalier might or he might not realize. The power of attorney, which, as we have seen, had been filled up with the name of the chevalier, had a clause, usual in similar papers, authorizing him to substitute another in his place, to execute it. This Teed filled, with his own name as the substitute; and Smith, who was only found after much trouble, had furnished him with the needed receipt, with Frank's name appended to it. And so all parties and matters went over to the developments of the next day.

CHAPTER LV.

MR. SMITH'S LAST APPEARANCE.

At sharp twelve of the ensuing day, Teed was placed on the track of his case, and pushed it with such energy as the methodical course of business permitted, which never lies in the line of great dispatch, and which to the anxious, imperiled Teed seemed slower than usual—" Slower than cold molasses," was his expression. At length the check was ready for delivery, and the chief of the bureau, having taken Teed's receipt, power of attorney, and also Frank Warbel's receipt, in his hand, accompanied the expectant Teed to the office of the Treasurer for its final delivery.

General Spinner was one of the remarkable men of the capital, at this remarkable period of its history, and often more conspicuous than many a nominal chief of the department—able, stern, inflexible, and tender, with the most marvelous face and the most wonderful signature on the continent. How relentlessly he prosecuted defaulters, and how heart-brokenly he wept over their misfortunes! To prevent agents and attorneys from wronging claimants, and claim-

ants from defrauding their agents, whenever it came to him
that such a thing was likely to occur, he unhesitatingly intervened; and, when the claim was paid, so far as he was able
he saw the matter of compensation adjusted between them.
The chief conducted Teed to his office, opened the door,
and as the latter entered, the cause of the delay, so embarrassing to him, was made quite apparent to the again surprised lawyer. Of its genuineness, in fact, there could be
no doubt this time. There in front of him sat General
Spinner, to be sure, but on his right was a very unusual
group: no others than Mrs. Vane, Miss Brand, Lucy, Grayson, and Colonel Gordon; while in a more remote part
of the large room were two or three gentlemen, among
whom he recognized Major Richards, chief of police, and
Jones, the seedy divinity student of Baker's force; and he
passed a policeman, apparently on duty at the door. One
or two others, cut off partly by a screen, were also noticed
by him as with an unchanged countenance he went forward to Spinner's desk. The chief laid the papers before
him, and explained to him what they were. Looking them
over a moment he called out, "Colonel Warbel, step this
way a moment;" when, stepping from behind the screen
which cut off a part of the room, Frank came forward, drawing the eyes of everybody. "What a change!" each lady
mentally observed. The fresh comeliness of youth had gone.
The face was thinner and graver, but still expressed the
frank manliness which usually governed him. Something
touching they saw in it, but the abstraction and coldness
which marked it two days before had disappeared, and
something of its old winningness was about it. And so he
had sat, all these waiting moments, within twenty feet of
Alice, and had not come forward. Nor did she before
know that he was there. Then, he may not have known
that she was in the room; and the three ladies drew three
long, quivering breaths. He came forward with his hat in

his hand, and as if the general and himself were alone. As he approached the official desk, he seemed aware of their presence, and carelessly threw his unconscious eyes over the group, with a graceful but cold inclination of the head toward them. At his appearance, the red skin under the red beard of Teed turned ashen, and subsided into the cadaverous, and he heard as one dead may be fancied to hear.

"Colonel," said the Treasurer, extending the receipt with Frank's signature to him, "is this your receipt?"

The young man took it and looked at it carelessly. "It is not," he replied, "though the signature is remarkably like, I think," with a slight smile; "that Mr. Jones, here, might throw some light upon it."

The general called that gentleman forward, which was a signal for the other gentlemen to approach, and among them young Bardlaw.

"Well, Jones, what have you to say—do you know who wrote that name?"

The youngish old man, or oldish young man, came very gravely forward, set his hat on the desk, pulled out a large pair of old-fashioned, green, brass-rimmed spectacles, which he wiped with much care, and, adjusting them to his eyes, he took from his hat a rusty-brown wig, which he fitted to his head; and, shrinking and bending, transformed himself into the veritable Jeduthan Smith, Esq. So complete, perfect, and instantaneous was it, that men looked about to see where Jones had disappeared to, and what wonder had so suddenly before their eyes substituted Smith for him. Not a mortal present, save the horrified Teed, but smiled, and in most it rose to a laugh. It was too much for the hitherto silent Grayson, who stood half a head taller than when we made his acquaintance; and he called out: "Sallee Salli, Sal Sally!" Mr. Smith, when arrayed, turned to the prostrated Teed with a bow—"Square, Mr. Smithers with the ers left off"—and proceeded to investigate the paper submitted to him with much care. "'Pears to me I've seen this ere little dockeyment somewhere, ginral," he observed.

"Do you know who wrote the name Francis Warbel?"

Before answering, Mr. Smith edified himself with reading the paper aloud:

"'WASHINGTON, *December* 24, 1866.

"'Received of Miss Alice Brand thirty thousand dollars, in full of all demands and claims due me from her, on account of services in prosecuting her ejectment case *vs.* Rymer, in the Supreme Court of the District of Columbia, and prosecuting the case of Brand *vs.* the United States, in the Court of Claims of the United States.

"'Witness my hand, FRANCIS WARBEL.'

"Wal, ginral, that's my signatoor," he said, very decidedly.

"Yours! How the devil came you to write it, I'd like to know?"

"Wal, you see, ginral, things kind o' hitched in this ere old consarn o' yourn, and, jest to help the square out on't, I clapped in and writ it, you see; that's all."

"Well, I should think that was enough," remarked Spinner. "Mr. Teed, what have you to say to this?" he asked of that worthy.

"It's all a d—d lie," he answered, doggedly, having already seen the hopelessness of attempting an escape.

"Wal, square," responded the imperturbable Smith or Jones, "as that starlin' old Roman, Pont'us Pilot, observed, on a momentuous leetle occasion, 'What is writ is writ,' is all I have to remark." He laid the paper down, replaced the wig in his hat, and removed the brass-rimmed spectacles. Presto! exit Smith and reappears Jones; and this transformation, to the observers, seemed more wonderful than the former, and perhaps this sell was the severest blow that Teed received.

"Major," said General Spinner to the chief of police, "I fear your attention must be directed to Mr. Teed."

The major and an officer came forward, with whom Teed passively retired to the back part of the room, when the business proceeded.

"Colonel," addressing Frank, "what are your charges against Miss Brand? How much are you entitled to of this fund?" asked the Treasurer.

"Me! What are my charges against Miss—Brand?" in surprise that anybody could ask the question. "I have none; was to receive no fee, under any circumstances. I can take nothing."

"Who advanced the money for all the expenses?" asked General Spinner.

"He, the most of it," answered young Bardlaw, "and spent very much for traveling expenses, and some months of time."

"It's no matter. I kept no account of time or money. I presume this is all"—looking hastily around. "Good-by, general; good-by, Bardlaw"—and with just a sweeping, proud bow to the ladies he stepped a little one side, where Grayson stood, to whom he gave his hand. "Good-by, I want to leave one who"—his voice was soft at the "good-by," trembled and broke at "who," when he rapidly passed out. To him it was a final adieu. Something of it seemed to flash on the ladies, who arose as he went out, while his sudden departure created surprise in the minds of the others. At this moment Grayson stepped forward and picked up a small paper that fluttered from the person of Frank, who jerked his watch from his pocket just at the door. The youth glanced at it, and with an exclamation rushed out after him. When he gained the outside, he saw an open carriage, rapidly driven, with Frank in it, turn from Fifteenth Street down New York Avenue, and he dashed off with reckless speed toward home, not a fourth of a mile distant.

After the departure of Frank, the Treasurer asked Mr. Bardlaw what the claim of their firm was, who answered that it was twenty thousand dollars—a contingent fee—which was confirmed by Colonel Gordon, and assented to by Miss Brand. General Spinner directed a teller to pay Mr. Bardlaw, who counted out to him twenty one-thousand-dollar notes. The general said that, if there was no other claimant, the remaining three hundred and fifty-odd thousands would be paid to Miss Brand, when he was told by her that 'she had promised to pay Mr. Teed twenty thousand dollars for procuring a dismissal of the appeal, and the payment of the money.

"The whole thing is an outrage, full of fraud, bribery, and, finally, forgery!" exclaimed Spinner, with a haughty energy; "and he sha'n't have a dollar!"

It was then arranged that Miss Brand's money should remain, subject to her personal order, on deposit in the Treasury. Poor child! her heart and soul went out with Frank. She saw his emotion when he took leave of Grayson, and had she known—oh, had she known—had she known indeed! The gentlemen gathered a moment about the ladies, and discussed his sudden disappearance, and the non-return of Grayson; and Alice hoped he would bring Frank back, but he did not return himself; and, after waiting a few minutes for him, they went home. When they gained the portico on the Avenue, Grayson dashed past on his blooded Madge Wildfire, at nearly full speed. He turned down New York Avenue, and the astonished women, attended by Gordon, went home to a new surprise.

CHAPTER LVI.

MRS. HARBECK EXPLAINS.

On reaching home, Mrs. Vane was told that there was a lady in the library who wished to see Miss Brand, in the presence of some of her friends, and the party proceeded to that room at once. Alice was surprised to find that the waiting lady was Mrs. Harbeck, whom she had not met since the last day of her service at the Treasury, and of whom she had the kindest recollection. She took her hand and introduced her to Mrs. Vane, Lucy, and Colonel Gordon, when Mrs. Harbeck addressed herself at once to her message.

"Mrs. Vane, I am about to leave Washington forever, and I feel that I ought to say some things about Colonel Warbel before I go, unless I am mistaken in supposing that at least one present," looking at Alice, "is much interested in him."

"I am—we are all interested in him very deeply," that young lady answered.

"Very, very deeply," added Mrs. Vane, "and nothing will gratify us more than to hear some more good of him, for such I feel it must be; we have labored under a most painful misapprehension about him."

Mrs. Harbeck was silent a moment, as if gathering her purpose and powers well in hand, and then proceeded:

"I am the wife of the man known in Washington as the Chevalier St. Arnaud." It was said with much effort, but was well said, and produced an impression almost like a spasm on some of her listeners. "Having been in Washington before, he came here early in the autumn of last year, and organized an extensive company to collect claims and speculate generally." This last quite low.

"He secured a large number of rooms on the Avenue, between Twelfth and Thirteenth Streets, and fitted them up in an extravagant manner. I never met many of his associates, although I was obliged to know more of his affairs than I wished to; but men in both Houses of Congress, and in responsible places elsewhere, were, as I suppose, among them. He was wholly unknown in connection with this organization, or as my husband, and more than once he has been introduced to me, by some of his associates whom I knew, as a stranger. In his supposed character of a man of society some of you have met him, and, I believe," with a smile, "he claimed Colonel Gordon as a valuable friend" (the colonel shuddered), "whose introductions were of much service to him. His associates, by their various—speculations, I will call them—received almost fabulous sums of money, which were recklessly squandered, I don't know for what. As Miss Brand may remember, I held at one time a place in the Treasury, where I met her, and was very much impressed by her; and there also I met Colonel Warbel, and fancied that they became interested in each other.—I knew all about your final escape, Miss Brand, and felt assured that you were aided by the one you would have selected." The words "escape" and "assisted" drew wondering eyes upon Alice. "To me," turning to Mrs. Vane, "there was something exquisitely touching in the meeting of these beautiful young people, and in fancy I saw them growing up in a rare love and faith, the belief in which is the last to leave the heart of a woman; and I cherished for these two this belief, or I would not have made this humiliating confession." And how humiliating the shame, her wondrous eyes, as they fell, best declared. After a pause—"The wealth of Miss Brand attracted the association, and her beauty, as I suppose, attracted St. Arnaud," without raising her eyes.

15

"St. Arnaud has the reputation of being capable of managing large enterprises, and is a master of all the—the means that are necessary to success, and an adept in all intrigue, I fear. It was thought necessary, as I have since learned, to detach Colonel Warbel from all his friends, and especially to have him driven from Miss Brand's side, and in a way that would utterly destroy him in her estimation. Of the means employed I know something. All manner of disreputable persons were sent to him with pretended engagements and appointments, and he was induced to go to all manner of places to meet persons, where he was seen and reported. It was supposed that he had possession of, or could procure, the will in dispute, in Miss Brand's case, and a beautiful and dangerous woman was employed to procure it from him by—by any means. She was young, artful, and distinguished for those personal attractions which are said to appeal most powerfully to—to the—the natures of men. She managed to secure a call from him at her then luxurious rooms, and to me was assigned the honorable task of playing a '*soubrette*' part—a woman in waiting upon the lady. Mrs. Croly proved to be a better woman than—than some women, for there are different degrees of bad ones, even among not good women. I was quite willing to take this part in this—this intrigue, for I might, after all, be of some service on its better side.

"Well, the young colonel came, and Valerie, who had already seen and was more than half in love with him, was at once completely taken with him. Something about him appealed with great force to her better nature—something which I can understand but not explain. He was no better than the good of his sex; nor quite so bad as the average, which is a little below par, I fear," smiling. "He neither preached nor prayed, exhorted or talked of virtue and sin, and the moral staples of the Young Men's Christian Association, with mistresses in the far background. He was a man of a high nature, purified and ennobled by a deep and fervent love for a pure and noble maiden," with enthusiasm, " and his heart and senses were, to all others, hushed in a charmed sleep by that spell. I was present at the interview, sometimes in the same room, or in the adjoining, with the door open. Mrs. Croly received him in shoulders, but long before he left her she came in where I was and covered them, as if ashamed; and, as I believe, they were never again given to the eyes of men." A pause. "I was present at the following three or four interviews—I think I was always present at every meeting of these parties after that first, which lasted an hour. Mrs. Croly became impressed with a real love for Warbel, and, notwithstanding his uniform dispassionate coldness, she dreamed of an escape with him from the life she lived and the worse which awaited her. She almost lost sight of her original object, only as it was a means of securing his presence. The result was, she received from him a copy of the will instead of the genuine. In this we were deceived, and I believe that he was chagrined and mortified with himself for this deception of the deceiver. I was present when he delivered it, and he seemed depressed and dejected. My confidence in him was then shaken—was lost. I thought he had surrendered all, and was under the remorse of a noble nature that had fallen. I remember the night well; it was the night of a great party at General Lozier's, to which St. Arnaud was not invited, and for which he was much chagrined.

"I afterward heard the full secret of Warbel's whole conduct in this intrigue with Mrs. Croly. It seems that this awful Teed, the lawyer against Miss Brand, as of course you know, had abducted her two witnesses, and Colonel Warbel's purpose was to find their hiding-place. This in some way Croly won from Teed, and disclosed to him, and for which she received the sham will. He left

Washington that night, and I did not know of his return till mid-autumn. Meantime, the unfortunate matter of the pardons occurred. Mrs. Croly lost her health, was taken with dangerous hæmorrhages of the lungs, and is threatened with an early death. She kept up, animated with the hope of again seeing Colonel Warbel. When he came, I was present, and in my ordinary character as a friend of Mrs. Croly. Indeed, I think Colonel Warbel was never deceived by my little masquerade. When he came, he was cold and distant, and poor Croly was much distressed. She often asked him about Miss Brand, and while he unhesitatingly admitted his love for her, he would not permit her to be talked about. Poor Croly was prostrated by that awful Baker trial, and never recovered from it. She is poor and distressed, and staying temporarily on Fifth Street. My husband's fearful reverses left me with little means to aid her. Finally she wrote a pitiful note to Colonel Warbel, and night before last he came and spent an hour with her, in my presence. He was kind and considerate. She knew it was the last time she would ever see him, as she intends to leave Washington in a few days. It was at this interview that I came to have a full understanding of Colonel Warbel's position toward Miss Brand; and I was pained and shocked beyond measure, as was poor, heart-broken Croly, that, through her pursuit of him, he had, as he felt, forever lost the slightest hope, not only of Miss Brand's love, but of regaining her esteem for him as a man of honor. He didn't say much about it — it is not his way, it would seem — but he spoke with the despairing bitterness of a proud and high-strung nature, stung with the sense of the greatest injustice; and I determined to come and tell you how cruel it is."

Not a word or breath broke the intense silence with which she was listened to by her auditors. As she finished, she arose, and a dark figure, which had stood listening in the background, moved noiselessly away. Alice, with her eyes beaming through tears, came up and placed her arms about her neck, and would have kissed her lips. The moved Harbeck quietly withheld them, saying: "No, my lips should not touch yours. Keep them till they meet his, or press them to such as these," with her finger almost touching the red mouth of the quite entranced Lucy.

"Mrs. Harbeck," said Mrs. Vane, coming up to her, and taking her hand warmly, "I cannot express the deep obligation which your statement lays us under. We had learned somewhat of the wrong which has so unwittingly been done Colonel Warbel. I do believe that your impressions of him are true, and I know, if he has not been driven off beyond recall, that the amplest and fullest reparation will be done him."

"Oh, I would so like to stay and know of it!" she answered; "and now, you precious one," to Alice, "farewell, and God bless you and your true love!" and, with a silent adieu to the rest, she passed out to her carriage.

"Oh!" exclaimed Mrs. Vane, "but one thing more is required, and God will certainly order that—the return of this youth to you," turning to Alice.

"I know he will—and to-night, please," with uplifted eyes, addressing the last to the High Authority named by her mother, added the all-abiding, all-trusting Lucy.

While they were yet murmuring and wondering, a house-maid attracted their attention, and, when Mrs. Vane approached her: "Please, ma'm, Mr. Grayson has not come back. He came a-rushin' in, an' flew to his room, an' went out slammin' all the do's, and went off on Wildfire like mad; an' I seed 'im with 'is revolvers, an' they ain't in his drawer, ma'm." And as they all stood, not a little startled by this announcement, Madge herself dashed up to the sidewalk, bearing a stranger, gave one long blow out of her nostrils, and awaited the pleasure of her rider.

CHAPTER LVII.

GRAYSON'S RIDE.

THE paper which Grayson picked up had written upon it the following:

"*Saturday Morning.*

"COLONEL WARBEL: You struck me a blow, and I enforce my claim. Take the road up past Glenwood Cemetery and past Harwood; at the angle of the road at the top of the hill, beyond, a path will take you down through the shrub-oaks. One hundred yards from the angle is an open smooth space, where I will await you *alone*, from four to five this evening. After the last hour, I will hunt you.

"ST. ARNAUD."

The quick mind of the brave boy saw the whole. He knew, under the revelations of the last two days, that Warbel would be foully met, at this remote and lonely place. He rushed out, to see him taking the shortest route to the battle-field, and a few minutes later, armed, with teeth set and eyes suffused from the heroic emotions swelling his bosom, he dashed headlong to the aid of his imperiled friend. On his go-off, his impatience fretted the noble mare, sufficiently goaded by her own fiery spirit, and she chafed and consumed a little energy uselessly at first. It was a good three and a half miles from her stable to the point named, and over an indifferent track. It was now past four, and Frank had fully two and a half miles the start, and went off at a rattling speed, but Grayson was confident that he would overtake him. Down New York Avenue, deep with mud in some places, to its intersection with New Jersey Avenue, when turning to the north he dashed over the bridge, with the long hill, on the ridge of which is the beautiful Glenwood Cemetery, down the other side, past the road leading to Edgewood, horse and rider at their best—she with her quick, long, fast-going, powerful stride; he with eyes flashing and absolutely motionless. He hoped here to catch sight of the carriage on the hill beyond the beautiful valley before him, and was disappointed. Lord! how that valley fled from under the mare's spurning feet. At the foot of the then sharp hill, the impatient rider called out, "Madge! Madge!" and, as the last word escaped, his eye ran down and swept the way from the ridge to the top of the next hill, which was his goal; and, just as the road turned near its top, a carriage, rapidly driven, disappeared. For the first time he now liberated Madge's head, and committed her fully to the flying devil that possessed her. He lost his breath and closed his eyes for a moment, and seemed to hear the short roll fiercely beaten from a battle-drum. The third of a mile vanished, and like a mounting falcon he was borne up the hill. There stood the panting horses, empty carriage, with two Irishmen who attended it, by the fence, looking anxiously down into the thickly-standing shrub-oaks, much of whose dead foliage still adhered to them. Grayson knew one of the men, who had been his coachman, sprang from his steed, and at that instant two reports of a pistol, in quick succession, broke out from the thicket almost under their faces.

"Mike—boys, come on, a murder is being done here!" in a fierce, excited voice; and, clearing the fence at a leap, he sprang down the descent, followed by the two men, at headlong speed. At twelve or fifteen rods from the fence, he discovered to the right of the path, and twenty or thirty yards distant, a group of men, apparently in a deadly struggle, uttering low, fierce sounds, like fighting brutes. With a loud shout, pistol in hand, he dashed through the thinning shrubs, and gained the open ground, where was Warbel with his hat off, partly on his left knee, with a struggling wretch pinioned to the ground by the throat with his left hand, while, with a large bowie-knife in his right, he was confronting and defending himself against another, who was assaulting him with a bludgeon. More than one blow he evaded; and once, with superhuman strength and agility, he interposed the form of the struggling wretch between himself and his adversary. The ruffian with the club seemed frantic, and gave forth fierce animal half-growls, half-barks, while Frank, with blanched face and flashing eye, confronted him in that stern silence in which a high nature will go to death without a moan. With a loud cry as he broke from the cover, Grayson dashed furiously upon them, but too late wholly to save. Fighting at fearful odds with the half-strangled man in his left hand, still too dangerous to leave, with a weapon too short to reach his principal enemy, and from whom he could not withdraw it long enough to dispatch the other, he was at this moment wholly at disadvantage, and the whirling club met the parrying arm, that received its first force, much reduced by the fierce shout of Grayson, that pierced the assassin's ear with a sudden paralysis, just as the blow was dealt. Still it dashed down the arm upon the unprotected head, which, with the form that bore it so proudly, went to the earth. As he struck, the murderer sprang from his victim, turned and looked at the advancing succor, and Grayson recognized St. Arnaud. Without a pause he threw away the club, and leaped into the thick shrubs with a ball from Grayson's pistol perforating his clothes as he ran. Released from Frank's wellnigh fatal grasp, the other staggered, cackling, choking, and coughing, to his feet, and made off, Grayson being too much absorbed with Frank to heed him, and his supporters making their approach too prudently for effective service as captors.

He found Frank insensible upon the trampled ground, much stained with blood, which came from a severe wound, two or three inches above the left knee, and accounted perhaps for his position in the fight, and greatly increased the odds against him. The boy at once bound his handkerchief tightly about the wounded limb, and, with the now prompt assistance of the stalwart Irishmen, carried Frank, who was still insensible, up to the carriage, and taking him upon the back seat, in his arms, with the wounded limb on the wraps and robes, so as to save it as much as possible, he directed his acquaintance, Mike, to mount Madge, and let her go back to town at speed; call at the police-headquarters and alarm the police; thence to Dr. Bland's and tell him to be ready; and then take the mare home and see that she was cared for. "And, Mike, don't say a word about what has happened, to mother, or any one about the house. Be sure and not alarm them. Tell them I'm down-town, all right."

"Yes, yer honor," and off he went. Frank's team was a good one, the carriage light, and Grayson went rapidly back with the still unconscious Frank, although he knew that he was alive, and hopefully and impatiently he called to the driver to increase his speed, while he tenderly and faithfully sustained the drooping form of his friend.

CHAPTER LVIII.

HOW MIKE EXECUTED ORDERS.

MIKE reached the town in advance of the carriage, and proceeded to the execution of his commissions, in the most Hibernian way. The police were thoroughly alarmed, and, had they only known the scene of the conflict, or who or what was engaged in it, very effective action might have ensued. Dr. Bland put things in readiness for the wounded of a regiment, and, having delivered Madge to her own groom, Mike approached the house of Mrs. Vane, to not alarm the inmates, as directed. The return of Madge was known, and Lucy, who recognized Mike, called him.

"Was it the young gintleman ye war after askin' fer, miss? It's meself that can till ye all about 'im, bliss yer two eyes."

"Where is Grayson?" asked Lucy.

"Oh! he's all right, and tould me not to alarum a blissed one o' yez!" was the prudent reply.

"Not to alarm us! Mother! Alice! Grayson told him not to alarm us!" which brought them with pale faces about him.

"Where is he?" asked Mrs. Vane, with apprehension in her voice.

"Him? Who? Master Grayson is it? Well, an' ye say—he's a-comin' in wid the body, mum."

"With the body! What body? Who? Where?" turning paler, and growing distracted, when Alice came forward, with face blanched and eyes a little distended, and placed her hand on his arm and looked him steadily in the face in a way to restore a maniac. "You won't alarm us any more," in a very quiet voice; "who is killed?"

"Is it who is it that is kilt, that ye mane—ye want to know, miss?"

"Who is killed?" steadily.

"Well, an' ye'll know, I s'pose; it's the young cunnel, miss."

"Colonel who?" firmly, with the pallor growing about her lips.

"I don't rightly remimber 'is name, miss," abashed and hesitating.

"Colonel Warbel!" with a great effort, said Alice. "Is it Colonel Warbel?"

"Indade, miss, I'm lookin' at yer great eyes; I fear it is, the howly Vargin kape 'im!"

A half-shriek from Lucy—a gasp from Mrs. Vane—"Great God!" from Colonel Gordon, and just a quivering breath from Alice.

"Is Colonel Warbel dead?" she asked.

"Only kilt, miss—howly Mouses, bless 'im, only kilt, an' not intirely. Grayson, the Lord bliss 'im, said he'd come out av it," with his eyes starting in alarm at the uncomprehended effect of his communication.

"Where is he—Colonel Warbel?" asked Alice, in unchanged tone.

"Wid Master Grayson, as brave a b'y as was iver born out av auld Ireland."

"Tell me all you know about it, from the beginning to the end," with her hand still on his arm.

"It's meself will do that same, miss. Ye say, Pat Kirly drives for Fowler, an' the cunnel had the little bays—theys the hosses, miss—well, the cunnel had the bays, fer half-pas' three sharp, fernenst the Treasury bildin', an' says Pat to me, sez 'e, 'Are ye after wantin' to drive out wid me, Mike?' sez 'e? Sez I to 'im, 'I don't care if I do,' sez I; an' so I got in, an' we waited on the strate more'n an hour, win the cunnel came tearin' out, an' jumped in an' said he was late, and tould Pat to go, an' aff we wint as though the blessid saints was afther us. We druv' out past the Catholic Cimetry—Heaven rist their sowls!—an' so on, an' niver a bit stopped till on the top o' the hill, beyant the Ould Souldiers—an' the cunnel threw aff his top-cut, and tould Pat to wait fer 'im; thim's 'is last words, miss, and all he said afther he got in the strate, an' 'e wint down the hill in the woods—thim's 'is very words—an' me 'n Pat got out, and was a-luckin' down the hill, when Master Grayson—the saints bliss 'im!—with his face blazin', came with Madge a-foamin', an' jist as he lit, two pistils went aff in the wuds, and we seed the smoke. 'B'ys,' siz Grayson, siz 'e, springin' ouver the fins, 'there's a murtherin' 'sassination, burglary, an' rape'—thim's 'is very words, miss—'a goin' on in these wuds,' siz 'e; 'come on,' siz 'e, an 'e draun a pistil, an' we all rin, togither, Grayson a good bit ahead, an' jist as I seed 'em, the cunnel 'ad his knay on the buzzim of one o' the burglars, an' 'ad 'im choked to death wid 'is lift han', an' wid the ither he was a cuttin' an' slashin' wid a big butcher-knife at this French spalpeen av a St. Arnoo—divil a saint is 'e at all at all—'oo was a-strikin' at 'im wid a big shilalah. An' jist thin Grayson was cluss to 'im an' yil'd at 'im, an' the St. Divil fitched 'im a wallop 'cross the arum, an' doun on 'is head, and 'twas all ouver. Two to wun, the rapin' divils! an' that is the hull o' it, miss. An' thin this divil of a St. Arnoo, when Grayson wint fer 'im, was feared, an' drapped 'is shilalah, an' rin, an' Grayson sint a pistil-ball after 'im—may the Vargin direct it into 'im, an' fix it in 'im! An' thin the ither thavin' divil, that was choked to death, instid av stayin' dead, like a dacint gintleman, as soon as the cunnel let up on 'im, craul'd aff, an' thin me 'n Pat came up, an' there lay the cunnel dead-like, wid a pistil-ball through his lig; an' Grayson boun' it up, and me 'n Pat an' Grayson put 'im in the kerridge, an' Grayson hild 'im, an' I driv on to start the p'lece an' git a docthor riddy intirely, an' not to alarum yez," with much which the reporter omits.

And Alice heard it all; then asked: "Where is he—where will he be taken to?"

"Dr. Blans, on If—jis' below Furtinth Strate, miss."

"He must be brought here—and at once!" said Mrs. Vane.

"He must stop at the first roof that will take him," said Alice, decisively.—"Take me to the place at once, good man." And, without heeding a word that was said, accompanied by Millie, and attended by Mike, she went to Bland's. She was shown into the inner office, where, with the lower part of her face enveloped in a twist of veil and soft stuff, her steady, unwinking eyes seemed to the polite young man in charge to have a strange power. "Was Colonel Warbel there?"

"He was in the adjoining house," was the answer.

"Is he—alive?" with a voice forced to steadiness.

"Alive? Of course. I think his wounds and hurts must be cared for by this time, and the doctor will be down in a moment," unable to withdraw his eyes from hers, that burned on in their light of weird but steady splendor. She wrote three words on a card, and handed to him—"Will he live?" "Please take that to the doctor, and bring me word." And he ran with alacrity. A moment later, Grayson came flashing in.

"Bully for you, Alice! You're a brick all through."

"And you're a hero—a true, brave hero, Grayson, and a true woman shall love you some time, as you deserve."

"All right—no doubt. No hurry about that," was his reply.

"And the doctor?" she asked.

"Oh! of course he'll live. He's pretty well come-to now, and the best man in the world, by two full regiments of Indian-fighters!"

"Thank God! oh, thank God!" with fervor. "And he is conscious, and knows things?" anxiously.

"Well, a little cloudy, perhaps; says some words, and I heard him say 'Alice' once, I'm sure "—the thoughtful boy!

"Did he! Indeed, did he?"

"I'm sure he did," said Grayson, with a liberal translation of a very indistinct utterance, but then, with a smile: "He's a little abroad, you know, so that it don't count for much." Then in came Mrs. Vane, Lucy, and the everlasting Gordon. When they were assured of Frank's safety, Grayson had to submit to being kissed, and said, rather ungraciously: "A woman's one thing, for all possible cases, is a kiss."

"Well, you ungrateful boy, that is about all you men have left us that we can give," said Lucy, with spirit.

"Well, why not have a little silver paddle with a handle to it, and carry it about to pat your mouths with, when the right time comes, and not bother a feller?"

"Do you think that Colonel Frank would prefer to have a certain mouth patted that way, eh?" asked Lucy.

"Well, that's a different thing entirely—ain't it, Alice? There's business in that, or will be, I hope." And then Dr. Bland came in, with his dark face aglow, holding Alice's card in his hand, and, going straight to her and taking her hand, read off, "'Will he live?' Why, of course he will. His hurts are not at all dangerous, and only just make him interesting. His right hand and arm will be disabled for some time, and somebody must feed him. His wound will keep him in hospital some weeks, and somebody will have to keep the blues from him. The effects of the rap on the head will pass away by morning, and in a few weeks I'll hand him over to you, as handsome a lover or bridegroom as maiden ever wished for. Is that satisfactory?"

"Perfectly. And, doctor, are there some rooms near, where I can take my old nurse and Peter, and where I can stay?—Mrs. Vane, I don't care for the world—for nothing but his sending me away; and he need not know—I shall not personally trouble him. His honor has been lied away; he has been betrayed into the hands of murderers for me; and what I can do I will, to satisfy my own conscience. That is settled." This was said with a quiet firmness which permitted no words of answer.

"I honor your determination from my soul," responded the doctor, "and every thing shall be placed at your disposal. I've observed that a young lady's conscience is often located next her heart, and, when it is, it is apt to be exacting."

"Is that a physiological or a psychological fact, doctor?" asked the now radiant Lucy.

"Tautological," answered the doctor.

With a great peace, almost a joy, and full of sweet, religious trust, Alice, accompanied by the party, went home. All the way back Grayson never spoke, and, while awaiting supper, he walked moodily and with troubled face up and down the parlors, and finally, casting his head down into his hands, burst into great sobs, while his whole person shook with his emotion. Mutely the wondering women gathered about him—a woman could hardly comprehend the cause of his emotion. "Only think!" he exclaimed— "just think, if you can, and realize—this man, going utterly alone into that solitary place, to be waylaid and murdered by those miscreants, with nothing this side of God in the whole swarming world—no hand to strike a blow for him! It is too bad—too bad! Oh, a woman can't comprehend it! It is something in the brute part of man, I s'pose. Oh, I would gladly have given all the rest of my life to have been there, even unarmed, to have grappled with that dastardly Arnaud. Where's Margie? There's something I don't yet understand: Warbel's pistols were both in the inside vest-pockets, and all the chambers are full in both. He could not have had a knife. That he must have got in some way from the miserable devil that he only just failed to choke to death. They must have sprung upon him when wholly unprepared and unarmed; and mortal man never made such a fight, at such dreadful odds. Oh, it is too bad—too bad!" giving way again for a moment. "Lord! he lifted that man with his left hand, and pushed and pitched him about as if he had been a rag baby! Dr. Bland says he never saw so fine a form. Oh, dear! Margie ought to be here, to stick pins into me—a great crybaby, because I didn't get in and have my head broken, too; she'd say it is too soft for that, I s'pose. Oh dear, again! what would my old father, the commodore, who fought with the fiery Decatur, say, if he knew how I was going on about my first skirmish?"

"He'd say you were his own true son," said Alice, "growing up to be like him." Laying her hand on his shoulder, "I'm not going to kiss you," she said; "don't be alarmed."

"Don't; there is one who has earned all that you can ever do in that line," was his answer.

That night there was, after all, a very happy household at Mrs. Vane's, and Lucy only wanted to have one good, whole night to tell up every thing to Kate Lozier; and the rather proud and not unhappy Grayson wanted much to see Sam.

CHAPTER LIX.

MRS. HARBECK HAS A CALL.

She had completed all her arrangements; all her trunks were packed. The portraits of her husband and child were removed from their frames, and carefully put up, and all were ready. She received a message late in the afternoon from St. Arnaud, saying that he would see her before eight, and, unless she saw or heard from him, she was to remain over; and she sat until eight, half-past, till nine— and no word or message. And so she sat on, waiting and thinking. What a waste and ruin was her whole life! A person of rare attraction, with intellectual powers superior to most, educated and admired, of a wayward, willful turn, delighting in its perversity, yet ever contrite for its follies, tender, and with a man's firmness and courage, intensified with a woman's electric energy, that may for an hour venture and do, where a man dare not; early wedded to a man she had only within the last few months learned to know and love, mother of a beautiful child, which never fully entered its place in her heart, till it ceased to be; delirious with a sudden passion for St. Arnaud, which drove her husband to suicide, already stung with remorse for his treason to his flag, followed as this was, with months of a wild whirl of fiery illusions, that cheated her, for the ecstasies of preternatural love, from which she was only startled by the death of her child, she—whom we know as Mrs. Harbeck, sat brooding over the intervening wreck from that awakening day to the present moment. How the real character of her husband was revealed, trait by trait, as one illusion and delusion after another was dissipated! How he descended from a veiled nobleman to a Mephistopheles of unknown origin, and fell from an embassador of the new Emperor of Mexico to the new President of the Confederacy, to a nameless adventurer, intriguing on his own account! and still his old fascination remained, to persuade and seduce others; and still he held control over her imagination and senses! The close of the war opened Washington to him, and here she was made, for the first time, to play a part, she hardly knew what, yet how that new character grew upon her, until he who called her wife made known to her that she was the price of a senatorial vote! In the storm which ensued, something of his schemes and associates escaped him, and she was startled at her own powers of dissimulation, never called into play before; and she grew silent, wary, and politic —seemed to lend herself to his purposes; went into the Treasury, met Kramer, and became his decoy; obtained from him his secrets and the details of transactions, with which she taunted him. She met Alice, and saw through the designs upon her, watched over her, and became interested in the loves of Alice and Frank; suspected St. Arnaud's designs upon her, but she did not fear for her, and ceased to care much on her own account. From time to time he had placed considerable sums of money in her hands, much of which he had reclaimed; and yet she had managed to retain quite sufficient for her needs, with reference to present and future; and was providing wholly for Croly, for whom she had a sincere regard.

Steadily the memory and love of her former husband, which dawned upon her like a new discovery, arose and grew on the memory and heart of the unhappy woman, until, like a fiery star at times, it hung in the heavens burning her eyes and searing her heart, while the pale face of her dying child, made ghastly and as if bathed in blood, would come palpably before her; and at times their beautiful faces, looking from the canvas, would seem to turn with supernatural power upon her, until, in self-defense, she turned them to the dead wall—all this now came back to her. She would go—she would separate from St. Arnaud, and bury herself in some town in the remote West —some obscure nook or corner, away from any thoroughfare, and where memory alone could connect her with the past.

The time ran on till ten, and finally eleven. She had heard nothing of the rumor of blood and murder just let loose upon the town, and sat self-contained and collected till the latest hour of departure lapsed, and she knew she must remain till the next day.

At about half-past eleven, a knock came to her door, and, upon her opening it, there tottered in unbidden an old and seemingly-palsied beggar-man, in tattered garments, who at first peered doubtfully around, and then himself closed and bolted the door. As Mrs. Harbeck drew back in surprise, with some approach to alarm, he threw open without removing his soiled coverings, and, lifting his fell of white beard and shaggy brows, revealed the form and heavy eyes of St. Arnaud, with something more sinister, haggard, and reckless in his look than she had ever seen before. He regarded her for a moment in silence, and then broke into a low and exceedingly unpleasant laugh.

"Why, St. Arnaud! what has happened?" still surprised.

"The proud descendant of an old aristocracy is now doubly eclipsed, ha! ha! ha—a—a! Reduced to his original elements," surveying himself in a large mirror. "My dear," approaching the lady, "what do you say to me, now? Do I look like the descendant of an earl? or the son of a broken-down French waiting-woman, maid to a wandering singer—otherwise no maid at all, and never was—ha? What do you say, for one of them I certainly am, and may be both, though I've had my doubts as to which it was? When I recall the gutters, the sinks and slums, of my first memory, a *gamin* in Paris, I think it's one. When I recall the *ruse* imposed by my mother on an imbecile old man, as a grandson by some sort of a marriage with his son, and recall the ten years of this successful *ruse*—followed by—the successful tuft-hunting—my association with Bazaine and Max—I'm ready to swear it's the other. Have me either way, my dear; though, for the present, the old ways must hide me."

"It may be either, for what I care; either is indifferent to me," with weariness, and a disgust which she did not care to conceal.

"How now, my Lady Pangborn, are you weary? doesn't it get invitations to state dinners, *entrée* to Washington high life? I think I must call over my cousin the duke to dispel the cloud—ha! ha! ha! By-the-way, where is the festive and frolicksome Pang? I haven't seen him lately."

The lady's eyes flashed.

"What do you mean by using that name to me?"

"Oh, nothing. I didn't mind the horns so long as nobody knows the head that wears them."

"St. Arnaud—St. Arnaud! I'll not endure this."

"Well, after enduring the Pang, I should think this might be borne. What will my lady do?"

"What will I do?" stepping forward, with her form quivering, her eyes flashing, and a small, two-edged dagger, burning with a quivering blue sheen, in her hand—"what will I do?"

St. Arnaud shrank.

"Hear me. You came, and, fool that I was, seemed to compromise me with my husband, whom I had already betrayed into treason. When he would have called you to account, you made him understand that my person had been yours; and, in a paroxysm, he turned the pistol, which should have killed you, against himself—and I forgave—with indecent haste—married you; when what had been a lie became true. So horrible was this union, that its atmosphere polluted and poisoned my child, and I saw him die, gladly. You, my husband, bargained my honor to this senator, and used arguments and persuasions, made opportunities, and multiplied inducements; and yet, pander that you would be, you know that I am as untouched as ere marriage. Now, St. Arnaud," advancing a step, and raising her hand with the dagger, with every fibre of her lithe person strained for a spring, "take back your filthy lie!" only looking the threat that he knew she would certainly execute.

"Oh, come, come, Marie, you do it well. What's the use? I was only joking—come."

"Take it back this instant."

"I do, I do. It is not true. I know you evaded him. I got the vote, though—ha, ha! By-the-way, Marie, one thing more—our marriage—it was too bad at the time, but it is now too good to keep—chaste wife that you are—we were not married at all. The license was a forgery, the parson a fraud, and the whole thing a sell! O Lady St. Arnaud!"

The form and face of the woman fell into softness as well as surprise.

"Is this really so?"

"Of course it is. Did you suppose I'd tie my wings with a real marriage for less than a million? D—d if I don't believe you're glad," a little piqued.

"Gladder than I can say," with a real joy on her face. "Thank you—thank you. And you were then quite in earnest with Miss Brand—and she refused you? Ha! ha!"

He turned as if stabbed, as well he might—it was a woman's guess, but from a woman's intuition.

"Much good may it do her!" with his face darkening. "I've killed her lover, this boy-colonel."

"How—what! killed him?"

"In a fair duel," putting his hand to his disguises.

"It's a lie, black and cowardly! If he is slain at all, it was treacherously done;" and, approaching the bell, "I will denounce you to the police!"

"Hold, one moment! it is true. He fell, but may not be mortally hurt. You are too noble and brave to betray me, after all, and I came to you for money to escape with." In silence she produced from her pocket a roll of bills, from which she took five, of one hundred each, and handed them to him, and opening the door, with a silent motion of her head, he passed out, with his disguise adjusted; and so they parted. Persons late on the street saw an aged man toiling on, with incoherent mutterings to himself.

The early train for New York bore Mrs. Harbeck, with her trunks, memories, and fortunes, from the capital forever.

CHAPTER LX.

FRANK.

THE next morning, bright with sun and Sunday, came over the capital, broken by noisy newsboys vociferating in the silent streets: "Sunday mornin' *Char-oni-cal!* full 'count o' the murder!" "*Her-ol, G'zett,* 'n *Chr-n-cal-l-l!*" "*G'zett, Herol,* etc., 'count the mer-ur-derer!" Mistily and hazily it stole, or was formed some way, in a dim room on F Street, where, steeped in the mingled vapors of sleep, dreams, unconsciousness, and wakefulness, hovering over the wavering line that vaguely divided light from darkness, with a pinion showing now in the former, and then melting into shadow in the latter, lay Frank Warbel—now catching the sound of his own half-groans, and wondering what noise it was, and with a vague half-idea that somebody was suffering; lying with a brick oven on his head, and an arm screwed into a vice, and wondering who it was; and somehow, queerly enough, suspecting who it might be; and lazily following out the idea, till something like certainty grew upon him, and then all faded off into cloud-land, from which he would half arouse, and he wondered where he was—where he last was, and what filled the intervening gap, and what ailed his right arm, his left leg, and what was sitting on his head, closing down one eye; then a fragrance as of mignonette and heliotrope stole over him, and then every thing grew indistinct, and somebody groaned, which must be himself; and he thought he had heard the same sound before. Somebody else must also have heard it, for a soft, sloppy step approached him, and a hand was laid upon him, and a voice whispered, "'E's awake, bress 'im, praise the good

Lord! 'ow's 'e feel, 'oney?" It was the voice and hand of Aunt Nancy; and slowly a bitter consciousness throbbed back, through wound and bruise, upon him. His mouth tasted badly, and his lips were dry.

"Aunt Nancy, where am I? What happened? Oh!"

"Ye's all right, 'oney, bress God! 'Ere's a drink," lifting his head and putting a glass to his lips. The water did not taste good, but was cold, and refreshed him.

"Aunt Nancy, what has happened?" putting his left hand to his knee, that had a wet bandage on it, and to his head, and groaning.

"Ye's shot, and was smacked over yer head; ye's 'ad a fight, yer know."

"Yes, yes, yes, I remember," as things which seemed to have happened a year ago came to him with a sharp pang; and as he fastened his mind upon them, they grew distinct and seemed to be the present. "Aunt Nancy," a little confused, "is this to-morrow morning or yesterday in the afternoon?" Poor boy! if a night had elapsed it was to-morrow morning; if not, it was still yesterday.

"Yer quare, bress ye; it's this mornin'," which of course was satisfactory, or seemed to be, for, with a grave thinking over it, he expressed his pleasure at having an important point settled.

"Oh, it's this morning. Well, it may be. Where am I? Oh! I see, in this room; is this a hospital?"

"Lord, 'ow quare ye are!" laughing.

"How came you here, Nancy?"

"Oh, I's fotched 'ere, 'oney, to take kear on yer. I com'd with Miss Alice."

"Alice — Miss Brand!" starting up with an "oh!" and finding he couldn't do it. How the image of that sweet girl came to him, and as it used to come, and the one unimpaired eye gave out its tears; and then all the hard, bitter past, like awful phantoms, trooped into his memory, and stood grim and defiant between her image and him; and some time he lay in silence and reached out his hand, and, taking up a small bouquet, he brought it to his face and smelled it, and hastily put it back. It seemed exactly like the one he sent her one morning, oh, ever so long ago!

Aunt Nancy seemed to divine his possible thoughts. "She'll not come to see yer till ye asks fer 'er," and there was the note of woman's pride in her tone.

"Aunty, don't! don't speak of her, please!" with a helpless pathos in his voice. He lay musing a moment. "Did Grayson Vane bring me here? I seemed to hear his voice shouting in my ears."

"I 'spec's 'e did, Masser Wa'bel." She was not a little hurt at his reference to Alice, and called him master. Then the door was thrown open, and the quick step and the cheery face and voice of Dr. Bland, which always brought a tonic into a sick-room, came together. He opened the blinds and turned off the gas, and sat down brightly by the side of his patient, when the hovering vapors disappeared, and Frank soon came to a full understanding of himself and his surroundings. The doctor was entirely satisfied with his patient, and Aunt Nancy was with every thing but one. "This yer young cunnel," she had come to understand, handsome and perfect as he was before that blow, that put an eye and half of his head and face in mourning, was at feud with Alice, and it was all his own fault, she knew. It always is the fault of the men, and she, sweet thing, was just "a-breakin' on 'er 'art fer 'im, as she could see."

CHAPTER LXI.

FRANK'S STORY.

AT ten or eleven, he was quite himself, and Grayson and he had a very hearty, touching interview; and Gordon came in, and Frank mentally rushed into the old man's arms, and asked his pardon for the stuff he had talked to him; and the colonel shed tears over him, and then Mason, to whom he joked about having Pike's Peak on one side of his head.

"And the blind Samsons, Frank, are they still turning the mills of the gods?"

"'No more of that, an' thou lovest me, Hal!' Don't remind me of the balderdash that I spouted by the square league, Charley. After all, it would not have hurt me had I bled a little more. The lower depths are still in shadow. Don't awake 'em now."

"And George's small-clothes and monument?"

"Oh, I can't see them for a month, unless it is with an eye single, when half their ugliness will be hidden. I think, for a totally blind man—born blind, so that memory would not torture him—Washington would be tolerable; but it would be awful to consciously blunder around even in the dark, haunted with all the horrors of this doomed town."

Stooping over him, Mason whispered, "And Alice, Frank?" and a mute spasm of pain was the answer.

And then Drybow—or Dryup is perhaps better—and General Baker, and young Bardlaw, and Jones, and the reporters, and others, were coming and going all day.

Frank was not disposed to say much of the transaction of the evening before. To Mason, Baker, and Bardlaw, he briefly explained that where the path at the battle-ground reached an open space on the right, he saw St. Arnaud, a few yards in that direction, standing with his arms folded across his chest, and who beckoned him to approach; and that as he turned in that direction, and just as he passed a tree, a man, whom he had not seen, sprang suddenly upon him and attempted to clasp him about and pinion his arms, and in part succeeded; that he extricated his right arm by a sudden effort and seized him by the throat, and liberated himself in an instant, when he threw this ruffian down and twisted his left hand into a strong tie about his neck, which gave splendid leverage for a compress; that the wretch drew a large bowie-knife, which he wrenched from him; and that, at about that moment, St. Arnaud, or Le Grand, fired two shots, one of which—the second—took effect, and brought him to his knee, as he thinks, when he exploded a cap, with the pistol so near his face that, with a sweep of his knife, he knocked the pistol from his hand, when he assaulted him with a bludgeon, which he must have had in the other hand; that a moment intervened, when he might have killed the poor nearly-choked devil, and he thought of it, but could never strike a man when down. Besides, he did not give him much trouble, doubtless for fear of being dispatched; that this man got in one or two blows about Frank's neck at first; that just an instant later he heard Grayson's voice, and described the rest of the conflict till he was knocked down.

When asked why he did not shout and alarm the Irishmen, he answered that the reserves were raw militia, and would have been more apt to advance on the capital. Baker told him that a revolver had been found that morning on the ground, but that neither party had been arrested, and he feared would not be; that he had just heard of a half-crazed old man who was in the streets the night before, who was undoubtedly St. Arnaud, whom he described as an adept in all the lighter graces of disguise, and cool and intrepid; that a man of his class would seldom risk his life in a fair fight, and that even the practised duelist always endeavored to secure an advantage. He had watched Le Grand since his first arrival in Washington, and was for a long time at fault. He was educated in Europe, and had some tactics not known in this country. That he should certainly have pulled him, had not Leibenthal been prematurely arrested in New Orleans, which was the only matter he could with any probability connect him with, and that could not be established with certainty, on either him or Teed, as the case finally stood.

Much excitement was produced in non-political circles by this attempted assassination, and *Harper's Weekly* and *Frank Leslie's* gave imaginary portraits of the principal parties, using for Frank the portrait of Heenan. A supposed likeness of King Theodore had the honor of standing for St. Arnaud. The fashionable circles and leaders "thanked God that they never were on terms with St. Arnaud and wondered how he ever obtained a footing in official society. One couldn't be too prudent."

I may not be complained of for the escape of this man, nor for that of Teed, who subsequently forfeited his bail of twenty-five thousand dollars. I am narrating a tale of life as it is lived, in which the small, weak villains alone suffer what is virtuously called condign punishment. The great ones are too huge; they dwarf the ordinary machinery of the law, and its administrators; and to recite the conviction and punishment of one of them would be a fiction so absurd as to render a tale unnatural and improbable, and destroy all interest in it.

CHAPTER LXII.

THE TABLES TURNED.

FRANK was early left to himself and the kindly devices of Aunt Nancy, abundant in stores of womanly kindness and sympathy, and with every device of art and luxury, to soothe, ease, and solace the poor patient, who was the pet son, strong, handsome, brave, and wayward, and who sorely grieved her mother's love, and outraged her woman's sense of right. Never was a man so uncomplaining, docile, patient; as heroic in enduring the pain of his wounds, as reckless in receiving them. He relapsed into a reverie, and meandered into a drowse, and was at last awakened with the spasm of a bruised or wounded muscle, and opened his eyes, brought back from the land of broken fragments to the commonplace world, only to have the light fade out, and his drooping lids close again. The latest distinct memory, as he finally sank into oblivion, was of the fresh flowers brought in by Millie, and her bright face over him, who asked if he had "no message to send her?" A sudden long breath, and a look of pain, with a tear coming into his eye, and, finally, "Thank her," was all; and somehow, as he shut his eye, Millie seemed to be Alice sitting patiently by him, and the to him absurd fancy soothed him to sleep.

When he finally came to distinct wakefulness, toward morning, the idea of that young lady was with him in a new aspect. Surely she had behaved toward him no worse than the rest, and all were really without fault. It is true they ought to have known better, but they didn't; and, however much he might admire their discernment, he could not complain of any intentional wrong. Still, it is just as bad for a man to be killed accidentally as to be murdered. But here was this young, friendless orphan, to whom he rendered important services, and she asked him to call, that she might at least thank him, and make him such acknowledgments as would be grateful to herself. Of course, she would not offer him money, for she would certainly have too much delicacy and sensibility for that; and, like a great booby-boy, who couldn't have the cake, he was sulky and mad, and wouldn't go; was preparing to run off. Of course, she and all the world would know that he not only loved her, which nobody would blame him for, but had the presumption to expect her love in return. What claims could he have that this proud, gifted, beautiful, and rich maiden should love him? Oh, dear, how humiliated he was! Had he gone and met her, it would have been all over now; and now he must meet her, and with this added humiliation. Well, when he did see her, he should acknowledge his fault, and ask her pardon. But she must despise him. Of course, she would see that he was nursed and cared for; and would, had he been her colored instead of her white servant. Possibly, had he not been hopelessly in love, he would not have thought himself at such long range from her, but he had a despairing lover's estimate of himself, though he did not look upon himself now as a lover, but merely as a man who had behaved toward a woman in a very unmanly way. It strikes me as very funny—this sudden turning of the tables on himself—but, then, I can recall several rather funny things which some of my people have done in spite of me. But the fault is theirs, and not mine. By broad morning his mind was fully made up, and, with him, his judgments went into execution at once. He would send a message to Miss Brand, and ask her, at her convenience, to come and see him. It was so common for American ladies to visit the wounded in hospitals, that the idea in itself need not occasion surprise.

She might not come, but, if she didn't, it would be some relief to do his best to excuse himself. He would ask Mrs. Vane to come with her.

Aunt Nancy noticed his restlessness and depression, and hurried Dr. Bland up, who pronounced him doing well, and said that the restlessness was not unusual, etc. Nancy, however, had misgivings.

"Aunt Nancy," said the young man, "will you do an errand for me? I want you should go and ask Miss Brand if she will come and see me, and say that Mrs. Vane, if she will, had better come with her."

"De good Lord bress yer soul, in course I will; and wen shall I say?"

"Whenever it pleases her."

Aunt Nancy looked at him a little anxiously, and he seemed to divine her thoughts.

"Oh, it will make no difference, aunty. My face, what they'll see, will shock them, but we'll keep it covered. I've no market to ruin."

Aunt Nancy went out, and was gone for but a moment, and returned, and employed herself about the room, as Frank supposed, putting it in condition to leave on her errand. A moment later, and there came a little tap at the door, which Nancy opened, and there was the exquisite rustle of soft draperies, and the lightest of footfalls, and, turning his face toward the front of his low couch, there stood Alice, and he could hear her breathe. Shocked she was at the little which the bandage disclosed of his very pale face, and moved by the sadness in his uncovered eye. Frank lifted his one hand toward her, and she took it in both hers, to which it seemed feverish. For a moment neither spoke.

"Miss Brand, I—I did not dream that you were in this neighborhood. It is very kind of you, and I hope you will pardon my request. The truth is, there is a matter which may not interest you, but which pains me much. I—I want to make you an apology, Miss Brand, for my recent conduct."

"You—apologize to me, Colonel Warbel!"—in surprise.

Without noticing this, the preoccupied young man, with his face turned coldly from her, went on: "It was natural enough that you should want to see me, and General Mason said that you requested him to ask me to call. I was so unmanly"—with still averted face—"as to refuse. I know not how to explain this, nor how to apologize." His voice was still steady, but very sad. "I somehow felt that I could not then meet you, and I intended to have left the city, in a day or two, without seeing you."

"Why should you leave me—why would you go?"—with her face bent over him, but eyes bashfully from his.

"Would you have me remain?"—the voice still sad and cold.

"And why not?"—in the softest of sweet little voices, and a flood of rich, warm color, which he did not see.

"I will remain, if you wish it. I will rebuild Magnolia for you; will gather up your scattered people, and plant them on your estate, and educate them; be your steward and servant, in all fidelity and honor, and will never, never utter one word of my great love. Mutely and unaskingly I will do this, and seek no reward, if indeed this is your wish." The voice was still firm but low, and exquisitely plaintive. The beautiful girl sank upon her knees by the low couch, and, leaning over him, said:

"Francis, turn your face to me," in a voice that would have reached the ear of death, and he turned, with the light more in his face. "I do not want that alone, I want more," low and sweet.

"What?"

"This," putting her full, ripe, virgin lips, with their

otherwise unutterable story of love to his. His breath of course stopped, and his soul wellnigh went, when he spoke: "Oh! if our two souls could now exhale from this wretched world, and rest, two dew-drops, in the bosom of some flower, in the paradise of God, and there unite in one." And Alice undoubtedly sympathized with this exhaling and condensing process; and, as no other apparatus was at hand, whereby the experiment could be performed, she put her two lips to his again, as the next best thing.

"You love me?" said the glorified Frank, with his broken head, broken arm, and perforated limb.

"I love you! Oh, how could you ever doubt it!"

"Tell me so—a thousand times—and then I shall famish to hear it again—will spend all my life hearing it!"

"Then hear me, Frank. I learned to love your voice, though heard only in battle. Then you came to me, in my saddest day, with kindest eyes full of sympathy, and I knew you; and you carried me out of that prison in your arms"—pulling his arm around her waist—" and cared for me, and took up my cause; and I had this one precious little sentence: you hoped I would not win my cases, for then you would dare love me; and you should have known why I called that a foolish speech; you did love me, I knew you did, and Lucy told me all your precious words to her. Then came those days of lies, and we cast you out. I was to blame, Frank—awfully to blame; in my heart I knew better, and loved you still. How noble you were and how true, suffering for me, never tempted, going down into pestilence, and faithful everywhere, in darkness and lies; you wouldn't even let me drive you from me, and you saved me when my own stupidity betrayed me, and it was on my account that you were entrapped by assassins, and are brought back bruised and wounded"—putting one hand under him, and clasping his neck gently in her arms—" and I never, never will be separated from you more—there!

Now, do you pardon me for my doubt, and distrust, and cruelty?"

"I was not offended. I could not blame you. I only had not your love, as I thought, and did not blame you for that; and how strange it seems, like a man who receives a stunning blow here, and comes-to in heaven!" And so with glad, happy tears, and murmuring words, and pressing of young lips, they came to know their happiness; and all the time Aunt Nancy, who saw and heard it all, and who seemed to regard it as a high religious festival, in which others could take a part, made it the occasion of a refreshing. "Amen—yes, bress the Lord! Bress his mighty name! Hallalewyer, glory to de Mos' High! I hears 'im wisperin in de mulberry-tops. De Lord is shorely come, an' I rises an' opens de do'," and so on through the superlative forms and manifestations of ecstatic shakings and clapping of hands.

Mrs. Vane and Lucy came after Alice, having some woman's plan of campaign against the enemy, under the leadership of the former, who thought it now time to demonstrate in support of the advance. The "do'" was opened, sure enough, by the glorified Nancy. "Come in, come right in an' see de marblous doin's ob de Lord!" and all that Lucy saw and heard was a kneeling maiden, an arm fast about a bandaged head, and an unrolled mass of golden-brown, wavy, hair, with low, murmurous sounds and half sobs, and to the maiden it did indeed seem that the Lord was there, and the room was sacred and holy. Just at the door the two sweetly-awed women stood, until Alice arose and turned with her transfigured face toward them, when they moved forward. They went straight to the bed, and Mrs. Vane bent over and kissed Frank, with blessings and tears. The coy Lucy hesitated, and then put her peachy cheek to his lips, and arose and threw her arms about Alice, and half smothered her. "I know how it was: you just went down on your knees and put your arms around his neck, and kissed him—didn't she Frank?"

"On the contrary, I sent for her, and went on my knees to her for my rudeness," said Frank, gayly.

"Mother, do you hear that? Do you suppose there is such another delicious goose of a man in the world?"

"I fear not," said the happy matron.

"I wonder what you asked her pardon for?" said Lucy.

"He wouldn't come to see me, and was going to run off," said Alice, in explanation.

"He sees now," said Lucy, "what he got for it; an awful warning to all young men inclined to run from young maidens." And to Alice, suddenly—"Oh, have you told him?" with a look of fearful import.

"She told me all I want to know," said Frank, innocently.

"Yes, I know; that which all the world but you knew before, and it was so lovely for you not to know that—so that she could tell you. But, Frank, there is really and truly a real woman's secret, that I'd like to tell, only it's Alice's to tell: you'd never guess it in this world, if you couldn't guess hers. How delicious that a lover don't know any thing! what delightful, precious fools they are! Come, Alice."

"It is about Mrs. Harbeck. We met her the night before last."

"The deuce!" exclaimed Frank, a little disturbed.

"He's thinking of Mrs. Croly—the bad boy!" said Lucy. "If he weren't 'kilt intirely,' as Mike says, he ought to be tortured."

"Lucy, Lucy!" interposed her mother.

"You see, Frank," said Alice, "after that dreadful row, and your flight on Saturday, we went home, and found Mrs. Harbeck waiting for me. She was a good, very good friend of ours, and came to tell me how cruelly you had been misrepresented about Mrs. Croly, and made us half in love with her, as well as with Mrs. Harbeck. All about Mrs. Croly," noticing the pain that came into poor Frank's face.

"I hoped all my punishment was over," he said, in a depressed tone.

"Frank," said Alice, in tenderest voice, with her lips close to his face, "this is not punishment, it is blessedness. She told me how true and noble you were." Then, putting her lips to his: "I wouldn't pain you for the world."

"He ought to be pained a little, on her account, stealing her heart, and Teed's secrets, and putting her off with a forged will," said Lucy.

"That last I am a little sore over," said Frank, quite seriously.

"How did that all come, Colonel Warbel?" asked Mrs. Vane. "That's the unexplained thing to us."

"It was the handiwork of Mr. Jones, Mrs. Thompson's Smith," said Frank, trying to laugh, and only scowling. "What does she say about him now?"

"Oh," answered Alice, laughing, "she declares that there are ever so many Smiths, and that hers is another one—"

"Entirely," added Lucy.

"And having forged this for us, he went over and forged it back again for the other side," Frank went on to say. "It was found that we were shadowed, and Mr. Drybow took me to Baker. Under his advice we determined to keep our secrets very close."

"Yes, you couldn't trust even me, Frank. How much would have been spared us!" said Alice, a little sadly.

"Alice, I disobeyed, and went to you, to tell you all about it, and—and you were in a society way—not at home to me," a little hurt.

"I remember, Frank, and will tell you all about it, and all about every thing, some day."

"I met you but once after that, when I began to comprehend what was said about me, which I was too proud to contradict even," Frank said, further.

"I would have been," put in Lucy, decidedly.

"That time was in the Congressional conservatory. I approached you then, determined to tell you my whole plan, and I much wanted some information also; and when I ventured to hope that you would not think ill of me, you, in a cold, proud way, merely hoped that 'I would not compel you to.' My lips were closed with that. Oh, dear, it's all over, and I'm half angry at myself now, that I can't call up a bit of pride against you."

"Frank, these are all you have against me; some time, when you are better, we will talk it all over. You know, now, that I loved you all the time," seating herself on the edge of the bed, bold in the presence of her friends.

"What a perfect romance it has been, and is!" said Lucy, with fervor; "and Kate—oh, I wish she was here—and Kate and I shall be the bridesmaids," at which, a little laugh from her mother, a good deal of color from Alice, a bright look from Frank, and a fervent "Amen! bress de good Lord," from Nancy. "And after all, only think!" exclaimed Lucy, "you have not told him Mrs. Harbeck's secret. She's the wife of this dreadful St. Arnaud—there!" excitedly.

"What!" in utter amazement, from Frank.

"She's St. Arnaud's wife," she repeated; "she told us so herself, and all about a good many things."

"Is there any other thing to reveal, I wonder?" said Frank.

Alice compressed her lips at the thought of one other, but it remained with womanly tact in her own bosom; and, with this last explanation, the party stood looking with a sort of happy wonder in each other's face, when the cheery voice of Dr. Bland was heard at the open door, and then came Millie, for whom a way was at once opened to the patient.

"This is one of the two," said Frank, extending his hand, "who never doubted me, and whose feelings I hurt so at Indian Neck, in my dark age.—Forgive me, Millie."

"So you remember it?" pleased more than she could say. "I knew all how it was 'tween you two, an' that it would all be right some time; an' I wanted you to know all how Miss Alice was. Oh, I'se so glad!" Frank had to explain the incident, and undergo a gay fusillade from the vivacious Lucy.

Toward evening of the following day, Frank received two communications, one from the hand of Bardlaw, senior, with many kind words, and the other from a messenger of General Spinner. The first contained the conveyance of an undivided half of the property recovered from Rymer, executed by Alice Brand; the other, a certificate of deposits in the Treasury of the United States for one hundred and seventy-eight thousand four hundred and fifty dollars. When he comprehended these, he turned his heavy head and wept, with the *abandon* and helplessness of a child. What help was there for it? They had a long time over it. Alice was inflexible, and, after all, what difference did it make to any but her, in whose name it was? At last, he came to recognize her right to have it so.

Was there ever such a docile, happy, patient patient, or such wonderful nursing? and the generous girl, in her *abandon* of self, was less careful than was her lover of her, as they went up the flower-strewed way of suffering, to Frank's recovery.

CHAPTER LXIII.

ELLEN AT THE CAPITAL.

It was after New-Year's, and the Berwicks were in Washington for the winter—Ellen, more womanly, and hence more beautiful than before, with the fuller development of person and powers, under the ripening influences of her happy love. With the wise instincts of her sex, she had rooms and made her home at a house other than that of her lover, somewhat to his chagrin and against his protest. She knew exactly what their relations were, and looked forward to what they were soon to become, with the sweet forecast which secured to that whatever belonged to it, with its freshest aroma. Affianced lovers—and her aunt agreed with her—had better dwell apart, was her notion, and they did, with many comings and goings; and almost every day she looked down from the ladies' gallery upon her lover in "the pit," where "bad men go;" and she usually remained to walk home with him when the weather was fair, or with a carriage in waiting when it was foul, as it sometimes was in Washington, and there was at least one happy member of Congress.

Society, on which she had made so pleasant an impression the winter before, smiled upon the ripened woman on her return, and at once recognized her as one of its real acquisitions. The Vanes, Loziers, and their set, made her acquaintance, and received her as one of theirs. She met Alice almost at once, having already learned her story, and was an old friend of Frank's; and the two young women, with so much in common, formed one of the possibly few genuine woman's friendships, which there was much to unite and strengthen, with nothing to disturb or mar. When

Mrs. Lozier gave her party, Frank was in attendance, and quite realized the romantic idea which the young ladies had formed of him. The first blush of careless youth had gone forever, but the manliness of his nature was full in his face, and something there was of thoughtfulness, which the events of the year past had prematurely written on it, which gave it that pensive cast so dear to the imagination of a dreaming young girl.

And at this party Frank's old classmate Moran, who had been struck by Lucy at Indian Neck the summer before, made his appearance in Washington society, and was very attentive to the conscious girl, to whom Alice quoted Aunt Sallie's estimate of Yankees: "'The good is very good, but quare.' Look out, Lucy."

As for that lady, she waited and watched for the unreturning Smith, and could not for a long time be made to realize his identity with the masquerading Jones. When that idea fully possessed her, she was true to the high nature of her mamma's family—the Biggses—and the high spirit of the sunny South. She tore the "compound extract" to shreds, and committed the spring inspiration to the fire which it needed, and revoked her favorable judgment of the Yanks. Luckily for the world, Grayson had secured a full copy of the former, and edited and annotated both with much learning and ability, which he and Mr. Lozier gave a large circulation, so that American letters suffered little from the just wrath of Aunt Sallie.

I have not the courage to take any reader I may have again to the two Houses, and will only note that in due time the Committee of Privileges and Elections, by its chairman, made a majority report in favor of Mason in his case of contest, and that Brasson brought in a minority report, signed by three of the committee, sustaining the claim of the contestant. When the case came up in the House, the chairman made an able *exposé* of its merits, and stated that, although the question was purely judicial, still, when the claim of a political opponent to a seat was involved, magnanimity would require every honorable mind to be jealous of itself in judging his case, and resolve doubts in his favor; that, as the proof was, the sitting member seemed to have a majority of the votes cast; that the doubt arose wholly through the misconduct of the conceded friends of the contestant, who purposely destroyed the only certain means of showing who had a majority; while the contestant was wholly exonerated from all imputation of complicity in this outrage, and the great mass of his supporters utterly repudiated it, still justice would require that the side out of whose misconduct the doubt arose should, if either must, suffer by it. Notwithstanding the strenuous exertion made by Brasson and a few partisans, the great bulk of the Republicans sustained the chairman; and it is but justice to say that, under circumstances favorable to a dispassionate consideration of a question, that majority was usually equal to an impartial disposition of it. Mason himself took no part in the presentation of his case, either before the committee or on the floor of the House.

CHAPTER LXIV.

A SPRING DAY ON THE POTOMAC.

It was a spring day on the Potomac. Not one of those warm, sensuous, languid days, which may come in midwinter, but a spring day, in a clime where spring—real spring—is a fact. From the southern sea, up the wandering Potomac, it came, lingering around and warming desolate Mount Vernon, which no vernal breath can recall to more than a mourning memory—touching the flag at

Fort Washington, throwing a gleam over lonely Alexandria, streaming up the Anacosta, flooding Washington, nestling warmly down on loved Arlington and the heights of Georgetown and Oakhill, bathing the Old Soldiers' Home with its golden flood, and lighting up all the romantic banks of Rock Creek and all the wooded hills and valleys, like a gilded setting for the city of the republic!

In a single night—from over the South it came, with voice of song, with color, and perfume—from all the hearts of living things and all the beginnings of new life, from the sources of motion and sound, the home of joy and hope, from the crystal dome of light and the casket of incense, stirring all the depths of earth, ocean, and air, and sending a pulsation—the premonition of the final coming forth—to the dead of Arlington and Oakhill.

In all the swelling buds, quickening through the tiny veins of the arbutus, trailing under the dead leaves, pricking out, here and there, with the tint of the rose and the fragrance of apple-blossoms, pungent with the winter-stored fragrance of the breast of Nature.

In the sky and air all men now felt, heard, and breathed it. In the heart and pulse of mortals, and they went forth in an atmosphere exultant with new electric ether; and caught dropping from blue-birds, lost in deeper blue, the notes of spring, like spangles from the buskins of God, still hovering, almost seen, over his new creation. Men turned frettingly in their garments, and would cast them, as snakes cast their skins. The heat, they said, when it was an unconscious impulse to escape from their old dead selves, and to take a new form from the kindling creation about them. The whispers of soft-voiced breezes from over the beds of budding flowers brought to them the passionate sighs for remembered childhood, that no spring shall renew. The choiring voices of happy school-children, in glad gushes from open window and door, came to them, with the wail of their own hearts.

Grave senators and the tribunes of the people lingered in the Capitol-grounds, hearing, as in boyhood, the rich note of the blackbird from the tree-tops; and the margin of some fair Northern lake or willow-bordered meadow-brook came to them longingly across dead years, bright with sun and life.

The old black crone sitting on the sidewalk by the market, in whose memory linger the traditions of Africa, wonders, as she ties little bundles of arbutus-flowers, whether the unwonted stir of her withered breast is not the footfall of the angel who shall bear her over the dark waters.

The young maiden, just awakened by the mysteries of her nature, lingers by the side of her boy-lover, with her eyes, in their liquid sensibility, flashing furtively toward the man awaiting her approach, and the poor boy feels that she is passing forever from his side to the new world which, to-day, has opened upon her, and toward which it so strongly impels her.

On that day, at eleven, in sombre, ivy-covered St. Johns, rich and soft within with flowers and color, at its altar stood a rare bridal-group—such, perhaps, as St. Johns had never seen. More beautiful brides, mayhap, but never one more assuredly lovely, and who so looked and felt a bride, and for whom all the beautiful ritual had such a deep and full meaning. Men and women looked on Alice's face, as she thus stood, feeling for a moment that there could be no man her peer. And then they turned to her bridegroom, whose face seemed to kindle like that of a young prophet, inspired by the vision of the new and sacred creation in which he was assisting—and they were content.

There was Ellen, in her ripened, virginal womanhood, more striking, and to whom the beautiful service appealed so powerfully; and the enchanted Lucy, and the beautiful Kate Lozier—such a group of young women, each a type of rare perfections, and each almost perfect in herself, as could hardly be rivaled out of America.

There was Charles Mason, with his face all aglow with the light of his high nature; and Moran, with eyes and thought for nothing but Lucy; and, the peer of the proudest, there also stood Grayson Vane, the model of young America, grave with the responsibilities of his position, and to whom Frank was still an object of more interest than any woman living.

The solemn hush came when, amid women's silent tears, a low, full voice spoke, hands were clasped, and the vows breathed.

On a May day, at her father's residence, Ellen also became a bride, surrounded by the old-time customs and observances of her New-England ancestors.

On a day of the seventh May succeeding, my eye lingers upon the last page regretfully, and my hand stays, loath to trace the last words that arise to my lips.

Seven years at the capital, and what changes do they not cover! Some so lightly, that through their dusky-growing veil so much is still present with us. Count up our great losses:

Stanton died one night, and the American world awoke to know, for the first time, how great a man it had lost, and never so seemingly great as when gone.

Seward came home from a triumphal progress around the world, and laid him down to final rest also.

Greeley, hunted with calumnies, until they fell on his beautiful, white dead face, which turned to reproach those who uttered them.

And Chase—mysteriously smitten—lingered, drooped, and passed from earth.

Then Sumner—the last of the great group—like a gray battle and thunder scarred tower, stood alone in the solitude of the American Senate—and fell.

It was but now that he lay in state through all the land, with common mortals pulling themselves up into notice by the dead giant's hair, to show the world how intimate they are with him when dead. I look out at the Capitol, and see the flags drooping, in the afternoon heat, over the two Houses, and I think of some of the changes in them.

Fessenden and Howard died long ago. Wade, who embodied more revolutionary force than any man in the Senate, is in exile from it. With that upward look of old, he is occasionally met solitary in our streets. Trumbull and Doolittle are practising law in Chicago. Many old warriors remain; and, of the newer, Sherman and Thurman are growing, while a new group of remarkable men have sprung up there, who have already reached the eminence of detraction—Morton, Schurz, Conkling, and Carpenter—while the younger Morrill has been permitted to reach distinction without that help. The Senate always has its Pangborns and Josephs.

I turn thoughtfully along the corridor toward the House, glancing a moment at the monuments in the old hall as I pass. I find an old door-keeper who remembers me, and I enter and cast my eye over the noisy, restless throng, so numerous and disorderly that the difference between its great and common men is lost.

Colfax went out through the vice-presidency. In the chair sits Blaine — handsome, able, and astute — already in the second, and seemingly not far from the first place.

Stevens, the greatest revolutionary force, save John Adams, which ever sat in an American Congress, sleeps with no column, national or private, save that erected by his own hand, and no biography but the *Congressional Globe* and Statutes.

Lovejoy died long ago, and the handsome and courteous Brooks passed more recently away.

Washburne is in Paris, Schenck in London, and Bingham in Japan, while Morrill, Conkling, and Windham, have gone over to the Senate. Dawes, a real tribune, is still in a House that has long ceased to follow any man. With him is that born leader and driver, Butler. Massachusetts is rich now in the House, for with these are the brothers Hoar and others. Shellabarger is gone, and Cox has been transferred to New York, and has lost nothing by the change. Ohio sends us Monroe and others, while Garfield has grown deepened and broadened into the proportions of real statesmanship. Poland is now at the head of the judiciary, and Orth comes back to head the foreign relations. New, strong names are rising on the horizon of the House, which still governs the republic.

The South is all back, and revives the memory of her old glory in eloquence, in the person of Lamar; while her new race is illustrated by Elliott and Rainey.

Then I recall the personages of these pages. The two brides, with their grooms, spent the first summer together in Europe, by arrangement.

Magnolia is rebuilt, the scattered freedmen recalled, and two-thirds of the estate divided among them. In their care and education, and the improvement of the residue, Frank finds ample scope for his admirably practical talents. Alice is realizing, with him, the hopes of the bride.

A bride's dreams are the programme of heaven.

Frank insisted that the oldest boy should be called Grayson Vane, and the mother has always regarded him as defrauded of his rights; and she half envies Ellen's, who rejoices in that of Charles Francis. Certainly a happy combination of names.

Mason served his second term, and found life in Congress too distasteful. He practises law, and contributes to the reviews and magazines, and furnishes lectures to more than one successful occupant of the platform.

Lucy sweetly submitted to inevitable fate, and, the spring following Alice's marriage, stood at St. John's altar, the bride of Moran.

Kate Lozier married an accomplished gentleman of the British legation. Grayson and Sam are with their mothers in Europe, and will return next autumn.

Margie came out of her cloud a little thinner, darker, more cautious, and bitterer than before. She never found the opportunity to tell Frank that St. Arnaud had offered himself to Alice, and, if she had, Alice anticipated her. She finally came to have much respect for Grayson. She was a woman to sour and sharpen under disappointment, but, if her qualities intensified to acridity, she also learned prudence, and, on the whole, seemed improved.

Mr. Drybow, who opened out somewhat promisingly in these pages, and whom the author perhaps found a little too voluble for his purpose, is rather at the head of what is known as "Newspaper Row," the "row" having become a figure of speech, rather than a locality—a new feature, almost a new power in journalism, impossible under every other government, and possible only at the capital city of ours; a set of gentlemen, numerous enough to become an association, and a distinctness of interest to form a class, with so much fraternity as to have an *esprit de corps*, with intelligence to secure respect, and ability to be formidable, as a whole, with integrity and independence, to be very useful. Among them are individual instances of rare sagacity, prudence, delicacy, and integrity. Standing at the lips of all who speak, potentially present at most council-boards, and penetrating the secrets of those who conspire; counting the throbs of the political pulse, while their duty is to report facts, they always go colored with the thoughts and characteristics of the reporter; and the columns of the great dailies, devoted to them, contain their gloss of the conduct of men, the current of events, the development of policies, the course of parties, which often mould and shape national politics, and are sometimes decisive of individual fates and fortunes.

One there was of this band, beloved of men, and for whom they had large hopes, who used to turn to me with that haunting, mysterious light in his wide, deep eyes, which we never understood until it was quenched. To us he came, with a tenderer and better revelation of each to the others; and when he departed, which was but yesterday, it was to light up and beautify the way. The world never more than half suspected its loss.

Bardlaw, senior, retired from active practice of the law, in the *nisi prius* courts, soon after the trial of Alice's case.

Mrs. Harbeck found pleasant and hopeful employment in a young ladies' school, in a thriving Western town, where her qualities and character ripened in many of the most beautiful and useful excellences of women.

Mrs. Croly never recovered her health, and died within the year near Albany, as she anticipated.

I have heard of Rymer. It was said that he was an inmate of a pauper madhouse.

I never heard of St. Arnaud, after his flight from the capital; but am sure I saw Ward here, about the time of the Red Cloud embassy.

I look out with wonder over the changed city, although it all occurred under my eyes. The great gangrened wound—the canal—is healed without a scar, and the Tiber decorously rolls its filthy tide underground, as a hypocrite should. Beautiful paved streets, park and lawn bordered, studded with trees, fountains, and flowers, everywhere invite the eye, foot, and carriage; and ample sewerage has banished the gutter trench and stench of the period of my story.

Some of the Bang-Borums probably still remain, driven to the debatable ground that surrounds and sometimes reaches near the hearts of great towns—links connecting them with their Saurian periods. True, a joint committee of the two Houses is now investigating Governor Shepherd and his board of improvements, and, whatever may be the result to them, the city has been boldly launched upon a career that it must pursue.

I close my eyes, and mentally open them upon the capital fifty years hence, when Grayson Vane and Sam Lozier, and the men of their time, will be passing away; and I see—"Papa," cries the blue-eyed Alice, "Chickasaw is waiting." I look out and see him eating sugar from the hand of Hattie, whose steed is also waiting, and I leave my vision untranslated, and go for an evening gallop over Meridian Hill and the Old Soldiers' Home.

THE END.

www.ingramcontent.com/pod-product-compliance
Lightning Source LLC
Chambersburg PA
CBHW030343230426
43664CB00007BA/517